'This is one of the most important books ever written by a Jungian analyst. Moving beyond the too-simple dynamic of self and other, Tyminski focuses on the shared reality of coming from different places. Offering cross-cultural examples both classical and clinical, he shows that theories of individual development that focus mainly on the need to establish identity have impeded our ability to engage with the way people's lives unfold. With uncommon clarity and compassion, he sees that we are becoming global citizens who will have to face the repeated crises of relocation and that we have in common both the duty and the drive to rethink our insistence upon boundaries.'

John Beebe is author of Integrity in Depth

'A rare, rich portrait composed of personal history and experience, psychological insight, mythic background and socio-political commentary is provided by Tyminski. He offers us a compelling overview of the many faces of migration, immigration and the refugee's plight. Empathic psychotherapy practice is amply demonstrated throughout, along with a deep understanding of the dilemmas, personal and collective, facing those who choose or are forced to leave their home country. A healing balm is offered for xenophobic injuries.'

Joe Cambray is President-CEO of the Pacifica Graduate Institute

'Robert Tyminski has written an extraordinarily compelling book on the key psychological issues affecting immigrants with great authenticity, and easily navigates the multi-layered issues of their prolonged and current struggles with belonging, identity, culture, language, pandemics, and more. Beyond an exhaustive and updated review of the literature on the psychological and clinical aspects of migration, Tyminski brings his insightful analytical experience of psychosocial counselling with young refugees in a reception center and patients in a more traditional psychotherapeutic practice. Adopting a Jungian perspective, he goes back and forth between mythical and clinical themes with great spontaneity, offering the reader an in-depth map to orient himself among the main issues affecting these patients, and the vital construct of psychological "perimeters." The presence of numerous autobiographical and clinical examples adds uniqueness, making the picture both *real* and *personal*.'

Monica Luci is a clinical psychologist and psychoanalyst with the Italian Refugee Council, Italy

'Dr. Robert Tyminski takes us on an epic journey through the heart and soul of immigrant experience, its traumas and psychological stressors. It is a book written from both a heartfelt personal and mythical perspective, and widespread practical and clinical experience. His vision is filtered through his unique conceptualization of perimeter and identity, and he unearths and challenges the roots of society's xenophobic and racist practices. It is a wonderful book of humanness and homecoming.'

Marcus West *is author of* Into the Darkest Places: Early Relational Trauma and Borderline States of Mind

'Robert Tyminski's book offers lively, full-blooded consulting room stories working with patients of all ages; the binding through-line has to do with immigration but, without a doubt, this book is a treasure trove for students learning the art/craft of psychotherapy. Further, he applies clinical skills as a cultural anthropologist exploring the very real struggles of refugees from Syria who have relocated to Germany. Tyminski coherently weaves well-told tales from the individual to collectives across cultural/geographical/generational divides and within our own country where gay people often feel like foreigners.'

Linda Carter *is a Jungian analyst in Carpinteria, California*

The Psychological Effects of Immigrating

Exploring immigration from psychological, historical, clinical, and mythical perspectives, this book considers the varied and complex answers to questions of why people immigrate to entirely new places and leave behind their familiar surroundings and culture.

Using research reviews, extensive case material, and literary examples (such as Virgil's The Aeneid), Robert Tyminski's work will deepen readers' understanding of what is both unique and universal about migratory experiences. He addresses the negative consequences of xenophobia, the acculturation experiences of children compared to adults, the trauma and psychological issues that arise when seeking refuge or relocating to a new country, and the more recent implications of COVID-19 upon border crossings. Tyminski also re-evaluates the term *identity* as a psychological shorthand, suggesting that it can flatten our understanding of human complexity and erase migrant and refugee life stories and differences. As one of few books to investigate immigration from a Jungian-oriented perspective, Robert Tyminski's work offers a new and broad perspective on the mental health issues related to immigration.

This book will prove essential for clinicians working with refugees and migrants, when in training and in practice, as well as students and practitioners of psychoanalysis seeking to deepen their understanding of migratory experiences.

Robert Tyminski is a Jungian analyst in San Francisco. He is a member and past president of the C. G. Jung Institute of San Francisco. His previous books were *Male Alienation at the Crossroads of Identity, Culture and Cyberspace* and *The Psychology of Theft and Loss: Stolen and Fleeced.*

The Psychological Effects of Immigrating

A Depth Psychology Perspective on Relocating to a New Place

Robert Tyminski

Routledge
Taylor & Francis Group

LONDON AND NEW YORK

Cover image: Juanmonino; © Getty Images

First published 2023
by Routledge
4 Park Square, Milton Park, Abingdon, Oxon OX14 4RN

and by Routledge
605 Third Avenue, New York, NY 10158

Routledge is an imprint of the Taylor & Francis Group, an informa business

© 2023 Robert Tyminski

British Library Cataloguing-in-Publication Data
A catalogue record for this book is available from the British Library

Library of Congress Cataloging-in-Publication Data
A catalog record has been requested for this book

ISBN: 978-0-367-63545-9 (hbk)
ISBN: 978-0-367-63547-3 (pbk)
ISBN: 978-1-003-11959-3 (ebk)

DOI: 10.4324/9781003119593

Typeset in Garamond
by MPS Limited, Dehradun

For my grandparents

Contents

Foreword

One of the most compelling things about this book is the way in which Robert Tyminski takes us on an impressionistic circumambulation around recurring themes. We travel alongside him, sharing in his discoveries. The book is built upon not only his clinical experiences with refugees and immigrants but also his own family's stories of immigration. Throughout the book he reaches many tentative conclusions about which he is not afraid to remain tentative. And he raises as many questions as he tries to answer. He is always the keenly sensitive participant witness of himself and others as he goes in search of the many different faces of the psychology of immigrants and immigration.

I follow in Dr. Tyminski's footsteps in choosing the word *mosaic* to describe the way in which the book is put together. Tyminski introduces the term in the context of a discussion about identity:

> Postmigration theory conceives of dismantling national labels that separate and oppress us. These so-called national identities are often imposed by mechanisms of power to divide human beings from one another. More likely, we are mosaics, not discrete identities given or handed to us; and these mosaics are, as Roger Bromley, a professor of cultural studies, writes, *bricolages*, a term from cultural anthropology that means improvised out of what is available, created out of various things.[1]

Just like Tyminski's suggestion that the notion of identity itself should give way to the idea of a mosaic, I suggest that the identity of this book is more like a bricolage than a straight-line narrative:

1   It follows Tyminski's inexhaustible curiosity by providing an extensive survey of the literature on many different aspects of the psychology of immigration. The references and their careful explications are always relevant to specific themes.

2   It is consistently and refreshingly revealing of the author's personal journey through his subject matter.
3   It includes twelve clinical vignettes from Dr. Tyminski's professional work that are stunning in their precision, elegance, and sensitivity to his own and to his patients' inner and outer lives, often as expressed in the transference and countertransference.
4   It takes on a broader set of reflections on contemporary themes in psychotherapy, which include provocative reflections on such topics as persona, identity, perimeters, mysteries, the uncanny, and the group skin-ego.
5   It always has in mind the more universal aspects or archetypal underpinnings on the themes of loss of home, the perils of finding a new place to call home, and the difficulties of adjusting to that new home. Virgil's Aeneid is Tyminski's archetypal touchstone, but it never prevents him from seeing the particular, the specific, the local—what makes each situation and person unique.

In short, this book is at once the record of an academic researcher's comprehensive literature review; the accounts of a treating analyst's clinical work on themes related to immigration in his private consulting room, as director of a child and adolescent treatment center, and as a cross-cultural consultant; multiple narratives from a seasoned lover of the world's literature; and finally the journal of a mensch, a real human being, who suffers empathetically to discover meaning in the suffering of humankind.

I want to comment on two specific topics on which Tyminski offers original insight: perimeters and identity. Each reflects Tyminski's opening the discussion of the psychology of immigration to broader reflections on our contemporary understanding and use of language to reflect the rapidly evolving individual and collective psyche of the twenty-first century.

Throughout the book, Tyminski speaks of *perimeters* rather than *boundaries*:

> Perimeters are both external demarcations of reality (such as societal regulations, laws, and national boundaries) and internal representations that we take from our experiences of them. Perimeters constitute a paradox about what we absorb from outside and subsequently believe to have made our own. For most of us, this is as if outer spatial lines wiggle inside us to then complete psychological puzzles about who we are, what makes us different, and where we belong. For example, borders with walls are external perimeters that affect how those on each side think of themselves and of those on the other side (p. 103).

This is an interesting shift away from the conventional use of *boundaries*, and when I queried him about his preference for *perimeters* over *boundaries*, he answered quite simply:

> I think "boundaries" is really dated, and as a term calls to mind various kinds of psychopathology such as "poor boundaries" or "inadequate boundaries" … adolescents routinely cross "boundaries" to see what happens, online and in games and with one another. I came upon "perimeters" as I thought about labeling, internalization, and the ways external lines come to categorize any of us. Perimeters seem to point toward a different idea about describing what gets inside us from outside and also about conceptualizing aspects of how we think about who we are.

I agree that *boundary* has come to mean so many different things to different people, both pejorative as well as prescriptive, that it has lost its precision as a psychological descriptor. Indeed the term *perimeters* enables us to see with fresh eyes what defines us from outside and what we take in as describing the edges or limits of who we are, depending on who is defining us.

Tyminski sees a similar process occurring with our use of *identity*. He even questions if one of our tradition's most sacred icons and ideas, Erik Erikson and his notion of identity, may have serious limitations:

> A criticism I have of Erikson is that his writing invoked many perimeters that were explicitly normative for the mainstream, that were bounded by what wider society deemed acceptable, and that seemingly recommended adaptation to more conventional values. … I believe that Erikson's definition of *optimal identity* referred primarily to existing safely inside the comfort of our perimeters, whereas his concept of negative identity meant being outside them. I don't believe, however, that being an outsider is necessarily unhealthy, suboptimal, or disturbed. In my view, these are dated aspects of Erikson's theory (p. 118).

Tyminski argues for a far more fluid understanding of how people, especially younger people, now understand themselves and the world. Neither boundaries nor identity can be thought of as fixed, as they once were, and rethinking their use implies a greater sense of experimentation and exploration. As Tyminski noted: "What I hear from adolescents and young adults about self-concept nowadays sounds quite different from what I heard even fifteen years ago. I hear now about playing and experimenting with who they are in ways that make 'identity' seem a bit fossilized."

In the spirit of amplifying Tyminski's preferences for the words *mosaic* over *identity* and *perimeter* over *boundary* I am reminded of a singular moment in my development as a Jungian. In 1978 I attended a conference that featured talks on the relationship between ego and Self by Edward

Edinger, the well-known Jungian analyst, and Mokusen Miyuki, who came from the eighteenth generation of a Pure Land Jodo Shinshu temple family and who had also become a Jungian analyst through training in Zurich. After their formal presentations, an informal group gathered in a circle of chairs to hear more from each of the presenters. Edinger went first and stood squarely in the center of the circle and spoke about the ego-Self axis, almost as if he and the circle around him had become a living embodiment of that notion. Edinger held the microphone stiffly and did not budge from the center. It was as if he was the axis, holding firmly to the fixed relationship implied by an axis. After Edinger spoke, Miyuki took his turn to speak about a more Buddhist/Jungian notion of the relationship between ego and Self. In stark contrast to Edinger, Miyuki almost swam around the entire space, encircled by the group as he spoke about the ever-changing relationships between ego and Self. Miyuki became a dynamic and fluid representation of how identity changes with changing environments and relationships. In comparison, Edinger appeared inflexible and unchanging in his physical embodiment of the ego-Self axis. The difference in more fixed versus fluid notions became indelibly embedded in my mind as I was able to visualize in the actual geometry of the audience and speakers the difference between a more open versus closed system of understanding the inner and outer movement of ego, Self, and identity. I suspect that the tension Tyminski notes in the consideration of specific words to describe psychological phenomena is always subject to a rhythm between more open and more fixed ways of describing the psyche. And so too there are surely open and closed systems for describing the psychology of immigrants and their hosts.

Finally, I would like to comment briefly on the notion of cultural complexes as it relates to the psychology of immigrants. Cultural complexes can lock both immigrants and their hosts in stereotypical modes of understanding themselves and one another with automatic, reactive emotional landmines that prefer simplistic black-and-white thinking and the collection of self-affirming memories that reinforce the complex. The transit to a more open state of mind is as old and arduous as Aeneas's journey in The Aeneid and as new as the most recent immigrants arriving on the shores of the United States and other lands around the world. Robert Tyminski takes us on that journey with an uncanny sense of mystery and a wonderfully open mind, heart, and soul.

Thomas Singer

Note

1 Wikipedia, s.v. "Bricolage," https://en.wikipedia.org/wiki/Bricolage; Roger Bromley, "A Bricolage of Identifications: Storying Postmigrant Belonging," *Journal of Aesthetics & Culture* 9, no. 2 (2017): 37.

Acknowledgments

From Virgil, we have a Latin phrase *mirabile dictu.*[1] It roughly means wonderful to say or tell. These acknowledgments are wonderful to tell you, the reader, about. Many people from various walks of my life contributed to this book through the kindness of sharing their stories with me. Because I have been able to travel, I could go to different places and stay for a while when I wanted to learn more. That has been a privilege that most migrants don't have. In that way, I've been fortunate. And because of that, I've tried to keep in mind the vastly different stories that immigrants and refugees have to tell.

I want to thank the patients in my practice who are immigrants and told me about their experiences with immigration. These stories were often difficult to tell because of the emotional pain they were associated with. I hope that their retelling has helped them form new meanings for what they have gone through. A central goal of analysis and psychotherapy is to alleviate mental suffering and reduce the intensity and scope of difficult emotions—I hope that this happened for those who were and are in my care. I have disguised identifying information in the cases I report in this book.

I want to acknowledge and thank the staff and clients at the Frei Center in Berlin, Germany, for opening their doors to me. I admire their work and the fortitude of the refugees in their care. I thank my German friend Norbert Hänsler, who helped arrange this visit.

The *Journal of Analytical Psychology* printed original material in Chapters 2 and 4 and gave me permission to reuse it for this book. *Jung Journal: Culture & Psyche* printed the article on which Chapter 6 is based. These professional journals are lifelines for analysts and psychotherapists because they help us to learn and see ourselves in a wider community.

I thank all the respondents to the study about immigration images that is the heart of Chapter 9 Their openness in replying helped to unravel many archetypal aspects of imagery that endures for immigrants after their resettlement. Special thanks to Marc Van Der Hout who let me interview him about his career as an immigration attorney in the United States.

The list of those who have encouraged my writing and taught me to write better is long. *Mirabile dictu.* John Beebe has been a terrific mentor and always pointed me in a better direction than the one I was moving toward. Others are Susan Calfee, Joe Cambray, Linda Carter, Elaine Cooper, Diane Deutsch, Tom Kelly, Phil Moore, Jeffrey Moulton Benevedes, Sam Naifeh, Katherine Olivetti, David Sedgwick, Dyane Sherwood, Ellen Siegelman, Tom Singer, Charlie Stewart, Til Stewart, Susan Thackrey, Dennis Turner, Marcus West, and Susanna Wright. They have read drafts, commented on half-finished essays, encouraged me to dig deeper, and told me when something wasn't ready. These are gifts of friendship and collegiality for which I am very grateful.

My copy editor for this and my other books is LeeAnn Pickrell. She has been excellent at bringing a trained eye to details that I would probably not see; she's made numerous suggestions for improving text that dragged on or was confusing. I count myself lucky to be able to work with her. I am thankful for having a great editor at Routledge, Susannah Frearson, who has seen promise in my ideas.

I have had encouragement and support from many friends through writing this book. Lauren Cunningham, Gordon Murray, and Susan Williams offered space for ideas to hatch and see how they might develop. My friends Hope Selinger and Kim Hettena have read drafts of my writing and offered thoughtful commentary. My friend Mary Brady is a delight to share ideas with and to think together about possibilities. Our collaboration always enriches my life and brings me deeper meanings. Her late husband, Carey Cole, was a terrific friend, a keen observer, and wise counselor.

My friend Candia Smith is a wonderful supporter of me and my writing. I feel blessed to have her in my life. Her sharp mind brings clarity to many questions a writer about psychology faces. My appreciation extends to her husband Jon Winge for his kindness, humor, and surprising intuitions.

My yoga group has been in my life for decades now. Our teacher, Barbara Wiechmann, creates a wonderful space for us to discover how to be healthier. She is a friend whose love and guidance have shaped me. Our yoga group has had many participants who are immigrants to the United States, and many have become friends.

I would not have written this book were it not for my family. Our immigration background has been a source of inspiration in my adult life, and I wish we had more openly embraced it when I was a child and teenager. Grandparents on both sides had stories to tell about migration, and these often did not get shared in much detail. My aunt Jane Fitch helped fill in missing parts about my Polish grandparents and what life was like for her and her ten siblings, my father among them, growing up on a farm in Upstate New York. Her daughter, my cousin Donna Holliday, facilitated my contacting Aunt Jane who was in her late nineties. I am lucky to have spoken with her before she passed away in January 2021. My cousin Marilyn Baker shows curiosity about my writing and has been enthusiastic about it. My cousins Kathy Abruzzese, Janet Cormier, and Cheryl Tyminski are relatives whose love is simply given, not measured. We have shared many helpful conversations about family and the past, keeping stories alive. My cousin in Poland, Teresa Tarnawska, provided me with valuable information about our family's Polish genealogy. I extend many thanks to all these family members.

For financial support, I want to thank the trustees of the Kristine Mann Library in New York City for a grant that helped me with the study in Chapter 9 I also want to thank the Scholarship Committee of the C. G. Jung Institute of San Francisco for a grant to assist me with other parts of my research. The librarians at the University of California, San Francisco, were super at helping to track down the occasional obscure journal article that I had to read.

My husband is the immigrant who has affected me most and opened my eyes to many things I knew only at the surface. Gady's parents were Romanian Holocaust survivors who immigrated to the young state of Israel and built a life there. Years later, Gady came to the United States to study Oral Medicine, and after we met, he decided to stay here. Like with many immigrants, his story had uncertainties to it. I am profoundly thankful he found a way to stay for both of us. And I have much gratitude that his love probably makes me a better writer—and definitely a better person. *Mirabile dictu.*

Note

1 Virgil, *The Aeneid,* trans. John Dryden (Project Gutenberg E-Book #228, 2008), 49; Robert Fitzgerald, trans., *The Aeneid by Virgil* (New York: Vintage Books, 1990), 19.

Credits List

The author also gratefully acknowledges permission to republish the following material:

Tyminski, R. (2020) 'Is Identity a Fiction?' *Jung Journal*, 14(2). Reprinted with permission © 2020 Taylor and Francis Ltd., http://www.tandfonline.com.

Tyminski, R. (2019) 'Just Black Sometimes', Part 2: Reflections on an Adolescent's Journey. *J Anal Psychol*, 64: 386–405. https://doi.org/10.1111/1468-5922.12504. Reprinted with permission © 2019 John Wiley & Sons, Inc. on behalf of the Society of Analytical Psychology.

Tyminski, R. (2018) 'Just Black Sometimes': Analytic Tools Applied at the Frontlines of Social Upheaval, Part 1 *J Anal Psychol*, 63: 619–640. https://doi.org/10.1111/1468-5922.12448. Reprinted with permission © 2018 John Wiley & Sons, Inc. on behalf of the Society of Analytical Psychology.

Chapter 1

Where Do I Belong?

Immigration has turned into a divisive topic in many countries, especially in the United States. Those of us who live in communities with a higher concentration of immigrants often find the conversations in the media and by our political leaders disheartening. Ugly rhetoric frequently characterizes the othering of immigrants by seeking to rile so-called natives against perceived intruders who will "take our jobs," "commit crimes," burden society," to name but a few of the oft-cited insults hurled at immigrants—essentially anything that attributes unpleasant human traits to them, such as criminality, poverty, illiteracy, disease, immorality, fanaticism, insatiable neediness, unpatriotic tendencies, and dangerous aggression.[1] Othering is a psychological process, both at the individual and group levels. What we don't like in ourselves is projected outward onto the people we dislike. Jungian psychologists call this an activation of shadow material that disposes unintegrated psychic contents elsewhere because we don't want to bear them ourselves. This process is both defensive, using more primitive defenses like projection and denial, and a kind of object relations stance that splits into concrete, simplistic categories, such as us and them, good and bad, and familiar and foreign. At a social level, group relations theory calls this *scapegoating*, something that, of course, can be a part of virtually any group when conflicts around differences are avoided and defended against. Othering, an externalization of what we don't want in ourselves, can further encompass rejecting what we don't want in our families and communities.

I grew up around immigrants. My paternal grandparents came to the United States in the early twentieth century, my grandfather (*dziadzi* in Polish) in 1910 and my grandmother (*babcia* in Polish) in 1911. Although they were Polish, the country Poland did not exist at that time; their country of origin was Austria, more specifically a part known as Galicia. They settled in Upstate New York, and my grandfather became a citizen, although my grandmother did not, probably because she never learned English. She had what was called an alien ID card. I recall seeing public service announcements on TV that encouraged aliens to register. This was during a time when my understanding of aliens was shaped by *Lost in Space*, Flash Gordon, and the

DOI: 10.4324/9781003119593-1

original *Star Trek* series. My father explained that Babcia was *not a citizen* and had to renew her papers every couple of years. That was why she was an alien. In my family, immigration stories were cloudy and obscure. (I will say more about this in the last chapter because I have found that, for many of us, migration stories are often cryptic.) When my grandparents were asked questions about why they had left, why they came here, and how they made many other essential life choices, the answers given were usually terse and unsatisfying, like a watered-down soda. This discomfort with describing such significant aspects of their past made it hard for me to appreciate the hardship and challenges that they had faced coming to the United States.

Exclusion and stigmatization

During the 1990s, I saw many gay men in my practice who were HIV seropositive. Some of them were foreigners who were in the United States on student or work visas. From 1987 to 2009, the United States banned visitors and immigrants who were HIV seropositive, and applicants for permanent adjustment of their immigrant status had to submit to mandatory HIV testing.[2] Hans was a thirty-five-year-old gay man who had been referred to me by a city health clinic because he was depressed.[3] He had grown up in Southern Germany with a single mother. His father had been a foreigner visiting Germany when he met Hans's mother, and he left them for his home country shortly after Hans was born. His mother died suddenly of a heart attack when he was eight, and a childless couple who were family friends adopted him. His adoptive father died five years later of a stroke, and Hans found it difficult to feel close to his adoptive mother, a volatile alcoholic. When Hans first met me, he said, "Problems, problems, everywhere in my life, problems." He looked visibly sad and added, "Where do I belong?"

That is a question many immigrants ask themselves. Hans had been in the United States for three years, and he was eligible for US citizenship through his biological mother's extended family. Knowing about the AIDS/HIV ban, he felt it was senseless to apply. Still, he liked living in San Francisco because of the acceptance he felt here as a gay man. He missed his friends in Munich, but he also found the social climate there stifling for gay people. During our work over a year, Hans vacillated between wanting to stay in the United States to feeling drawn to return to Munich. He often framed this choice as "escape," that he was escaping either from not getting permanent legal status in the United States or from the social conservatism of Southern Germany.

Midway through his treatment with me, Hans had the following dream:

> It was a nightmare. I was in Munich in the apartment where I lived with my [adoptive] parents. I argued with my father who said he was disappointed in me. He couldn't condone my lifestyle and said he'd expected more from me. My father was so upset he took a gun and shot me. I think I died.

Hans woke up panicked and couldn't fall back asleep. He told me his adoptive father had been a physician and an active member in a local conservative party. His father never knew that Hans was gay, and later, after Hans came out to his adoptive mother, she told him that his father would never have accepted this. Hans felt rejected.

Hans was saddened by his dream, because it reminded him of all the losses in his life and of his struggle for acceptance by his adoptive family. He said he never felt really taken in by them as a son because he wondered if they had done it only out of obligation to his birth mother. The dream placed Hans's central question—where do I belong?—within a family drama. Hans told me that his adoptive mother didn't know about his HIV status and that he couldn't imagine telling her because she'd react poorly to hearing about it. He went on to say that he left Germany largely to escape the homophobia of his family and of his local surroundings. He said that, although there was a gay culture in Munich, many gay people still preferred being in the closet to protect themselves, their careers, and their families from negative social consequences. He was profoundly disappointed, rightly so, that in coming to the United States, the freedom he sought was illusory because of our government's hostility toward gay people seeking to immigrate.

Hans's dream led him to associate to Germany as *Vaterland*, or father-land, although this connotation also made him uneasy in thinking about the Nazi's use of that for propaganda. I asked in this context how Hans understood his death by his father in the dream. He said that he wished he could be free of his father's judgments because they felt crushing to him. He added that perhaps he could let go of these memories of his critical father and of a rigid version of Germany because they depleted him and killed his hope. He began to wonder whether there might be a way to live in Germany that didn't feel confining and inhibiting. In this sense, Hans's death in his dream offered him a possibility for change by allowing him to let go of old attitudes associated with father and country, ones that drove his anxiety about his question, where do I belong?

Finding work in San Francisco was complicated by his uncertain immigration status. He began to consider returning to Germany for practical reasons and because he saw it less negatively than he had. He eventually decided to return to Munich. Several months later, he wrote, "I feel here already like at home, actually it is my home! Honestly, I don't miss San Francisco very much, perhaps the weather, the ocean and gay life. But there are possibilities here."

Hans had worked through a need to escape from himself, one that he had imagined could be solved geographically. Immigrants are usually searching for something better, something to turn their lives in new directions. So many make it that it is a testimony to human resourcefulness and resilience. But as Hans's story shows, they typically face many obstacles that relegate them to outsider status.

US immigration

As of 2013, more than 40 million people in the United States were foreign-born, a number that represented 13 percent of the population; by 2018, that number had grown to 44.8 million and 13.7 percent.[4] The historic high was reached many years before, in 1890, when percentwise, the population was 14.8 percent foreign-born. In terms of overall numbers of people, the United States has more immigrants than any other country in the world. Seventy-seven percent of immigrants are in the United States legally, with 10.5 million in the United States as unauthorized immigrants.[5] As of 2017, a plurality of US immigrants (25 percent) came from Mexico. However, since 2010, more Asian than Hispanic immigrants have come to the United States altering an historical trend. New immigrant arrivals overall have declined because of government policies, deportations, and xenophobia. In 2018, more than 22,000 refugees were settled in the United States, with the two largest groups (51 percent) coming from the Democratic Republic of the Congo and Myanmar. Almost half of all immigrants (45 percent) live in just three states—California, Texas, and New York. In 2015, more than a quarter (27.3 percent) of California residents were immigrants, approximately 10.7 million people, and in 2016, about 24 percent of the state's population were native-born with at least one immigrant parent.[6] The US Census Bureau projects most of the growth in the population of the United States in the coming decades will be due to immigration.

For a comprehensive overview of American immigration, the National Academies of Sciences, Engineering and Medicine (hereafter referred to as NASEM) has published *The Integration of Immigrants into American Society*, and it contains chapters about the historical, legal, political, and socio-economic dimensions of US immigration, which has become increasingly complex over the last hundred years.[7] Of note, they find that the overall well-being of immigrants and their descendants subsequently declines as they become more Americanized in the areas of health, crime, and family stability; this is sometimes referred to as "the immigrant paradox."[8] Interestingly, immigration restriction was one of the grievances against King George III in the *Declaration of Independence*: "He has endeavoured to prevent the population of these states; for that purpose obstructing the Laws for Naturalization of foreigners; refusing to pass others to encourage their migrations hither, and raising the conditions of new Appropriations of Lands."[9]

As an ideal for the signors of the Declaration of Independence, immigration appeared necessary, and yet, American history is strewn with deep conflicts illustrating how far short the country has fallen from what such ideals mean. For example, the immigration the founders sought came at terrible and unjust expense to the Native American population that had been in North America for thousands of years.

The first law regarding US citizenship was passed in 1790, and it allowed any free white person of "good character" to apply for citizenship after living in the United States for two years.[10] Inhumane blindness toward the role of slavery and willful ignorance of the forced migration of slaves were entwined with the founding of the United States and evident in this early law. In 1798, the first anti-immigrant legislation (Alien and Sedition Acts) passed Congress. This act made naturalization more difficult, allowed the surveilling of foreign nationals, and permitted deportation of anyone considered a threat to national security.[11] An immigration wave followed the War of 1812 and lasted until the Civil War, with many immigrants of Irish and German backgrounds coming to the United States, and these immigrants were both poorer and more Catholic than previous newcomers.[12] Anti-Catholic sentiment led, in part, to the formation of an anti-immigrant political party, the Know-Nothing Party, organized around various nativist groups, whose answer to questions about their activities was "I know nothing." They blamed immigrants for mass poverty, crime, and class conflict, and their populist approach gained support among skilled workers and shopkeepers who felt threatened by immigration. The party's peak was in the mid-1850s, and in the 1856 presidential election, its candidate, Millard Fillmore, won over 20 percent of the vote.[13] In 1868, the Fourteenth Amendment to the Constitution provided for birthplace citizenship for any person born in the United States.

With the Industrial Revolution and urban expansion, immigration again picked up. Between 1880 and 1920 more than 20 million immigrants arrived in the United States, many of them from Eastern and Southern Europe, including 2 million Jews. In 1881, however, the Chinese Exclusion Act was passed, racist legislation that barred Chinese immigrants. Prior to that, many Chinese immigrants worked in mines, factories, and on railroad construction. This law was the first to exclude a specific immigrant group. In 1892, Ellis Island, a port of entry into the United States, opened in New York Harbor. Peak US immigration occurred in 1907 with over 1 million people.[14] The Immigration Act of 1917 established literacy requirements for immigrants and restricted immigration from most Asian countries. In 1924, a quota system was passed into law with nationality limits based on a percentage of the 1890 census, which thereby favored white Northern and Western Europeans. The same year, the US Border Patrol came into being to halt illegal crossings.

During World War II, the United States and Mexico began a program to permit agricultural workers to come on a temporary basis to the United States. In 1948, legislation regulated refugees coming from Europe during the post-war period. The McCarran-Walter Act of 1952 ended the exclusion of Asian immigrants. During the Cold War, there were episodic laws and regulations to permit immigration from Communist countries such as Cuba, Hungary, and Vietnam. In 1965, the Immigration and Nationality Act ended most of the preexisting quota system and substituted a policy of preferences based on reunifying families and bringing skilled labor into the United States, although it did contain a limitation on immigration from the Western Hemisphere of 120,000. Between 1965 and 1985, more than 13 million immigrants were deported, the majority having come from Mexico.[15] An amnesty passed in 1986 that legalized more than 3 million illegal immigrants living in the United States. Other notable federal legislation includes a 1996 law (the Illegal Immigration Reform and Immigrant Responsibility Act) and the 2001 Patriot Act, both emphasizing enforcement, border protection, removal, and restrictions aimed at specific groups.[16] In 2012, President Obama instituted the Deferred Action for Childhood Arrivals (DACA) program to shield those undocumented immigrants who came to the United States as children and about 700,000 qualified. The Trump administration attempted to eliminate DACA, however, in 2020, because of a legal challenge to that move, the Supreme Court ruled that the government's rationale for stopping it was flawed, and therefore, the DACA program could continue.[17] Soon after taking office in 2017, Trump issued a Muslim ban aimed at stopping travel and immigration from several Muslim-majority countries to the United States. His administration also restricted refugees into the United States to only 18,000, dropping the number to historic lows.[18]

Some of the chaos in the US immigration history stems from a confusing legal framework that has changed over time. The previously mentioned book by NASEM finds that "For much of the nineteenth century, immigration and naturalization laws were primarily instituted at the state and local level, with little federal oversight or intrusion, with the notable exception of exclusions from citizenship based on race."[19] This racist ideology reflects both rigid systems of white privilege and white control over mechanisms of power that have plagued the United States since its founding and during colonial times as well. The early period of immigration history was characterized by a "relative unimportance of immigration status or citizenship."[20] A central problem since the 1970s has been the increasing complexity of the immigration system with a multiplication of various legal categories that, in turn, have their own distinctions attached to them. In brief, the main immigrant categories now include the following: permanent status, often called "having a green card" (without voting rights and without a right to remain); temporary statuses (seasonal workers, students, certain other workers); discretionary statuses (through executive action such as DACA); and undocumented status (illegal or unauthorized).

Individual states can assist with laws and policies to support integration for any immigrants in these categories. California, where I live, has created many protections for immigrants. Barriers to education and employment have been removed, for example, allowing undocumented immigrants to pay in-state tuition fees and receive financial aid for college and university. Immigrants have tended to settle in metropolitan areas around cities. As of

2010, three cities in California ranked among the top five nationally for having the highest percentage of foreign-born residents: San Jose (37 percent), Los Angeles (34 percent), and San Francisco (30 percent).[21] These vibrant, diverse cities thrive through integrating immigrants and supporting their local communities.

One debate about immigration often revolves around calculating its economic pros and cons. An entertaining 2019 book styled as a graphic novel by the economist Bryan Kaplan and illustrator Zack Weinersmith makes a convincing argument for open borders because economic research and data about immigration indicate its benefits far outweigh its costs.[22] Kaplan debunks many anti-immigration theories by instead showing that free immigration does not economically hurt societies, that it does not cause poverty to increase, and that it is compatible with the expenses of a welfare state because immigrants "ultimately more than pay for themselves."[23] He finds that many nativist ideas are based more on scapegoating than on data about immigration's economic impacts. Tackling anti-Muslim prejudice, Kaplan notes that the risk of dying from terrorism is less than one in over three million (that of being hit by lightning is about one in over a million). Likewise, he finds that by the second generation, immigrants are basically English fluent. Austan Goolsbee, a University of Chicago economist who advised President Obama, agrees immigration restrictions hurt the economy rather than protect it. He notes that immigrants start companies at twice the rate as native-born Americans: "Almost half the companies in the Fortune 500 were started by immigrants or their children...."[24] The foreign-born seem to believe more in the "American dream" than the native-born, when this dream is broadly defined as an aspiration for a better life, along with a belief that one's children's will become more prosperous than their own generation.[25]

As glum as the legal and political situation for immigration in the United States is, we are not entirely alone in making a mess out of immigration policies. *The Economist* reports that there are 270 million people living outside the country where they were born, about "3.5 percent of humanity," a percentage not much higher than in 1960.[26] From an economic perspective, their assertion echoes that of Kaplan and Goolsbee—freedom of movement has the potential to increase everyone's prosperity. But, they too find, isolationists and nativists have propagated a political narrative that many Western governments find persuasive, including much of Europe: "Brutality at the border is now a central feature of European migration policy."[27] What once was part of a nationalistic extreme is now practiced by many governments, as if Europeans are mirroring the lunacy of the United States. *The Economist* writes that the EU's "pretensions to moral leadership" are undermined by a reality of stalling and refusing refugees—only 65,000 have been admitted since 2015.[28] Although I will write about the situation in the United States, I mention this trend to show that it is part of a more general tendency among many high-income Western countries expressing hostility to immigrants.

Xenophobia

Webster's defines xenophobia as "an unreasonable fear or hatred of foreigners."[29] Compounding this psychological bias is the presence of racism. NASEM reports that racialized immigrants—those perceived as different based on race—face systemic discrimination that impedes their integration into US society; for example, those with darker skin earn much less than those with lighter skin.[30] Xenophobia functions as a social exercise of power that is based on a combination of shaming, hostile legal actions, discriminatory government policies, and exclusionary social maneuvers. It represents a group psychology of dividing people into binary categories of us (who are in) and them (who are kept out). Scapegoating is an aspect of xenophobic expression when undesirable characteristics such as criminality and disease are projected onto out-groups. Felice Blake, in a study of three manifestoes of mass murderers (Anders Behring Breivik, Elliot Rodger, and Dylann Roof), analyzes the contents of their writings, which espouse a virulent mix of xenophobia, racism, and misogyny.[31] She suggests that their incendiary expressions reflect wider tendencies in Western societies and "expose the ambivalent commitments to persons of colour evident in the current retreat ... from multiculturalist ideals in the name of post-racial integration."[32]

Oksana Yakushko writes that xenophobia is "a form of attitudinal, affective, and behavioral prejudice toward immigrants and those perceived as foreign."[33] She finds it is linked to nationalism, racism, and ethnocentrism; has many negative mental health consequences; and is multidimensional, as do others.[34] To account for xenophobia, some have looked at the social need to locate an inferior group to rationalize their own relatively low group status in society—excluding others so they don't have to perceive themselves as excluded, putting "the outsiders-them" on a lower rung of the social ladder.[35]

Pratyusha Tummala-Narra writes from a psychoanalytic perspective about the close linkage between xenophobia and racism in the United States.[36] She discusses defenses such as denial, projection, splitting, and dissociation that enable xenophobic manifestations making hate and prejudice acceptable. She comments on the primitive levels of object relations that are representative of such regressed psychological states, which rely on domination of others. Using case examples she describes how "humanizing the 'other'" within the transference-countertransference relationship comes to be felt as threatening to identity and personal power.[37] A challenge for psychotherapists and analysts working with immigrants is how to address injustice, othering, and aggression as they affect our patients and, specifically, in their relating to us and us to them.

Pew Research reports that "by 57 percent to 41 percent, more Americans say that the growing number of newcomers from other countries strengthens American society rather than threatens traditional American customs and values," a reversal from 2016 when by 50 percent to 46 percent Americans felt it was the other way round.[38] This more recent poll information perhaps indicates a turning point in the United States brought about by having seen our xenophobia in action through the Trump administration's blatantly cruel policies.

An opposite tendency from xenophobia is integration. NASEM defines it as a process through which "members of immigrant groups and host societies come to resemble one another."[39] The mutuality of this process implies a willingness to abandon xenophobic attitudes and their expressions. Integration is a psychological attitude as well as a social one. Here we are willing to own our shadow aspects and understand why it is important to have consciousness about them rather than project them. The centrality of aggression, power, and a necessity for empathy in this process makes it less of a sure thing than might otherwise appear. What effective actions will follow our well-intended words?

Psychological factors for immigrants: Their mental health and trauma

An extensive search of academic databases since 1990 using the keywords *immigration* and *mental health* produced more than 350,000 hits on Google Scholar. On PubMed, I got narrower results of more than 300 articles and on PsychInfo more than 340. An obvious pattern was the emergence of more articles across this time period revealing an increasing research interest in this important and developing topic. Although this recent upsurge in research is welcome and exciting, psychology has not always taken up immigration as a complex subject of study. Victoria Esses et al. note, "Despite the potential contributions of psychologists, however, they have been slow to enter this field of enquiry."[40] Maria Hernandez agrees, discussing the four acculturation strategies typically laid out: assimilation, separation, integration, and marginalization.[41] She defines *acculturative stress*, now a recognized experiential term for immigrants and refugees, as a stress response to the life changes accompanying acculturation, the psychological challenges of adapting to a foreign culture, and the psychological distress arising from unfamiliarity with cultural and social norms.[42] She also discusses the importance of language proficiency because it permits an immigrant to read cultural "social axioms" that would otherwise be indecipherable. I discuss the four acculturation strategies next, but first I want to emphasize that assimilation rests on a cultural presumption that can be experienced as a violent colonization by immigrants, a terrible cost to pay for joining the society of the receiving culture. This strategy potentially denigrates whatever unique contributions immigrants can make to changing a society. Assimilation in the United States is concurrent with the myth of the melting pot, in which immigrants have to soak in and absorb the cultural soup in which they have landed. Writing about her experiences with immigration,

Jungian analyst Lynn Franco emphasizes the emotional harm done by the melting pot myth, which renders immigrants' backgrounds invisible and alienates them.[43]

John Berry articulated a model for immigration from which the four above-mentioned categories come.[44] He too commented on the lagging position of psychology compared with other disciplines such as anthropology, economics, political science, and sociology. Applying intergroup relations theory, Berry wrote, "In any intercultural situation, a group can penetrate (or ignore) the other, and groups can remain culturally distinct from (or merge) with each other."[45] He used these group-level phenomena to explain the psychological routes for acculturation, which characterized immigrants' acculturation attitudes. The resulting two by two matrix of the degree (+/–) maintaining heritage culture versus the degree (+/–) engaging with each other created the four acculturation strategies. *Integration* is a situation of biculturality when immigrants socialize readily with the receiving culture natives and neither group abandons their heritage. *Separation* arises when an immigrant group does not mix socially with the native cultural group, instead maintaining high identification with its own heritage culture. *Marginalization* appears the worst possibility when an immigrant group neither mixes nor keeps alive its heritage culture. *Assimilation*, a kind of psychosocial colonization, comes from high social participation with native culture groups and relative disregard for the immigrants' cultural heritage. Berry noted that integration is characteristic of societies defining themselves as multicultural and valuing diversity with low levels of xenophobia.[46] In this context, resilience is also significant. Esther Ehrensaft and Michel Tousignant defined resilience, not as a coping skill or form of protection, but rather as a transformational process over time that depends on access to resources, such as community and mentors and that none of this happens "in a social or cultural vacuum."[47] There is also something called "the immigrant paradox," by which the first generation—the immigrants themselves—often report lower incidence of mental health problems than subsequent generations. David Takeuchi noted that many community studies "show immigrants to have lower rates of mental health problems compared to their US-born counterparts," although refugees are likely different in this regard.[48] However, as a trend, it is unclear how salient contributing factors, such as limited access to care and avoidance of mental health treatment for cultural reasons, are in this finding.

Seth Schwartz et al. emphasized that acculturation is a multidimensional process, which involves contact between culturally dissimilar people and groups.[49] They critiqued Berry's four-strategies model on two grounds. One, they stated that many of the existing categories might have subtypes that are not easily subsumed under a single category heading and might cut across them. Two, they cited research that the validity of Berry's category of marginalization was questionable for statistical reasons.[50] Schwartz and his colleagues emphasized the definitions of *ethnicity* ("membership in a group that holds a specific heritage and set of values, beliefs and customs") and *culture* ("shared meanings, understandings, and referents held by a group of people") as essential considerations for understanding acculturation.[51] They affirmed that biculturality appears to be the most adaptive strategy for acculturation, and they developed a different process-oriented model for acculturation that looked at the overlap between practices, values, and identifications of both the heritage culture and the receiving culture. "Something is assumed to change as immigrants and their children adapt to life in the receiving cultural context ... exactly what that something is has been difficult to pin down."[52]

The role of acculturative stress and of resilience in an immigration process remains central to contemporary research about the mental health of immigrants. Governmental policies, especially of late, have amplified this factor because of immigration restrictions and cruel procedures such as family separations and detentions, all despite widespread evidence that immigrants help the economy and do not lead to an increase in crime. Stephanie Torres et al. discussed the effects of trauma, violence, and governmental practices on immigrants from Mexico and Central America, of which there are 15 million in the United States and another 9 million who are undocumented.[53] They noted that the prevalence of premigration trauma is high for Latinx immigrants because of gang- and drug-related violence in their home countries. They further reported on the increasingly hostile and punitive policies of the US government at the borders since 2017, policies that have resulted in detention and deportation at will. Families are frequently torn apart, and there are long-term and immediate negative consequences for a myriad of psychological disorders.[54] A family separation policy and the internment of unaccompanied minors likely lead to a high incidence of posttraumatic stress disorder (PTSD), depression, and aggressive behaviors, with harm to the attachments of children and adolescents.[55]

In a study of immigrant families stopped at the US border, Yok-Fong Paat and Rachel Green commented on the prominence of acculturative stress, which they cited was "found to be associated with a range of mental health disorders and challenges that immigrants face."[56] They mentioned considerable social barriers for immigrants and refugees to obtain mental health intervention, circumstances including isolation, unemployment, limited English proficiency, stigma, and racism. Their interviewees spoke about economic hardship, fears for their safety, trauma they had been through, feeling low status, worry about their families, and problems with acculturation. One participant said, "Life in my country is very hard," a sentiment that certainly motivates many immigrants and refugees, namely, to hope for a better life.[57]

Pratyusha Tummala-Narra et al. affirmed the significance of acculturative stress for South Asian adolescents from differing immigrant backgrounds, some who are immigrants themselves and some who are native-born to immigrant parents.[58] They noted that acculturative stress has been associated with anxiety, depression, substance abuse, self-harm, and suicidal ideation. Major issues factoring into acculturative stress include a changing set of family roles, learning English, perceptions of minority status, and discrimination. Much research confirms that acculturative stress contributes to negative mental health outcomes.[59]

Immigrant trauma can be experienced at different phases of migration. Sean Cleary et al. looked at the consequences of trauma on mental health for Latinx adolescents in the United States with trauma occurring premigration, during migration, and postmigration, which can include forced stays in detention centers.[60] In this adolescent sample (more than 100), premigration trauma pertained to war and violence in the home country. Migration trauma happened when there was violence during transit and separation from family. Postmigration trauma included detention, poor housing, and acculturative stressors. Over two-thirds of these adolescents reported at least one traumatic event, and for most of them, it happened in their home country. The premigration trauma appeared more significant for this sample than what happened after their arrival in the United States.

Detention policies are in effect not only in the United States, but also in the European Union (EU) and the United Kingdom. Von Werthern et al. updated an earlier literature review with an analysis of twenty-six newer studies to assess current conditions that show the mental health consequences of immigrant detention on adults, adolescents, and children.[61] They found that anxiety, depression, and PTSD were most commonly reported as psychological disorders during and after detention and that the duration of detention was positively associated with an increased severity of psychological symptoms. Detention by itself is now recognized as a potential traumatic event. Younger children tended to exhibit signs of regression and externalizing behaviors, whereas older children showed anxiety, depression, and PTSD. The American Academy of Pediatrics, in 2018, issued a strong position statement opposing the separation of children and parents at the US border and noted the great harm being done to vulnerable families by the Department of Homeland Security.[62]

Sarah MacLean et al. remarked that the capacity for detaining immigrant and refugee families at the US borders has increased significantly in the last five years.[63] To date, there has not been a large study of immigrant children's mental health in detention within the United States. Their study included more than 400 mothers with at least one child and also included evaluations of 150 children (ages nine to seventeen) held in custody by US Immigration and Customs Enforcement (ICE). Over 90 percent were from Central American countries. They found the children had more than twice the rate of emotional and behavioral problems compared to the general US population of children and more than three times the rate of PTSD symptoms. Alarmed at these findings, they emphasized a need for immediate mental health interventions. Children were additionally burdened by learning a new educational system and a new language (English). Exposure to trauma has long been associated with effects on cognitive development in children, and their educational needs are complicated.[64]

Working with a large sample size of adults (more than 3,000), Cindy Sangalang et al. documented the effects of premigration and postmigration trauma among immigrants and refugees with Latinx and Asian origins.[65] The role of trauma for immigrants is less researched than for refugees, even when immigrants might have been exposed to traumatic events premigration but they are not coming to the United States as refugees. Trauma includes "direct exposure to or witnessing an event that involves an actual or threatened death or serious injury and violence."[66] Sangalang et al. found that pre- and postmigration trauma for both immigrants and refugees was associated with mental disorders and distress and that traumatic events were the most common premigration factor associated with psychological disorders for refugees.[67] Discrimination contributed to poorer mental health for both groups. Significantly, "The most consistent predictor of negative mental health across all refugee and immigrant groups was family conflict."[68] They also noted that traumatic events may be much more common among immigrants than is generally recognized.

In a review of research about the psychological effects of exposure to war and armed conflict on younger children (ages zero to six), Michelle Slone and Shiri Mann looked at thirty-five studies comprising over 4,000 younger children.[69] They commented on the many critical developmental milestones of this period, during which exposure to trauma can badly affect levels of trust, tendencies toward magical thinking, and self-blame. Young children experiencing trauma showed increased rates of tantrums, eating problems, sleep disorders, disrupted play, and psychosomatic symptoms. The authors found a dose-response relationship between the amount and intensity of trauma exposure and the subsequent severity of mental health problems.[70] They reported that studies on younger children tended to overlook the mediating effects of the parental relationships, and so it is not obvious when these are protective or when they are harmful.

Andrea Danese remarked on the connection between trauma in childhood and myriad problems in later life with education, employment, and mental health. She questioned, however, many of the explanatory models that are used to study trauma in childhood.[71] She explored methodological and descriptive issues that can lead to false interpretations about correlations, prevalence, and sequelae. However, she acknowledged that "traumatized children still often have poor long-term outcomes."[72] Other research argues that the health consequences of trauma and early life adversity (ELA) are associated with higher risks for disease as an adult.[73] ELA refers to experiences of parental separation, childhood maltreatment, and low socioeconomic status, and thus incorporates a broader category than exposure to traumatic events. Such later-life diseases can include autoimmune disorders, asthma, allergies, and type 2 diabetes. There is an "ELA immune phenotype" characterized by chronic inflammation and decreased immune vitality.[74] Further, brain-scanning techniques have found that childhood trauma has been associated with negative changes in the brain, such as decreases in the volume of the hippocampi and amygdalae and reduced gray matter in the prefrontal cortex.[75] These areas are all involved in emotional life and emotional regulation; gray matter contains the neurons that make us as humans who we are.

Posttraumatic stress disorder (PTSD) is defined by a set of responses to an exposure of actual or threatened death, serious injury, or sexual violence. These responses can often include the following:

- Intrusion symptoms such as flashbacks, nightmares, intrusive thoughts, repetitive memories, physical symptoms
- Dissociation in which conscious awareness is diminished
- Avoidance of situations that remind a person of the traumatic event
- Cognitive and mood disturbances such as amnesia, distorted beliefs about the traumatic event(s), negative self-worth, self-blame, shame, anhedonia, detachment
- Arousal symptoms such as hypervigilance, difficulty concentrating, irritability, sleep disturbances, recklessness, strong startle reaction

PTSD symptoms last longer than a month and cause great suffering in the psyche, impairing a person's social relations and their capacity to learn and work.[76]

Trauma is such a huge psychological topic that it extends beyond my scope other than providing this overview. Because trauma shapes many immigrants' stories from premigration to migration to postmigration, it is important for my current context. As noted, trauma is usually understood as experiencing a definable event of violence, death, or a life-threatening circumstance. *Complex trauma* refers to childhood exposure to multiple traumatic events, often invasive and interpersonal in nature, and having long-term psychological and physical effects.[77] For those interested in understanding trauma from a Jungian perspective, I highly recommend Donald Kalsched's two excellent books: *The Inner World of Trauma: Archetypal Defenses of the Personal Spirit* and *Trauma and the Soul: A Psycho-Spiritual Approach to Human Development and Its Interruption.*[78] Kalsched develops an idea about traumatized individuals carrying forth their traumatic experiences through the actions of a self-care system that initially seeks to protect them from terrors of encountering further trauma. This system shields them from psychic overwhelm but at a cost of also isolating and subsequently persecuting them with terrible affective and imaginal states, in a way perpetuating traumatic lived experiences.

Bessel van der Kolk offers a neuroscience-based overview of trauma, its dissociative effects, the disruption of the brain-body connection, and the healing process, in his book *The Body Keeps the Score: Brain, Mind, and Body in the Healing of Trauma*.[79] He describes areas of the brain that are strongly affected by trauma (amygdala, parts of the prefrontal cortex, hippocampus), using brain imaging scans to illustrate what happens from exposure to trauma. Psychological effects include the loss of a time horizon that something will end and be over, the reliving of traumatic events, severe memory distortions ("traumatized people … remember too little and too much"), dissociation, and depersonalization.[80] Van der Kolk discusses the many body-based symptoms of trauma leading not only to autoimmune disorders and various musculoskeletal ailments, but also to difficulties in somatic self-regulation and bodily self-awareness. His message is clear: with a loss of reliable mind-body feedback, "the body keeps the score." He finds eye movement desensitization and reprocessing (EMDR) to be an effective intervention for treating trauma survivors that allows them to gain a type of closure, relegating their trauma to the past.[81]

Jungian analyst Margaret Wilkinson also details in a highly readable book the neurobiological underpinnings of trauma.[82] There, she discusses the importance of the brain's right hemisphere for processing emotions, relationships, and implicit memories, which belong to a kind of automatic memory that bypasses thinking.[83] Wilkinson helps analysts and psychotherapists to appreciate the many challenges of working with trauma survivors because typically their experiences of the traumatic event are hidden within implicit memory and not easily accessible, much as van der Kolk confirms.

Returning to trauma research, Theresa Betancourt et al. conducted a study comparing refugee youth with US-born youth and immigrant youth to ascertain what the differences are for trauma exposure and mental health outcomes.[84] Refugees showed higher rates of exposure to community violence, dissociative symptoms, traumatic grief, somatization, and phobias; they also showed higher total numbers for types of trauma (sexual abuse, physical abuse, assault, emotional abuse, neglect, domestic violence, serious injury, kidnapping, traumatic loss, impaired caregiver). Looking at a sample of more than 300 children and adolescents, she and her co-authors noted, "Few refugee youth who need mental health services receive care."[85]

Lloy Wylie et al. discussed the difficulties that medical and mental health providers have in assessing complex trauma.[86] They also found that there were huge barriers to care such as a lack of information about medical and mental health treatment for immigrant and refugee populations, stigma associated with mental health care, and a limited knowledge base among clinicians about how to engage helpfully when someone with an immigrant or refugee background that includes trauma shows up. Others too have researched variations in trauma, such as continuous traumatic situations (CTS), which clinicians may not know how to handle.[87] These refer to ongoing wars and social violence that a person may not be able to escape from.

A somewhat more recent approach to understanding trauma and its physiological and behavioral impacts considers its epigenetic effects. Epigenetics looks at environmental and chemically mediated factors that influence gene expression without changing our DNA.[88] For example, trauma survivors frequently show changes in their immune and endocrine systems, such as dysregulation of the hypothalamic pituitary axis (HPA), and this disturbance can persist over time.[89] In this way, external occurrences like exposure to a traumatic event can shape biology by altering what our genes instruct our bodies to do. This is actually not a bad thing in that it allows people to adapt to their environments, essentially "fine-tuning" their neural networks as they develop out of infancy.[90] Nicole Gröger et al. noted that mammalian brains usually have critical periods in development, and two of these, for humans, are the perinatal period and the peripubertal one, when there is more plasticity in the brain's neural networks.[91] These could be times of increased learning and also heightened vulnerability if exposure to a traumatic event occurs. Most interestingly, epigenetics also provides evidence that behavioral patterns (phenotypes in a strict sense) "can be transmitted to following generations" and that the mechanisms for this are epigenetic via the family environment.[92] The transgenerational transmission of trauma is something that many immigrant and refugee families struggle with.

Literature on growth after trauma is somewhat sparse. The role of spirituality is one area that has been studied, however. Justyna Kuckarska reviewed seventy-nine studies that addressed the role of religiosity and outcomes to trauma.[93] Religiosity was loosely categorized as attitudes toward religion, religious beliefs, various behaviors that include spiritual rituals—a wide net. There was some evidence suggestive of a positive association between religiosity and general mental health, but it was unclear whether religiosity shapes a person's reactions to trauma much. Nonetheless, having some previous inclination toward a religious attitude does seem to correlate with posttraumatic growth.

Theory

Jungians have made significant contributions to understanding culture, beginning with Jung himself and his concept of the collective unconscious.[94] In a lecture he gave in 1936, he stated that the personal unconscious consists mainly of complexes, whereas the collective unconscious houses the archetypes.[95] Complexes can generally be understood as highly individual and affectively charged expressions of our early attachments, drives, conflicts, and object relations that have been acquired throughout our personal developmental histories, for instance, showing up in a father or mother complex, a power or erotic complex, to name but a couple.

Critically, complexes manifest at the group level as well as at a social level. Jung believed archetypes to be emergent tendencies or "preexistent" forms often seeking conscious expression, for example, through images, myths, collective stories, art, fairytales, and folktales—many of the components of what we call culture. Aside from the personal unconscious "there exists a second psychic system of a collective, universal, and impersonal nature."[96] Jung thought that our dreams provide evidence of archetypes at work; "we must look for motifs [in a dream] which could not possibly be known to the dreamer and yet ... coincide with the functioning of the archetype...."[97] I once dreamed about Pindar. I had little conscious knowledge about Pindar, and I would have guessed he was an ancient poet. I looked him up and discovered he was a Greek poet from the fifth century BCE, who had written an ode about Jason and the Argonauts.[98] That set me off into exploring the tale of the Golden Fleece and eventually led to my first book. Jung's thinking was ever evolving, and he continued to write about archetypes and the collective unconscious throughout his lifetime.[99]

Jung was fascinated by mythology. This aspect of his writings has always been central to my appreciation of Jung. In the book I just mentioned, I wrote about a pivotal role for myth in understanding theft and stealing. There, I summarized some of Jung's ideas about myths, which are cultural manifestations of our collective psyche.[100] One quote essentially captures Jung's emphasis on the importance of myths for cultural traditions and their transmission:

> The man who thinks he can live without myth, or outside it, is an exception. He is like one uprooted, having no true link either with the past, or with the ancestral life which continues within him, or yet contemporary human society.[101]

Ironically, this describes a lot about our current state of affairs, in which so many are alienated and adrift because they long to connect with something larger and meaningful, yet find this difficult or impossible.

Immigration is a bit mythical too. Immigrants bring their cultural traditions and identifications with them to the receiving country. This potential interchange between immigrants and natives can enrich the lives of all who participate. However, when immigrants feel compelled to discard their heritage culture, then, as in Jung's quote, they will likely experience alienation and loss at a deep level of the psyche. In Chapter 3, I explore Virgil's The Aeneid as a kind of mythic story about migration and resettlement. Although centered within Roman—and therefore Western—tradition, I hope to show that aspects of the story capture archetypal layers of an immigrant's journey, such as heroism and defeat, acceptance and hostility, and preservation and loss.

Thomas Singer and Samuel Kimbles have made a crucial contribution to contemporary Jungian thinking about culture with their seminal work on the cultural complex.[102] Early in their book, Singer notes that Jungian analyst Joseph Henderson originated a notion of a cultural unconscious as a space operating between the personal unconscious and the collective unconscious.[103] Within the cultural unconscious, elements of the cultural psyche proliferate, such as social norms, aesthetic values, philosophical beliefs, and spiritual traditions. From this area, our cultural complexes arise, forming what Singer terms "an inner sociology."[104] Cultural complexes tend to repeat, function autonomously, and gather what already confirms their points of view. Often, they are activated whenever a group feels something like a traumatic injury, and they seemingly offer protection for the group, while surreptitiously persecuting it—these are terms that Singer applies from Kalsched's model of the self-care system. Singer notes the analytic importance of addressing cultural complexes because we all exist in relation to groups throughout our lives.

Kimbles expands on the group dynamics surrounding these cultural complexes. He observes that such complexes can come to define an individual's identity in relation to a specific group. His emphasis on the parameters of inclusion and exclusion accords with my thinking about perimeters that separate us in more concrete ways. Kimbles discusses what happened with an analytic patient of his to creatively illustrate the emergence of cultural complexes within analysis. He explains that in part, these cultural complexes "bind anxiety related to differences."[105] That insight reminds us that those anxieties are usually considerable, especially in the territory of intergroup relations.

On the psychoanalytic side, Julia Beltsiou edited a fine volume with contributors addressing immigration, weaving in many stories from their own personal experiences.[106] In her introduction, she notes a lack around this subject in psychoanalytic literature: "The existing psychoanalytic literature on immigration has some catching up to do to reach the wisdom, nuance, and psychological sophistication of autobiographical and fictionalized accounts of immigration."[107] Francisco González, in the opening chapter, comments on a pathologizing tendency within psychoanalytic writing about immigration; he finds this has obscured immigration's positive effects at creating new possibilities. Further, "Place is a category largely neglected by psychoanalysis," which has come to prefer intellectual ideas about space, and he adds, "place matters."[108] His commentary draws attention to the environment and to how we interact with it, often amid conditions of suffering, stigma, and discrimination as well as those of hope, vitality, opportunity, and emotional growth. Ghislaine Boulanger also mentions a lack of a growth-oriented perspective about immigration within psychoanalysis—that analysts either ignore the topic or equate home country with mother.[109] This latter point contrasts, for example, with how my patient Hans viewed his home country as linked to father. I will return to more essays from Beltsiou's edited book later in Chapter 8, when I discuss the role of language and return to the topic of othering.

Some psychoanalytic writers have approached immigration by examining particular aspects of it. For example, Ricardo Ainslee discusses how an immigrant's social position and class in their home country comes to affect their self-perceptions in the receiving country, especially when there is a change in status.[110] In a subsequent article that also echoes Beltsiou regarding the topic of immigration having "little interest among analytic writers," Ainslee et al. look at the roles of mourning, language, racism, trauma, and generational differences across immigrant family experiences.[111] Luis Vazquez comments on the impact of colorism, which he defines as our perceptions and biases about the intensity of skin color, from light to dark, and how these in turn influence an immigrant's self-perceptions, biases, social attitudes, views of ethnicity, and acculturation.[112] For example, as he notes, "Shades of light skin color among racial/ethnic groups have been associated with greater wealth and accomplishments."[113] Such discrimination hurts not only an immigrant's self-image, but also their potential contributions to the receiving country. Frank Summers uses a case example to illustrate the pitfalls and gaps in experience that Latinx immigrants can face when their ethnicity is perceived as practically invisible.[114] Analysts can be blind to such areas and overlook attachments that an immigrant has to their home country, especially when an immigrant looks more like the analyst and less like someone the analyst imagines a person from their country to be. A lack of analytic curiosity in this regard can be hurtful to a patient's feeling safe and thus being open to exploring difficult material about their culture and immigration. Andrew Harlem cites an analytic case example of when dissociation becomes an expression of feeling exiled, a situation sometimes evoking a chasm between the country of origin and the receiving country.[115] As a result, there appears to be a loss of memory and selfhood from before migration. These psychoanalytic writers often seem to grapple with the newness of immigration as an area of psychoanalytic interest.

The American Psychological Association recommends that clinicians and teachers of psychology remain mindful of the numerous layers to multicultural perspectives when working with patients, students, and trainees with diverse backgrounds.[116] They suggest seeing an individual in their fullness as nested within concentric circles starting at a *microsystem* level of immediate family, friends, and institutions to which they belong.[117] A *mesosystem* refers to the interrelations of the groups from the microsystem. An *exosystem* contains social, cultural, and governmental influences that directly affect an individual. A *macrosystem* encompasses the broader cultural norms and values, and a *chronosystem* marks the passage of time and history. These guidelines reflect the complexity of when multiple intersecting variables contribute in different ways to a person's individuation.

My own ideas about the many strands of immigration that I hope to develop in this book are related to thinking specifically about perimeters, which I explore in more detail in Chapter 6. Here, I want to raise the idea about what happens when we use external markers to define aspects of self. For example, citizenship seems to be an easy perimeter to explain because it is based on governmental procedures and laws that define a person's legal status. Although these policies and laws grant access to legal standing and provide an amount of freedom when a person has passed the criteria to be included, they have nothing to do with who a person actually is. They do not reflect substantive qualities about an individual's history, their current situation, or the stories that make up their lives. Perimeters ironically define us and have little to do with who we really are.

I believe that there arises something of a psychological problem when we rely on perimeters to characterize what we have been accustomed to calling identity, because we are then using a concrete piece of external reality to portray ourselves in what is a simplification and even an obfuscation. Identity, as historically understood by most traditions of depth psychology, is mostly a category of ego attributes that document, or label, our adjustment to external systems. For example, an economics professor once told a class I was taking that being a college graduate was essentially shorthand to employers that a person is trainable. What he was saying is quite intriguing. A piece of identity that belongs to having graduated from college has a value for forming an external perception about worth, potential skills, and trainability, all of which can be internalized when we think of ourselves in those ways too. Thankfully, not everyone does so, although a focus on getting a return on college, like an investment, is more typical nowadays than it was thirty years ago.

Immigrants confront numerous identifying labels that, I believe, flatten our understanding of who a person is or might be. Identity makes sense as a kind of checklist of externally validated categories. However, I am less inclined to think that it still makes sense psychologically because this flattening effect takes away our depths. Identifying ourselves does not make us unique individuals. I will discuss perimeters throughout much of this book, and I hope to convince you as a reader that they compel us for confusing reasons but that we ought to consider what they rob us of.

A related and useful Jungian contrast to identity is the term *persona*. Jung calls the persona a mask: "The man who identifies with this mask, I would call 'personal' as opposed to 'individual.'"[118] The mask is not unimportant, for it helps us deal with various social situations in a nearly automatic way without having to reinvent our responses. I think of it as what we bring of ourselves to a gathering where we know few, if any, people. Deploying a persona is a way to manage social interactions by routines that we have learned throughout our lives. Jung also remarks, "The persona is exclusively concerned with the relation to objects."[119] I understand him to mean that persona is essentially preoccupied with matters of concrete reality. It is not viewed as an aspect of creative imagination, although certainly a person could fantasize about fame and fortune and acquiring an even more impressive persona. Adolescents often engage in this process when they describe their aspirations to become a part of celebrity circles, whether in sports, film, television, or art. They are playing, however, with different masks and wondering what it would be like to wear them. Immigrants too may dream of achieving flashier personas once they settle in a new country. The value of our masks often corresponds to how they help us navigate the perimeters of existence. But when we rely on such perimeters just for inclusiveness, then I believe persona is a better descriptor than identity for what we are doing psychologically.

Overview

In Chapter 2, I discuss what happened during my consultation with a nongovernmental organization (NGO) in Berlin, Germany. This organization was involved in resettling unaccompanied minors from Syria and Afghanistan who had come to Germany during 2015. This experience afforded an opportunity to look at immigration from outside an American context and to reflect on circumstances of trauma and vicarious trauma in caregivers.

Chapter 3 provides a discussion of Virgil's Aeneid. After summarizing the story, I examine heroic aspects of migration, which can include overcoming life-threatening obstacles. A threat of inharmonious cultures becomes pivotal to this story, and this piece of the plot relates to how many populist movements and nativist prejudices currently treat immigration. A mythical dimension of immigration is considered from the standpoint of how people move in search of something better for themselves and their families.

Chapter 4 looks at the coping of refugees in an unfamiliar environment. I discuss details from some of the stories that I heard during my time consulting for the NGO in Berlin and the psychological difficulties that many of the adolescents faced there. Chapter 5 contains clinical examples of immigrant children having to live out problems that their parents have not solved, especially pertaining to differences. Children can then be subjected to painful and cruel discriminatory acts.

As mentioned, Chapter 6 examines psychological terminology and theory related to identity, persona, and self. I discuss a model positing fluidity of self as juxtaposed with older views on identity that now seem more rigidly determined. Chapter 7 offers a preliminary evaluation of the coronavirus pandemic on immigration. I discuss psychological issues around threats and safety, disease, and othering, while considering what happens when a microbe does not abide by our many perimeters. Chapter 8 continues with clinical cases for when immigration occurs suddenly, and the relocation seems traumatic and imposed. There are huge psychological challenges in suddenly having to adapt to unfamiliar cultural values and norms. Chapter 9 summarizes results from a survey about images that respondents associate with their immigration experiences. Many of these images cluster into categories that appear unique to perceptions about the receiving and home countries.

Chapters 10 and 11 are concluding chapters reviewing much of the conceptual territory covered in this book. Chapter 10 examines what happens when a migration has to continue because of difficulties in resettlement. Chapter 11 reconsiders the evolving legal and political framework, while also discussing in depth what happens to our stories when they contain missing pieces. How do we make sense of them when there are big gaps, omissions, and deceptions? Many immigrant families describe the secrets and mysteries that have become integral parts of their migration story.

Hans and perimeters

Before ending this chapter, I want to look at Hans's predicament in terms of the perimeters that he faced, which were considerable. First, there was a visa that regulated his stay in the United States, a legal perimeter. Second, there was a terrible government policy that excluded him from becoming a citizen, another legal perimeter. Here we can see the constraints that begin to box an immigrant into something that imposes identity on them, especially when they are seen as undesirable.

Third, there was his adoption in Germany after his mother's death, yet another legal perimeter pertaining to how families are defined. In this instance, Hans surely needed a perimeter to be included somewhere. However, his question "Where do I belong?" expresses an essence of what I call a perimeter problem, namely, feeling excluded even when appearances seem to show a person is supposedly included as part of something. A consequence of this problem is that it invites lying, deceiving, and hiding to survive within a given perimeter. Fourth, there was a social perimeter, for what Hans described about perceptions of otherness, related to being out as a gay man in Southern Germany at that time—"stifling," to use his word. Perimeters operate anywhere, and Hans's discomfort with his prior life in Germany had to do with his feeling identified in ways he did not like.

His dream reveals an operative function of perimeters: their power to exclude and get rid of what is unwanted—when he is killed by his father. At the time, I would not have thought this, but now, I believe Hans's dream illustrates how perimeters can turn what is unwanted into something eraseable to make it invisible. Hans confirmed that he never really felt part of his second family, voicing a fourth perimeter that existed within that family. He spoke about homophobia as a discriminatory mechanism that excluded him and made a hard barrier for the social and familial perimeters he felt. His father's judgments, like a gun shot, worked oppressively to keep Hans quiet and in hiding.

Fifth, Hans associated to an historical perimeter, one especially fraught with destruction and horror, a "fatherland" that specialized in using perimeters ruthlessly and murderously. Discussion of twentieth-century German history is not going to fit into this chapter, but most readers likely have an appreciation for how its perimeters separated, devalued, and murdered people who were on the other side of religious, ethnic, cultural, and national perimeters. This period constituted a violent use of perimeters. I believe that the US HIV ban mentioned at the beginning, like the family detention policy now, are both violent applications of perimeters.

Hans returned "home," and although I wondered whether he had idealized his eventual choice to make peace with it, he apparently felt better, "like at home." He expressed a sense of inclusion that made him also feel freer. This "like at home" seems to encapsulate an attitude about ourselves in which perimeters have less sway and less power to say who we are. "Like at home" may also indicate what an immigrant hopes for in having a self that is not boxed in by the state, by the norms of the welcoming country, by cultural constraints, or by the past and history. "Like at home," at its best, implies a future to choose without being told what to do, and any immigrant would likely desire some of that.

Notes

1 Use of the word *native* can be misleading. It could mean the original inhabitants of a land, and in the case of North America, that means Native Americans and First Nations peoples. Here, for lack of a better choice, it refers to those who are citizens or longer established residents of a contemporary country.
2 Susanna E. Winston and Curt G. Beckwith, "The Impact of Removing the Immigration Ban on HIV-Infected Persons," *AIDS Patient Care and STDs* 25, no. 12 (2011): 709–711. https://doi.org/10.1089/apc.2011.0121
3 All patient identifying data is disguised to protect confidentiality. This applies throughout the book.
4 Fred Dews, "What Percentage of the U.S. Population Is Foreign Born?" Brookings, October 3, 2013, https://www.brookings.edu/blog/brookings-now/2013/10/03/what-percentage-of-u-s-population-is-foreign-born/; Abby Budiman, "Key Findings about U.S. Immigrants," *FactTank*, Pew Research Center, August 20, 2020, https://www. pewresearch. org/fact-tank/2020/08/20/key-findings-about-u-s-immigrants/
5 US numbers in this paragraph, up to the statistics about California, were excerpted from Jynnah Radford, "Key Findings about U.S. Immigrants," *FactTank*, Pew Research Center, June 17, 2019, https://www.pewresearch.org/fact-tank/2019/06/17/key-findings-about-u-s-immigrants/.
6 American Immigration Council, "Immigrants in California," August 6, 2020, https://www.americanimmigrationcouncil.org/research/immigrants-in-california
7 The National Academies of Sciences, Engineering and Medicine, *The Integration of Immigrants into American Society* (Washington, DC: The National Academies Press, 2015). Cited hereafter as NASEM (2015).
8 Ibid., 3.
9 Declaration of Independence, July 4, 1776.
10 History.com editors, "U.S. Immigration Timeline," *History*, May 14, 2019, www. history.com/topics/immigration/immigration-united-states-timeline

11 Sean Wilenz, *The Rise of American Democracy: Jefferson to Lincoln* (New York: Norton, 2005), 78.

12 Ibid., 679.

13 Wikipedia, s.v., "Know Nothing," revised September 23, 2020, https://en.wikipedia.org/wiki/Know_Nothing.

14 History.com Editors, "U.S. Immigration before 1865," *History,* updated July 25, 2020, https://www.history.com/topics/immigration/u-s-immigration-before-1965

15 David Nasaw, "Open and Shut," *New York Times Book Review,* May 24, 2020, 16.

16 NASEM (2015), p. 64.

17 Adam Liptak and Michael D. Shear, "Trump Can't Immediately End DACA, Supreme Court Rules," *New York Times,* June 18, 2020, https://www.nytimes.com/2020/06/18/us/trump-daca-supreme-court.html?searchResultPosition=7

18 Jens Manuel Krogstad, "Key Facts about Refugees to the U.S.," *FactTank,* Pew Research, October 7, 2019, https://www.pewresearch.org/fact-tank/2019/10/07/key-facts-about-refugees-to-the-u-s/

19 NASEM (2015), 60.

20 Ibid., 62.

21 Ibid., 216.

22 Bryan Caplan and Zach Weinersmith, *Open Borders: The Science and Ethics of Immigration* (New York: Roaring Brook Press, 2019).

23 Ibid., 78.

24 Austan Goolsbee, "Sharp Cuts in Immigration Threaten U.S. Economy and Innovation," *New York Times,* October 13, 2019, section BU, 4.

25 NASEM (2015), 307.

26 *The Economist,* "A World of Walls, Special Report," November 16, 2019, 4.

27 *The Economist,* "Pour décourager les autres," March 14, 2020, 42.

28 Ibid.

29 *Webster's Unabridged Dictionary,* s.v., "xenophobia," https://unabridged.merriam-webster.com/unabridged/xenophobia

30 NASEM (2015), 51.

31 Felice Blake, "Global Mass Violence: Examining Racial and Gendered Violence in the Twilight of Multiculturalism," *Ethnic and Racial Studies* 40, no. 14 (2017): 2615–2633.

32 Ibid., 2616.

33 Oksana Yakushko, "Understanding the Roots and Consequences of Negative Attitudes toward Immigrants," *The Counseling Psychologist* 37, no. 1 (2009): 36–66.

34 Gal Ariely, "Globalization, Immigration, and National Identity: How the Level of Globalization Affects the Relations between Nationalism, Constructive Patriotism and Attitudes toward Immigrants?" *Group Process and Intergroup Relations* 15, no. 4 (2011): 539–557; Wolfgang Frindke, Fredrich Funke, and Sven Waldzus, "Xenophobia and Right-Wing Extremism in German Youth Groups: Some Evidence against Unidimensional Misinterpretations," *International Journal of Intercultural Relations* 20, nos. 3 and 4 (1996): 463–478; Andreas Wimmer, "Explaining Xenophobia and Racism: A Critical Review of Current Research Approaches," *Ethnic and Racial Studies* 20, no. 1 (1997): 17–41.

35 Nilüfer Aydin et al., "Social Exclusion and Xenophobia: Intolerant Attitudes toward Ethnic and Religious Minorities," *Group Process & Intergroup Relations* 17, no. 3 (2014): 371–387.

36 Pratyusha Tummala-Narra, "The Fear of Immigrants," *Psychoanalytic Psychology* 37, no. 1 (2020): 50–61.

37 Ibid., 59.

38 "Views on Race and Immigration," *U.S. Politics & Policy,* Pew Research Center, December 17, 2019, https://www.pewresearch.org/politics/2019/12/17/views-on-race-and-immigration/

39 NASEM (2015), 19, 293.

40 Victoria M. Esses et al., "Psychological Perspectives on Immigration," *Journal of Social Issues* 66, no. 4 (2010): 635–647.

41 Maria Y. Hernandez, "Psychological Theories of Immigration," *Journal of Human Behavior in the Social Environment* 19, no. 6 (2019): 713–729.

42 Ibid., 716.

43 Lynn A. Franco, "An Immigrant's Transit: From a Multicultural Complex to a Multicultural Mind," in *Cultural Complexes and the Soul of America: Myth, Psyche, and Politics*, ed. Thomas Singer (London: Routledge, 2020), 199–218.

44 J. W. Berry, "A Psychology of Immigration," *Journal of Social Issues* 57, no. 3 (2001): 615–631.

45 Ibid., 617.

46 Ibid., 619.

47 Esther Ehrensaft and Michael Tousignant, "Immigration and Resilience," in *The Cambridge Handbook of Acculturation Psychology,* eds. David L. Sam and John W. Berry (Cambridge, UK: Cambridge University Press, 2006), 481.

48 David T. Takeuchi, "Vintage Wine in New Bottles: Infusing Select Ideas into the Study of Immigration," *Journal of Health and Social Behavior* 57, no. 4 (2016): 425.

49 S. J. Schwartz et al., "Rethinking the Concept of Acculturation," *American Psychologist* 65, no. 4 (2010): 237–251.

50 Ibid., 239.

51 Ibid., 240.

52 Ibid., 245.

53 Stephanie A. Torres et al., "Immigration Policy, Practices, and Procedures: The Impact on the Mental Health of Mexican and Central American Youth and Families," *American Psychologist* 73, no. 7 (2018): 843–854.

54 Ibid., 848.

55 Daniel Upchurch and Donna Gibson, "Strange Situation at the Border: Examining the Importance of Attachment and the Consequences of Forcible Separation," *Global Social Welfare* 7 (2020): 257–261, https://doi.org/10.1007/s40609-019-00154-3

56 Yok-Fong Paat and Robin Green, "Mental Health of Immigrants and Refugees Seeking Legal Services on the U.S.-Mexico Border," *Transcultural Psychiatry* 54, no. 5/6 (2017): 785.

57 Ibid., 788.

58 Pratyusha Tummala-Narra et al., "South Asian Adolescents' Experience of Acculturative Stress and Coping," *American Journal of Orthopsychiatry* 86, no. 2 (2016): 194–211.

59 Andres J. Pumariega and Eugenio Rothe, "Leaving No Children or Families Outside: The Challenges of Immigration," *Journal of Orthopsychiatry* 80, no. 4 (2010): 505–515.

60 Sean D. Cleary et al., "Immigrant Trauma and Mental Health Outcomes among Latino Youth," *Journal of Immigrant and Minority Health* 20 (2018): 1053–1059, https://doi.org/10.1007/s10903-017-0673-6

61 M. Von Werthern et al., "The Impact of Immigration Detention on Mental Health: A Systemic Review," *BMC Psychotherapy* 18 (2018): https://doi.org/10.1186/s12888-018-1945-y

62 Collen A. Kraft, C. "AAP Statement Opposing Separation of Children and Parent at the Border," American Academy of Pediatrics, May 8, 2018, https://docs.house.gov/meetings/IF/IF14/20180719/108572/HHRG-115-IF14-20180719-SD004.pdf

63 Sarah A. MacLean et al., "Mental Health of Children Held at a United States Immigration Detention Center," *Social Science & Medicine* 230 (2019): 303–308, https://doi.org/10.1016/j.socscimed.2019.04.013

64 Ida Kaplan et al., "Cognitive Assessment of Refugee Children: Effects of Trauma and New Language Acquisition," *Transcultural Psychiatry* 53, no. 1 (2016): 81–109.

65 Cindy Sangalang et al., "Trauma, Post-migration Stress, and Mental Health: A Comparative Analysis of Refugees and Immigrants in the United States," *Journal of Immigrant and Minority Health* 21 (2019): 909–919, https://doi.org/10.1007/s10903-018-0826-2

66 Ibid., 909–910.

67 Ibid., 912.

68 Ibid., 915.

69 Michelle Slone and Shiri Mann, "Effects of War, Terrorism and Armed Conflict on Young Children: A Systematic Review," *Child Psychiatry and Human Development* 47 (2016): 950–965, https://doi.org/10.1007/s10578-016-0626-7

70 Ibid., 958.

71 Andrea Danese, "Annual Research Review: Rethinking Childhood Trauma—New Research Directions for Measurement, Study Design and Analytical Strategies," *Journal of Child Psychology and Psychiatry* 61, no. 3 (2020): 236–250.

72 Ibid., 236.

73 Martha M. C. Elwenspoek et al., "The Effects of Early Life Adversity on the Immune System," *Psychoneuroendocrinology* 82 (2017): 140–154, http://dx.doi.org/10.1016/j.psyneuen.2017.05.012

74 Ibid.

75 Casey Paquola, Maxwell Bennett, and Jim Lagopoulos, "Understanding Heterogeneity in Grey Matter Research of Adults with Childhood Maltreatment—a Met-Analysis and Review," *Neuroscience and Biobehavioral Reviews* 69 (2016): 299–312, http://dx.doi.org/10.1016/j.neubiorev.2016.011

76 National Center for Biotechnology Information, "DSM-5 Criteria for PTSD," https://www.ncbi.nlm.nih.gov/books/NBK207191/box/part1_ch3.box16/

77 The National Child Traumatic Stress Network, "Complex Trauma," https://www.nctsn.org/what-is-child-trauma/trauma-types/complex-trauma

78 Donald Kalsched, *The Inner World of Trauma: Archetypal Defenses of the Personal Spirit* (New York: Routledge, 1996); and *Trauma and the Soul: A Psycho-spiritual Approach to Human Development and Its Interruption* (New York: Routledge, 2013).

79 Bessel Van der Kolk, *The Body Keeps the Score: Brain, Mind, and Body in the Healing of Trauma* (New York: Penguin, 2014).

80 Ibid., 181.

81 Ibid., 257.

82 Margaret Wilkinson, *Changing Minds in Therapy: Attachment, Trauma, & Neurobiology* (New York: W. W. Norton & Co., 2010).

83 Robert Tyminski, "The Substrate of Transformation in Psychotherapy and Analysis: Review of Wilkinson's *Changing Minds in Therapy: Emotion, Attachment, Trauma & Neurobiology, Jung Journal: Culture & Psyche* 5, no. 2 (2011): 128–132.

84 Theresa S. Betancourt et al., "Comparing Trauma Exposure, Mental Health Needs, and Service Utilization across Clinical Samples of refugee, Immigrant, and U.S.-Origin Youth," *Journal of Traumatic Stress* 30 (June 2017): 209–218.

85 Ibid., 209.

86 Lloy Wylie et al., "Assessing Trauma in a Transcultural Context: Challenges in Mental Health Care with Immigrants and Refugees," *Public Health Reviews* 39 (2018): https://doi.org/10.1186/s40985-018-0102-y

87 Orit Nuttman-Shwartz and Yael Shoval-Zuckerman, "Continuous Traumatic Situations in the Face of Ongoing Political Violence: The Relationship between CTS and PTSD," *Trauma, Violence, & Abuse* 17, no. 5 (2016): 562–570.

88 Laura Ramo-Fernández et al., "Epigenetic Alterations Associated with War Trauma and Childhood Maltreatment," *Behavioral Sciences and the Law* 33 no. 5 (2015): 701–721, https://doi.org/10.1002/bsl.2200

89 Nicole R. Nugent, Amy Goldberg, and Monica Uddin, "Topical Review: The Emerging Field of Epigenetics: Informing Models of Pediatric Trauma and Physical Health," *Journal of Pediatric Psychology* 41, no. 1 (2015): 55–64.

90 Nicole Gröger et al. "The Transgenerational Transmission of Childhood Adversity: Behavioral, Cellular, and Epigenetic Correlates," *Journal of Neural Transmission* 123 (2016): 1037, https://doi.org/10.1007/s00702-016-1570-1

91 Ibid., 1038.

92 Ibid., 1045.

93 Justyna Kucharska, "Religiosity and the Psychological Outcomes of Trauma: A Systematic Review Of Quantitative Studies," *Journal of Clinical Psychology* 76, no. 1 (2020): 40–58, https://doi.org/10.1002/jclp.22867

94 C. G. Jung, *The Archetypes and the Collective Unconscious,* vol. 9i, *The Collected Works of C. G. Jung* (Princeton: Princeton University Press, 1959). Hereafter, references to Jung's *Collected Works* will appear as Jung, title, date, and volume number in the *Collected Works* (CW).

95 Ibid., para. 89.

96 Ibid., 43, para. 90.

97 Ibid., 49, para. 100.

98 G. S. Conway and Richard Stoneman, trans., *The Odes and Selected Fragments: Pindar* (London: Orion, 1997).

99 Robert Tyminski, *The Psychology of Theft and Loss: Stolen and Fleeced* (London: Routledge, 2014), 37.

100 Ibid., 34–37.

101 Jung, *Symbols of Transformation* (1912/1956), CW 5, xxiv.

102 Thomas Singer and Samuel Kimbles, *The Cultural Complex: Contemporary Jungian Perspectives on Psyche and Society* (New York, Routledge, 2004).

103 Ibid., 19.

104 Ibid., 4.

105 Ibid., 210.

106 Julia Beltsiou, ed. *Immigration in Psychoanalysis: Locating Ourselves* (London: Routledge, 2016).

107 Ibid., 6.

108 Francisco González, "Only What Is Human Can Truly Be Foreign: The Trope of Immigration as a Creative Force in Analysis," in *Immigration in Psychoanalysis: Locating Ourselves,* ed. Julia Beltsiou (London: Routledge, 2016), 25.

109 Ghislaine Boulanger, "Seeing Double, Being Double: Longing, Belonging, Recognition, and Evasion in Psychodynamic Work with Immigrants," in *Immigration in Psychoanalysis: Locating Ourselves,* ed. Julia Beltsiou (London: Routledge, 2016), 55.

110 Ricardo Ainslie, "Immigration and the Psychodynamics of Class," *Psychoanalytic Psychology* 28, no. 4 (2011): 560–568.

111 Ricardo Ainslie et al., "Contemporary Psychoanalytic Views on the Experience of Immigration," *Psychoanalytic Psychology,* 30, no. 4 (2013): 664.

112 Luis Vazquez, "Integration of Multicultural and Psychoanalytic Concepts: A Review of Three Case Examples with Women of Color," *Psychoanalytic Psychology* 31, no. 3 (2014): 439.

113 Ibid.

114 Frank Summer, "Ethnic Invisibility, Identity, and the Analytic Process," *Psychoanalytic Psychology* 31, no. 3 (2014): 410–425.

115 Andrew Harlem, "Exile as a Dissociative State: When a Self Is "Lost in Transit," *Psychoanalytic Psychology* 27, no. 4 (2010): 460–474.
116 Caroline S. Clauss-Ehlers et al., "APA Multicultural Guidelines Executive Summary: Ecological Approach to Context, Identity, and Intersectionality," *American Psychologist* 74, no. 2 (2019): 232–244.
117 Ibid., 233.
118 C. G. Jung, *Psychological Types* (1971), CW 6, para. 800.
119 Ibid., para. 801.

Chapter 2

"Just Black Sometimes"

"I walked at night. Always in the dark, no lights. It was hard to see. Just black sometimes." A seventeen-year-old Syrian refugee told me this as he described his flight from Syria. He walked from Syria, through Turkey, across the Balkans all the way to Austria. He was fifteen and a half when he made this night-time journey.

Like others, I find myself struggling as an analyst to make sense of the interface between the private workings in my office and the chaotic happenings in the world. Many of my patients come in deeply troubled by current political events, social and health problems, such as the coronavirus pandemic, racial injustice manifested by the horrendous murdering of black men by the police, the rabid politics stoked by demagogic leaders, and gun violence in schools, which not coincidentally has decreased because of school closures during the pandemic. Patients frequently report nightmares of doom and apocalypse. One young man told me as wildfires then raged around the San Francisco Bay Area, turning the sky orange-red and blocking out the sun, "We're living the apocalypse." Many of them appear increasingly anxious and troubled about what to do—how can they make their voices heard in meaningful ways? I try to understand their sufferings and to explore the unconscious factors contributing to them. Yet an immediate experience of chaos can feel so real to us that it often defies just maintaining a psychological attitude of integrating it without also acting on it. Not too long ago, another patient asked me with visible worry, "Do you think we'll survive Trump?" Realizing that there are many approaches to this question, I replied, "We are in a mess, and I really don't know." We sat silently for a bit.

Before becoming an analyst, I had studied and lived in Berlin and still have personal contacts there. In 2017, I decided to go to Berlin to offer consultation to a program that provides housing and social services to refugees who had entered Germany as unaccompanied minors. Previously I worked as director of a mental health center for youth and their families, and later, I provided organizational consultation to NGOs (non-governmental organizations) that treated the severely mentally ill, homeless families, and children with special needs. Importantly for this topic, my analytic practice includes a

DOI: 10.4324/9781003119593-2

great deal of work with children and adolescents, many of whom are in immigrant families that came to the United States. At the mental health center in San Francisco where I had worked as director, I supervised clinical and educational services for refugee families that had fled from Central America and Southeast Asia.

Before my trip to Berlin, I read news stories about the ordeals of Middle Eastern refugees coming to Germany; I reviewed many articles about psychological trauma; and I spoke with others who had worked with refugee populations. Once there, I met with the organization's staff, administrators, and the adolescents they worked with. In this chapter, where I focus on my encounters with staff and administrators, I discuss some of the compelling and memorable experiences that made me more aware that migration is a never-ending piece of human history.[1] It will always be with us, and how a society handles it is decisive for whether we side with humane outreach or whether we retreat behind fences and walls.

At the time, I was curious what someone like me, a Jungian analyst and psychologist, could offer to this program. Would it be helpful? How was I going to feel switching from the relative safety of my private practice to the frontlines of a complex and fraught social situation? Which analytic tools would be useful to me and which would not? I went with some anxiety, knowing that it probably would not be easy for me coming in as an outsider, a foreigner, both to Germany and to Middle Eastern cultures.

Analysis out there

After my return to San Francisco, when I tried for a long while to metabolize the experiences I had in Berlin, I read an essay by Andrew Samuels with great interest.[2] He reinforced for me that we can be active in many creative ways that make use of our analytic skills outside the frame of our private practices. In this piece, Samuels quotes Jung's short introduction to his *Essays on Contemporary Events*. I find Jung's preface to be especially applicable to our current troubled times when we are beset with many epidemics:

> We are living in times of great disruption: political passions are aflame, internal upheavals have brought nations to the brink of chaos ... the doctor must follow its effects with more than usual attention ... he feels the violence of its impact even in the quiet of his consulting room and in the privacy of the medical consultation. As he has a responsibility towards his patients, he cannot afford to withdraw... Were he to remain aloof from the tumult, the calamity of his time would reach him only from afar, and his patient's suffering would find neither ear nor understanding.[3]

Jung emphasizes here that analysts, who insulate themselves from real contact with social and political forces such as discrimination, marginalization, health disparities, government-sanctioned violence, and the consequences of in-equality, risk offering a half-baked experience to their patients. Withdrawal from these realities would transport any of us, intentionally or not, into a position of privilege and entitlement. It further communicates an elitist no-tion that psyche exists separate from social and political occurrences. Using Jung's alchemical language, it would be as if I were working only within the vessel, keeping myself isolated from anything else happening in the sur-rounding laboratory, even if it were on fire. Younger patients and consultees find this attitude of what I call "psyche in isolation" particularly hard to relate to, because it is too separate, too cordoned off. Samuels, however, encourages analysts to view Jung's warning as solid counsel for becoming involved in the social arena. He argues that Jung's ideas are "expressive of a collective ago-nizing over what is meant by 'the West,'" and that Jungians can provide insight into the cultural dimensions of this problem that include alienation, excessive rationality, and continued attacks on the ecosystem.[4] After Berlin, my hope is not only to help patients discover how to express their outrage, but also to support organizations promoting awareness for multiplicity, integra-tion of shadow, and bridging differences.

In Berlin, the staff were interested in what "fresh eyes" might see that they couldn't. Thus, they expressed a value in my otherness, a freedom that consultants have when their assignments are temporary and they are not part of the organizational culture. I was impressed by how administrators worked to smooth my way, as various bureaucratic approvals were necessary to make my participation happen. I liked the idea of "fresh eyes" because it seemed to welcome bringing in something unknown to create a possibility of change. I also considered the shadow side of "fresh eyes" as being whatever cultural complexes I would bring along. As I spent time with the staff, I wanted to create a space where they could express their experiences with the refugee youth. I had hoped we would think together about what feelings came up regarding the emotional currents within their daily routines. Clearly trauma would be a central theme.

Context for meeting

After introducing myself via email to a team leader at this organization, we arranged the details of my visit and how I would provide consultation. I indicated that I would like to write about this experience, and the organi-zation gave me permission to do so, asking that I avoid using their actual business name. I will use a pseudonym referring to it as the *Frei Center*. *Frei* is the German word for *free*.

The Center provides residential apartments and social services to ado-lescents who are separated from their families. Since 2015, they have mostly been serving a refugee population. Previously, many of their clients were German; however, they made an abrupt transition to handle the flurry of placements needed for refugees. Their referrals came through city's *Jugendamt* (youth services for the city of Berlin). Their client base included twenty adolescents, 75 percent of whom were boys, settled in shared residential apartments throughout the city. To qualify for intake, they must have been separated from their parents.

Most of them were refugees from Syria and Afghanistan. There are over 80 million forcibly displaced persons worldwide, of which more than 25 million are officially designated as refugees.[5] A refugee is someone whose claim for asylum is recognized under international treaties from the 1950s, whereby he or she is "someone who has been forced to flee his or her country because of persecution, war, or violence, and has a well-founded fear of persecution for reasons of race, religion, nationality, political opinion or membership in a particular social group."[6] Their status usually means that their lives are at risk. Over 5 million refugees have come from Syria, with the second largest number coming from Afghanistan, with over 2 million.[7] Turkey hosts most refugees, with nearly 3 million. Asylum seekers, although having much in common with refugees, do not have the same legal standing within receiving countries such as Germany and the United States. An asylum seeker must have their claim for asylum substantiated.

Unaccompanied minors—children and adolescents separated from their parents—accounted, in 2016, for about 75,000 asylum applications, and Germany received the largest number, more than 35,000. For all ages, Germany received more than 720,000 asylum applications in 2016, and Syrians composed the largest group, with more than 260,000.[8] By comparison, the United States received the second highest number of asylum requests, just over 260,000. Asylum is a legal form of protection or sanctuary granted by the host country to refugees and is not easily obtained.[9] In Germany, refugees from Syria are usually granted an initial three-year permit to remain. Those from Afghanistan receive a permit for one year. Afghanis do not qualify for asylum in Germany because Afghanistan is regarded as a secure country of origin, therefore many of them may try to gain a psychological exception to prevent deportation. Because of a backlog, it can take two to three years to obtain an appointment for a hearing about an asylum application.

Adolescents at the Center ranged in age from sixteen to eighteen; anyone older than fifteen was eligible for the program. Afghanis usually speak Dari, a language similar to Farsi. English was used as a bridging language because most clients knew little or no German. The Syrians speak Arabic, and on average they seemed to have more years of formal schooling before their arrival in Germany. The Center assessed their social and educational needs and provided referrals to programs and schools to support the clients in meeting these. Clients often did not want to leave their apartments—a recurring obstacle—and so follow-through with attendance at school and for other appointments was erratic.

In my initial meeting with the Center's director, I asked her to describe a typical day for a client. She told me that residents were expected to attend school or vocational training. Many, however, reported severe sleep disturbances and frequently missed. They also described feeling fatigued secondary to panic and fear about their new circumstances. Staff at the Center estimated that only 50 percent were able to complete the demands of German schools or job training. The others did little, staying in their apartments, or hanging out on the streets with other refugees. The behaviors the director described—insomnia, nightmares, intense anxiety, and apathy—indicated a high incidence of psychological trauma and its aftermath.

I inquired about drug use, which was reported to be very high; possibly 90 percent of clients smoked marijuana. Of these, the majority were thought to be regular users. I wondered, as I heard this, about self-medication and a need for many troubled adolescents to dissociate from psychological pain. I asked where clients got the funds to purchase their drugs. Apparently they obtained them through a kind of barter economy, doing favors for others and possibly engaging in sex. Only one refugee had completed the most rigorous form of German schooling for teens, the Gymnasium. Others who went to school mostly attended a less demanding type of school where they could leave after tenth grade with a German diploma of *Mittlere Reife*, meaning "middle maturity." This diploma is sufficient to find work in various service-sector jobs.

The Center hosted a weekly community meeting at the main office, and attendance varied. Topics included aspects of German society that the teens found confusing, such as a preference for formality in everyday conversations. One of the Center's goals is to help refugees integrate into German society. As such, they were sometimes placed in apartments with German teenagers, who themselves were part of the social services system. The purpose of this arrangement was to promote peer adjustment and socialization. Clients were expected to take classes that the Center offered on German society, for example, about sexual norms and gender equality. I asked how effective these classes were. Staff reported that an adolescent's cultural background outweighed an appreciation for what more commonly held, modern German attitudes may be, but there was a hope to foster increased tolerance for how German society has different perspectives on gender and sexuality. The high point for placements was in 2015, when circumstances were chaotic and boys slept on streets and in parks across the city. Many were placed in youth hostels at the time.

An ongoing difficulty for the Center's staff was the prevalence of wide-ranging psychiatric problems in the refugees. Suicidal thoughts and self-harming behaviors were challenging to detect and, when discovered, to manage given the limited staffing. The Center's staff tried their best to monitor alarm signals, such as isolation and threatening behaviors. Between 2015 and 2017, the Center had to hospitalize three residents for serious psychiatric reasons. Many received outpatient psychiatric care for suicidal thoughts, depression, and trauma from before their flight, mistreatment during their flight, and physical and sexual abuse from traffickers. As we discussed these psychological problems, I noticed a heaviness in me and a sense of being overwhelmed from the staff. It was like facing a gaping hole without any possibility of crossing it. The staff most likely held in themselves a variety of negative and destructive projections emanating from their close work with the young refugees. How did they cope with such suffering? The staff expressed an interest in my facilitating a workshop on adolescent development and trauma. Before discussing this workshop, I will provide a brief description of the asylum process and relevant staff-client interactions, because the clients depended on the staff to help them make it through the bureaucratic hurdles to remain in Germany.

Becoming a refugee

To qualify for legal status as an asylum-seeker, a teenager must have a convincing narrative that he can communicate to the authorities.[10] As this process creates much anxiety, the Center tries to help adolescents prepare. The young refugees must be able to report the following in detail: (a) what happened in their country of origin that caused them to leave; (b) what happened during their flight; and (c) how they are adjusting to German society. An incomplete story can result in a determination that they do not qualify for asylum. Their stories commonly involved descriptions of having been transported with many others, crammed into trucks during a trip that was dark and cold.

Many of the young people did not have papers and claimed to be younger than eighteen, even when they looked older. Those who look older are asked to obtain a health examination to verify that they are not lying about their age. There is a legal exception available for psychiatric disturbance that can support an asylum application, but this requires an evaluation and treatment by a mental health professional.

Staff described what, based on their experiences, a boy from Syria might face in this legal maze. He must ask for asylum before his eighteenth birthday in Germany to obtain a three-year residence permit. Within the German legal system, there is absolutely no latitude around this cut-off date. If a Syrian boy's parents eventually hope to follow him, they must apply for a visa at a German embassy in Istanbul or Beirut, not an easy journey to undertake because of the ongoing war. At first, a boy separated from his family has considerable freedom. However, if his family succeeds in making it to Germany, then this freedom would be abruptly curtailed. Staff described how, in these refugee families, father is boss, and that family reunification tended to bring strife for those young men who had arrived earlier.

I asked how the staff assisted the adolescents with their asylum interviews. Staff have learned not to intrude in asking too much about each client's history, since the boys especially would become uncommunicative. They did not aim for a therapeutic intervention; instead, they used an active listening approach as well as motivational interviewing techniques. Among the clients, there was significant mistrust of staff, whose authority was regarded with suspicion. A relationship must be built before an adolescent would tell a staff member what he had been through. To hear about this mistrust did not surprise me. Adolescence is a period of development when mistrust of parents and elders is normative, and this usually plays out in an adolescent's navigation of autonomy and dependence issues. Yet, as an analyst working with adolescents, I was aware too that, when there has been a history of abuse, violence, and mistreatment, this mistrust can become impenetrable. I wondered how the Center's staff addressed problems when the young refugees were avoidant.

The staff mostly faced real problems as they arose, for example, specific conflicts that the refugees had around school, drug use, or with roommates. Their approach was geared toward being matter-of-fact without implying negative judgments. Nonetheless, they found that many adolescents reacted to them with shame and pulled away. Staff modeled sensitivity and empathy, and they hoped this would reduce avoidant behaviors. There was, however, an inherent conflict dynamic because the young refugees regarded the staff's influence as both positive and negative, and they feared the repercussions of someone in power retaliating against them. To their credit, the staff were aware of this and strived to not act out an aggressor-victim dynamic, which many of the adolescents seemingly pulled for.

Personal narratives are regularly created and revised during adolescence. In the case of the Frei Center's clients, questions such as "why have you left your country?" and "why did you come here?" were woven into these adolescents' stories. I asked the staff what they understood to be answers to these questions. They replied that many adolescents came to Germany because their families had placed expectations on them; they were told to flee to find a better future elsewhere. This demand was expressed more often to sons than daughters. Often the family had communicated that they would not follow the son, and he would be on his own. This rationale has a fairytale quality to it, the wanderer striking out to find treasure while leaving the poor parents behind. Yet for these children who lived the "fairytale" it can be all too dangerous and entail suffering severe traumas.

A workshop on adolescence and trauma

For a June in Berlin, the weather is sunny, pleasant, and warm. It is late morning when I get off the subway, which I still know well from my student days. I walk along a familiar street, although it has become more commercialized and many buildings have been renovated in the intervening years. Along the street-level are businesses—cellphone and clothing shops,

Turkish grocery stores, florists, bakeries, and hip cafes. On each block large, leafy linden trees spring out the sidewalk. The Center director requests that the workshop include a discussion of trauma and dissociation during adolescence. The staff are interested in vicarious trauma that is passed on to caregivers and support persons, as they often report feeling like they are in the presence of something awful that is not communicated verbally. Early in the workshop, one staff member describes feeling like she is being given something she does not want, having it forced on her, and feeling repelled, yet somehow, being powerless. This is a good description of projective identification and shows the nonverbal transmission of deep suffering. I am aware of how disturbing their work often must be. I wonder how I might react to feeling some of this disturbance in myself. I've come prepared with an outline and pages of notes about adolescent development and an overview of trauma. I have spent hours preparing and wish I had a PowerPoint presentation to guide me, but that is not to be. But I do not want to lecture; my main goal is to have engaged conversation.

We sit in a large room adjacent to the street in one of Berlin's old buildings from before World War I. The Center is housed in what had probably been, at one time, a large apartment. There is coffee and cake on the table. I introduce myself. I explain that I am organizing the workshop into four segments, a choice that I realize is overly ambitious: the role of initiation in later adolescent development, a discussion of trauma, the effects of dissociation, and the passing on of traumatic affects (via projective identification). As I look at the expectant faces around me, I realize the scope of what I am planning reflects a great unmet need that I sensed from my earlier interactions with them, and I recognize that I will not be able to satisfy that need. As we begin, I comment that I can only offer a taste of these topics and suggest they might later desire to go into them more deeply. I propose we use the informal German *Du* instead of the formal *Sie* in addressing each other, commenting that they can attribute this to my coming from California. Heads nod in agreement, and many of them smile, although I later realize that I am managing my anxiety at this moment by suggesting we can be informal.

Initiation

There are ten in the group, a mix of administrators, support staff, social workers, teachers, and interns from local universities. I invite them to introduce themselves and encourage each of them to tell me a little about their backgrounds. Many identify as having grown up in the former German Democratic Republic (GDR); another is an immigrant herself; others are Berliners who had seen their city change dramatically within their lifetimes. I think about all the social and personal transformations they describe, all of which reflect migration, movement, and assimilation. East Germany was essentially absorbed into West Germany in 1990.

I begin by discussing what happens in the transition from middle to late adolescence, because this age range included most of their clients. I frame it as a time of initiation during which a young person begins to take stock of moving into adulthood. I tell them how Joseph Henderson's seminal contribution informs my thinking about initiation, specifically his ideas about an emergent process surrounding a point in time when perspectives about our past and our future change and reorient us.[11] Henderson, in *Thresholds of Initiation*, discusses how many myths and folktales depict a seven-step process of initiation that begins with separation and submission; crossing a threshold, a person realizes something is about to change and he will never be the same as before.[12] Afterward, trials of strength ensue that test whether he can make it through to the end. During these steps there must be some kind of containment. This model of initiation captures significant elements of a refugee's journey. About half of the group are taking notes, and I encourage them to ask me questions.

On arriving in Germany, a refugee is no longer the same as he was "before." Narratives about such journeys can vary across a spectrum of drama and detailed content. There might be a complete story about having been a child who grew up in a foreign land; or it might be one compressed and truncated with missing pieces; or it might even disintegrate into a few unrelated facts, barren of meaning. Regardless of spoken form, a migrant usually has a sense that he has departed from the known and will not turn back. Thoughts of what comes "after" generate questions like "What will become of me?" In later adolescence this question takes on urgency because it casts a view into the future conveying many pressures associated with breaking through to the next stage of life. I mention to the group an example from a paper in which I describe how many adolescent boys literally have to break something, a surface, as a manifestation of this passage.[13] A teacher then speaks up about a boy in the program. "Omar has made many holes hitting the wall of his room, and the doctor finally told him he had to see a psychiatrist."

I outline how initiation occurs within the context of a social group and is also culturally informed; this is an aspect of the containment that Henderson describes. Different groups, which encircle and envelop us, establish models for behaviors, norms, goals, achievements, and failure. Without a group, alienation sets in, and even when there appears to be a form of belonging to a group, this can be problematic if the group is organized to be psychologically anti-growth. (After my trip to Berlin, I was inspired to write a book exploring how many boys and men become alienated and what can go wrong.[14]) A central conflict in later adolescence pertains to a young man's orientation to the future and whether he perceives it as hopeful, uncertain, or discouraging. Often nostalgia and unresolved mourning can impede the redirection required at this time of life.

I invite the group in Berlin to talk about what initiation brings up that relates to their work. A teacher coordinating educational materials for the refugees at the Center mentions the difficulties they have with separation. I reflect how separation anxieties come to the fore when a developing personality navigates becoming a self with clear desires and ambitions. This process involves much trial and error, and I mention that Erik Erikson wrote about it in his work on identity crisis.[15] Risks are taken to explore how far a person can go. Choices have to be made about education, career, love, intimate relationships, and sexual orientation. Coping with separation entails balancing needs for dependence and independence. A young man might struggle with holding this tension. He might feel defeated, collapsing into helplessness or alienation, or he might assert an omnipotent belief that he can handle life totally on his own. Consciousness that this is not a choice of "either/or" but rather of "both/and" can be hard to gain.

The effects of trauma

I move the group into the next segment: what happens when trauma disrupts development? They are all well aware that trauma is psychologically devastating for development. I give a useful research-based definition of post-traumatic stress disorder (PTSD): it is "a condition that severely disrupts individuals' capacity to perceive, represent, integrate, and act on internal and external stimuli because of major disruptions in the neural systems associated with attention, working memory, and the processing of affective stimuli."[16]

This description emphasizes a psychosomatic interface of trauma that scrambles a person's capacities for stable relationships with himself and others. Although psychologists assess an ability for resilience, what a person needs to recover from trauma is not always apparent. Time can pass before a suitable approach is found that helps with recovery. Research shows that for children, a one-time trauma can be experienced without damage to development such as an impairment of perceptual or cognitive skills.[17] Two traumatic instances, however, impress an emotional complexity on the developing mind and require therapeutic intervention to recover and get back on track. Both educational and psychotherapeutic modalities may be necessary. And, when trauma is cumulative—multiple incidents over time—research indicates that damage to psychological and physical health happens more frequently and at clinically significant levels.[18] For example, Kira et al., in a study on trauma, conclude that "cumulative trauma dynamics have total negative significant effects on all of the four IQ components: perceptual reasoning, working memory, processing speed, and verbal comprehension."[19] Betancourt et al., looking at war-affected refugee children, have found that academic and behavioral problems are prevalent with high levels of PTSD, generalized anxiety, and somatization.[20] Discussing trauma in the refugee context, Rene Papadopoulos explores the topic of resilience and when adversity might activate development.[21] Most of these authors recognize that the needs of refugee children are intense and, if not addressed, the psychosomatic effects can become permanent. Many staff at the Frei Center believe that their clients fit the category of cumulative trauma. They also speak about the psychosomatic issues they have heard about, like headaches, skin conditions, gastrointestinal problems, and even neurological symptoms affecting memory and perception—they feel lost in trying to understand the wide array of problems their clients present them with on a daily basis. Midway through the workshop, we take a short break, although the group is eager to keep it short and resume.

Dissociation

Following our break, we venture on to a related phenomenon that they encounter regularly in their interactions with clients: dissociation. They all know that psychic fragmentation occurs as a result of, and as a way to cope with, repeated traumatic incidents. I explain that this fragmentation begins as a defensive maneuver; however, it can turn into a structural organization of the psyche. I introduce them to the work of Donald Kalsched, whom they have not heard of and who formulated the useful concept of a self-care system to explain what happens in states of fragmentation.[22] A self-care system both protects a person from further external trauma while continually subjecting them to internal persecution and agony. Anne Alvarez, a British psychoanalyst, discusses therapeutic challenges in working with children and adolescents who appear unreachable and hardened because of their chronic mistrust and withdrawal.[23] Both Kalsched and Alvarez explore the interpersonal deficits arising from fragmentation of the psyche. Whenever this happens, psychic growth stalls, as if a kind of anti-growth force has taken control of the personality.

I tell the group about an example of dissociation that has stayed with me since I worked at a mental health center and school where many children suffered from cumulative trauma. A nine-year-old African American boy, Gus, had witnessed gun violence that claimed the life of an uncle on their front steps. Gus often blanked out into dissociated states. In a session with his therapist, Gus described, "It starts in my belly. I think I'm getting a cramp, but it moves up into my chest. I feel like I can't breathe, and it moves into my head. My eyes go funny. Then, it's like I go outside my head, like I'm floating above it, just waiting up there." I was supervisor of Gus's therapist. When she told me that she had goosebumps hearing him say this, I said that was a clue that she had would have to help him get back into his own skin.

The workshop group nods as I share this experience, a remarkable description from a child of the psychosomatic unfolding of dissociation and his therapist's own somatic response. Several mention that they have witnessed episodes of dissociation when their clients seemed to disappear right in front of them: "He just blanks out"; "I can tell he's not with me"; "He's gone." A few in the group worry and ask if these observations indicate brain trauma or neurological injury. I reply that intense emotional pain can lead to someone wanting to be gone, far away and not even in their own body. Others in the group describe their clients speaking in a monotone, with no emotion, and how odd and unsettling this manner of speaking feels. Sometimes they are unsure whether these clients have heard them or re-member what they were saying.

Over time, severe dissociation consumes valuable psychic energy and puts a child or adolescent at risk for losing developmental opportunities. It affects learning whenever it happens during classes because attention and recall are impaired. Members of the workshop group express concern for how PTSD will affect a refugee's potential adjustment and integration. "Could it be severe enough to stop that?" A teacher in the group notes that many refugees struggle with learning problems. Clearly, they are not living up to their potential (compared to before the war in their country). Another in the group reports that refugees often find learning German extremely difficult. As language students, they seem caught by something that freezes their cognitive scope, as if they are emotionally hindered from learning a new language. Without oversimplifying this observation about learning German, I wonder if perhaps their mother tongue holds them captive, in a primal attachment to their original language. That frozen attachment can represent unresolved grief over losing so much. Some of the Center's clients start psychotherapy, but many do not because, culturally, they view it as a weakness; it is shame-inducing. There are relatively few practicing therapists in their home countries, and therapy is frequently perceived among them as both foreign and intrusive.

I encourage the group to consider the multiple implications of dissociation—that perception can be blocked, that it is disturbing to wit-ness, that it is disorienting. Time gets lost with little difference in yesterday, today, or tomorrow. Memory becomes compromised and the intake of new information limited. As a result there are holes in the fabric of experience, and between them there are no meaningful connections. Confirming this, staff describe how at times clients report vastly different stories about events in their lives yet do not appear to be lying. It is as if their fragmentation imposes various psychic realities on them, and this distortion controls what they communicate. As a defense this can appear to be splitting, for example, shifting without awareness between love/hate or idealization/devaluation. Yet, as a structure of the psyche, Jung notes that autonomous complexes "behave like independent beings" and, as he recognized, they might origi-nate in trauma after which they can "interfere with the intentions of the will and disturb the conscious performance."[24] Helpers understandably feel confused when this occurs, because they are unsure of the accuracy and consistency of what is being reported to them. Their clients may also not know whether something is true or not when they are in dissociated states of mind. Intense dissociation leaves voids in relationships and, when a basis for trust is necessary, these holes are disruptive to that.

Vicarious trauma

The final topic is vicarious trauma. By the last hour of the workshop, which is scheduled to last a total of three hours, I am feeling a bit of trauma myself, because the refugees' stories, which some in the group have related, are dire and horrifying. Vicarious trauma occurs when caregivers unconsciously absorb the psychic pain and disorientation of those with whom they are working closely. The entire workshop group confirms that they have had this experience. Everyone. I remark that empathy is for us an occupational hazard, when it creates deep and painful unconscious links between clients and their caregivers. Much of our analytic understanding about vicarious trauma comes from psychological studies of families with intergenerational trauma, for example, Holocaust survivors. Haydée Faimberg examines this intergenerational dynamic and the projective intrusion of a secret by a parent into a child, following which the parent regards the child with alienation and avoidance.[25] Attempting to explain how something that is unconscious and unspoken gets passed on to others, she hypothesizes an intrusion-alienation sequence to account for some cases when a child's psyche is appropriated by a parent to pass along traumatic experiences. Samuel Kimbles, in his examination of a similar phenomenon, finds that it can occur in groups, families, workplaces, and even societies, and he calls the unconscious aspect that emerges a "phantom narrative."[26] Because these things occur nonverbally, there is usually bewilderment in the psyche of the recipient of these projections. When they land, they often create over-whelming emotions for what feels like no apparent reason.

As I notice the clock on the wall and that we only have twenty minutes left, the workshop suddenly becomes strangely activated. Everyone in the group seems pressured to discuss more about vicarious trauma with their adolescent refugee clients. All at once, each of them has a story they want to share. One worker reports breaking into tears after work and not under-standing why; another says her insomnia feels confusing because she nor-mally sleeps well. Someone else mentions afternoon headaches that she vaguely associates with the morning routine of crises, missed appointments, and phone calls from police and other bureaucratic departments. Trying to find my own footing amid what seems cathartic, I offer that helpers' own previous emotional histories can resonate unconsciously around the wounds and suffering of our clients. I interject the idea of the wounded healer, and almost everyone in the group affirms that it applies to them. But this happens quickly, perhaps because we are coming to the end of the con-sultation and the group did not want to stop. I ask which feeling best describes their own experiences at work, and a social worker replies, "Helpless." The others in the group mutually endorse helplessness as a huge professional challenge in setting limits about what is reasonable to expect of themselves.

This final part, when we discuss helplessness, evokes parallels between what staff feel and what their clients feel. It is a form of projective identification, but I do not want to bring that term into the discussion because I prefer hearing about the group's feelings. Staff are frequently in the dark about details of how the refugees made it to Berlin, what happened in route. For many of the refugees, those stories are probably too upsetting to tell, and likewise, only a few of the adolescents are comfortable revealing much about what they had experienced of the war in Syria. However, the refugees eventually have to tell their story when their asylum claim is heard, and if their personal stories told to administrative judges are too thin, it could result in a negative decision about whether they can stay. A staff social worker from another Middle Eastern country who had immigrated to Germany as a refugee herself decades ago reports that clients often do not believe she was a refugee. She thinks that they cannot conceive of her having past hardship given her current position. Sadly, their disbelief expresses the depleting effect of trauma on an ability to foresee a better future for themselves.

Feedback

When the clock finally reaches the three-hour mark, I ask the group to take ten to fifteen minutes to give me feedback about the workshop experience. Nearly all say that they enjoyed the range of topics, especially an application of theoretical ideas to their work. Many note how the trauma of dislocation feeds into intractable help-refusal behaviors among their clients. There are many examples of what looks like self-sabotage. One person comments that clients often see that they are not learning and adjusting because of their emotional issues. Some refugees might feel resistance to learning German, especially because proficiency means they have a better way to communicate about trauma that they prefer not to speak of. Additionally, many clients do not like feeling dependent, which they are by definition of being in the program. Although developmentally still in late adolescence, they may perceive requirements contingent for their housing and securing their legal status as punitive restrictions on their autonomy. Many clients become resentful of staff, and they often demonstrate this through avoidant behaviors, including passivity and becoming uncommunicative. Their assertiveness and strength in fleeing to Germany through harrowing situations, to start their lives over, may have paradoxically reinforced a manic self-image of not needing others.

In speaking about what else might support their clients with their adjustment to Germany, I ask about the role of religion. Most of the clients are not religious and do not attend a local mosque, of which there are many in Berlin. They may, however, claim that they are practicing Muslims, but, as a staff member says, they do not "walk the walk." Spiritual concerns do not seem among their more pressing needs.

Staff struggle with the prevalence of lying, especially when it seems intentional. Lying is part of adolescent development, of learning to have privacy. Alessandra Lemma writes about lying and notes that it can serve as self-preservation and protection. I wonder whether staff are dealing with lying that helps a person to hide in order to feel safe.[27] They observe that lying occurs in discussions about money, belongings, appointments, school attendance, and drug use. They do not want to put themselves in a position of judging morality and truth and so they downplay any overt evidence of a lie. Naming the lie makes the mistrust all too apparent and staff feel this would be counterproductive. They prefer to sidestep labeling that could seem derogatory and instead speak about their clients "telling stories." They find that using this euphemism makes the numerous deceptions they encounter feel more normative and less manipulative. These linguistic acrobatics may help staff to not feel taken advantage of in doing what is extremely difficult work. I have great respect for the immensity of what they share with me and for what they carry, working on the frontlines of this international trauma.

Discussion

I want to address three aspects of my experiences consulting to the staff at the Frei Center: (1) a revealing countertransference reaction; (2) the consultant as an outsider to the group; and (3) a commentary about social activism during troubled times. Back to Berlin: when I leave the workshop, the sun is still shining on a late afternoon. I am aware of feeling exhausted and I decide that I will go to a neighborhood café that I visited just two days before. As I've mentioned, this area of Berlin is familiar to me. Walking here, however, I begin to feel disoriented and unsure of the location of the café. I look around, and although I recall seeing many of these stores and shops, they somehow provide me no reference, and I feel confused and lost. Thinking I might have to return to my hotel, I even become uncertain of where the subway entrance is. That is surprising because I still know the Berlin subways fairly well from when I lived in the city years ago.

After several minutes of feeling lost in a recognizable environment, I find the café. Relieved, I go in and order coffee and begin writing in my notebook about what has just happened. That I am tired makes sense. I facilitated the workshop in German, not my first language by any stretch. But I slowly realize that my feeling lost has something to do with a feeling left over from the workshop—one I find difficult to name exactly. There was a fleeting awareness of something jarring when I went from inside the Center to outside. Does this sense of losing my bearings have to do with the group's discussions at the end of the workshop? About when the familiar is unreliable and instead becomes disorienting?

Looking back at my emotional response, I believe that I might have carried a piece of a split that the refugees and the staff unconsciously felt in their interactions—that what should be normal is not, what should be clear is not, what should be familiar is not. Considering this chaotic experience of a rug being pulled out from underneath a person, I think it reveals something about the intense suffering brought on by violence that catapults a person from one dimension of experience into another without safety. Helpless and lost. Trauma is unpredictable and life-threatening, and it tears apart rational understanding as well as destroys narrative flow. Traumatic voids are full of human loss. No wonder these young refugees felt lost, or that the Center's staff felt lost, and that even I felt lost. Perhaps this experience that I had resonates with Jung's words, quoted earlier, about the doctor feeling a violence of impact from social upheaval.

I came to the Center as an outsider, and I became part of a group field that consisted of unconscious split parts that might have felt irrecoverable. It took me months to go through my notes from my trip, and only then could I write about my experiences at the Frei Center. I could feel various elements of my experience, but I struggled to put them into anything more whole, such as this chapter and the article it is based on. Perhaps that struggle defines a quality of working with refugees—searching for how to put the pieces of a life and a psyche together again, overcoming fragmentation, feeling helpless while struggling to get to know the unfamiliar in us.

Sverre Varvin, a Norwegian psychoanalyst, writes about helper interactions with refugees and notes that these "seem to represent an encounter with the 'Uncanny'—an unfamiliar but nevertheless known entity, whose human characteristics are diminished or completely denied."[28] Helpers whose job it is to care for refugees are exposed to an aspect of the deep unconscious that they may not understand or even be aware of. They unwittingly swim amid archetypes. Analytic psychologists have much to offer in helping them come up for air, especially when their situations might feel "just black sometimes," lost in the dark and looking for familiar ground. I will discuss an idea about the uncanny's relation to immigration more in Chapter 11.

I approached the workshop as a kind of group consultation, in which I encouraged every member to participate. Fortunately, they all did so, and this level of engagement made the workshop satisfying. I used Bion's ideas about group dynamics and group process as well as many other group theorists whose work I have read and used through the years.[29] This approach meant that I attended to moments when I noticed difficult emotions in the group that had not yet been verbalized. For example, when I encouraged a participant to tell us how she felt about a difficult situation with a client, she was initially tentative about naming her feelings. With encouragement, she indicated that she had felt embarrassed about her anger. I asked if anyone else in the group could relate to this, and of course someone did. Whenever a member joined our discussion in this way, the group quickly became more open and dynamic.

I did not have an impression of resistance from the staff. On the contrary, I felt they were hungry for this sort of experience that permitted exploration of hard feelings, connection with colleagues, and a space to think about what these feelings meant. Johan Norman and Björn Salmonsson, applying Bion's theories about group function to consultation, use the term "weaving thoughts" to describe the establishment of a safe, supportive group that permits members to think aloud about difficult clinical material.[30] Their model is based on Bion's idea of "thoughts in search of a thinker" and encourages connections between group members to locate common threads of experience.[31] I find this technique useful in consultation groups for encouraging members to explore together difficult client interactions that evoke defensiveness around unpleasant emotions.

As part of the group dynamics at the Center, I was there as an outsider, the "fresh eyes" in the original invitation to me. Although I had tried to inform myself as much as possible about the refugee situation in Germany, I recognized that there were many things that I did not know. I wondered when and where I had made false assumptions. I felt a responsibility for staying open to the shadow side of being an outsider, and I am sure I missed much in this regard.

An example of this shadow side was present when I introduced myself. The group was deferential and that made me slightly uncomfortable, because it felt as if it could run counter to the consultation model I hoped to use, described previously. Some of this deference I understood as a cultural attitude of German respect for age, educational credentials, and titles. When I asked the staff if they would be comfortable using the more personal *Du* in talking with me, rather than the more formal *Sie*, I probably blundered. I knew that this request was something of a breach of formality among us, an outsider's upending a cultural norm. Many of them had seemed pleasantly surprised, although a few appeared hesitant.

In looking back, I believe I was culturally naïve in not discussing this request more with them. I was imposing my desire for informality on them and, although well-intended, it replicated a parallel process of their experiences with the refugee youth. I was asking them for a cultural adjustment concerning something important, and in doing so, unwittingly threw myself into a field of cultural negotiation that many staff described to me as a challenging aspect of their daily routine with their clients. Although staff were gracious in accommodating this language issue, I nevertheless had not recognized that this apparently simple request regarding the way we addressed one another likely enacted an outsider's disruption and misunderstanding of the home culture.

At the beginning of this chapter, I mentioned that analytic activism felt more important to me. This advocacy will look different depending on an analyst's or psychologist's personal interests and background. I find myself thinking about consulting more to groups and organizations. To me, such work implies a cognizance of group and cultural dynamics, so that I can assist when I am outside the comfort of a traditional analytic frame. Samuels writes, "What is the state of the art regarding intercultural and transcultural work? Does immersing oneself in the culture of the other help?"[32] I would answer affirmatively, based on my short time at the Frei Center. I have to make sure, however, that I am open equally to what I do not understand and to the many things that I am ignorant of. In ways that Jung (and others like Bion) helps me to appreciate, a position of not knowing, of holding uncertainty, is something that potentially enriches what we might offer.

The Sigmund Freud Institut (SFI) in Frankfurt has been working extensively with refugees. In a paper summarizing some of their work, Marianne Leutzinger-Bohleber et al. ask, "Can psychoanalysis contribute to this current urgent and complex societal situation?"[33] In their important efforts, they find a critical contribution to be the consultation that analysts offer frontline workers, whether they be teachers, social workers, or lay persons. This consultation "helps to meet the danger of being over-filled and overtaxed ... to prevent burn-outs, depressions and psychosomatic reactions among the 'helpers.'"[34] This finding corroborates my impressions as well.

Several days after the workshop, the assistant director told me that he and the director scheduled a meeting with the administration of their parent organization because they wanted to request ongoing consultation as a result of how positive they felt about what had happened during the time we spent together. It astonished me to learn that they did not receive such support. It also made their invitation for "fresh eyes" that much more understandable and indicated how alone they must feel on the frontlines of the refugee crisis.

Communicating about the unfamiliar

Leutzinger-Bohleber et al. comment that "working with severely traumatized patients requires a modified psychoanalytic treatment technique."[35] This observation underscores an awareness of my responsibilities when I venture into new territory, namely, that I have to adapt to be helpful. Part of my adaptation concerned how I communicated with others who do not know much about Jung or psychoanalysis. How do I speak about projective identification or complexes to someone unfamiliar with my jargon? I recall that my husband once overheard me talking with a colleague about projective identification, and he later remarked, "You know most people don't talk or think that way."

In my meetings with staff at the Frei Center, I avoided analytic terminology. Instead of using the term "projective identification," I spoke about how we can feel unsettled—and hurt—by picking up something from another person without knowing how this happens. The group readily gave examples that confirmed they got this point. With that recognition, we could discuss what helpers can do when this occurs with clients. Self-care was one idea; another was consulting with a coworker to think together about it. There was general acceptance that these interactions mean something peculiar has happened with our boundaries and that it helps us when we sort it out with someone.

The analytic tools that I found most helpful in my work at the Frei Center included the following: (1) attention to unconscious group processes; (2) close observation of nonverbal interactions; (3) trying to be mindful of my countertransference reactions; (4) encouraging staff members to amplify their ideas; (5) making space for affective responses and normalizing negative emotions; and (6) translating analytic concepts to make them more familiar to the work they did.

In Chapter 4, I write about my encounters with the adolescent clients of the Frei Center. I thought for months about these conversations because I felt both impressed and disturbed by them. This polarity seems to capture an essential tension of the tragedy that these refugees face in seeking safety and welcome elsewhere. Their resilience is admirable; their trauma is nightmarish. Monica Luci confirms that "Refugees constitute a particular challenge to psychoanalysis and analytical psychology for a number of reasons," many of which she finds are related to the extent of their suffering from war-related traumas.[36] In an important paper, she documents some of these challenges and suggests how analytic process might adapt to help those afflicted by brutal circumstances. Here, I have offered a schema for another adaptation that provides organizational intervention, based on group relations, for those working closely with refugees.

Notes

1 In Chapter 4, I discuss my experiences with the refugees at the center.
2 Andrew Samuels, "The Future of Jungian Analysis: Strengths, Weaknesses, Opportunities, Threats ('SWOT')," *Journal of Analytical Psychology* 62, no. 5 (2017): 636–649.
3 C. G. Jung, "Preface to 'Essays on Contemporary Events,'" *The Collected Works of C. G. Jung* 10 (1946), *Civilization in Transition* (Princeton: Princeton University Press, 1968), 177. Hereafter, references to Jung's *Collected Works* will appear as Jung, title, date, and volume number in the *Collected Works* (CW).
4 Samuels, "The Future of Jungian Analysis," 644.
5 The UN Refugee Agency (UNHCR), "Figures at a Glance," accessed June 23, 2021, https://www.unhcr.org/en-us/figures-at-a-glance.html.
6 UNHCR, "What Is a Refugee," accessed June 14, 2018, https://www.unrefugees.org/refugee-facts/what-is-a-refugee/
7 UNHCR, *Global Trends: Forced Displacement in 2016* (Geneva, Switzerland: UN High Commissioner on Refugees, 2017), 3.
8 Ibid., 40.

9 UNHCR, "Asylum Seekers," accessed June 14, 2018, http://www.unhcr.org/asylum-seekers.html
10 Because most of the clients are male, I will use the masculine pronoun unless otherwise indicated.
11 Joseph Henderson, *Thresholds of Initiation* (Wilmette, IL: Chiron, 1967/2005).
12 Ibid.
13 Robert Tyminski, "Lost for Words: Difficulty Expressing Feelings in Work with Three Adolescent Boys," *Journal of Child Psychotherapy* 38, no. 1 (2012): 32–48.
14 Robert Tyminski, *Male Alienation at the Crossroads of Identity, Culture and Cyberspace* (London and New York: Routledge, 2019).
15 Erik Erikson, *Identity: Youth and Crisis* (New York: W. W. Norton, 1968).
16 Bessel A. van der Kolk, Alexander C. McFarlane, and Lars Weisaeth, eds., *Traumatic Stress: The Effects of Overwhelming Experience on Mind, Body, and Society* (New York, NY: Guilford Press, 1996), x.
17 James Garbarino, ed., *Children in Danger: Coping with the Consequences of Community Violence* (San Francisco, CA: Jossey-Bass, 1992).
18 Theresa S. Betancourt et al., "Trauma History and Psychopathology in War-Affected Children Referred for Trauma-Related Mental Health Services in the United States," *Journal of Traumatic Stress* 25, no. 6 (2012): 682–690; Kimberly A. Ehntholt and William Yule, "Practitioner Review: Assessment and Treatment of Refugee Children and Adolescents Who Have Experienced War-Related Trauma," *Journal of Child Psychology and Psychiatry* 47, no. 12 (2006): 1197–1210; Miriam George, "A Theoretical Understanding of Refugee Trauma," *Clinical Social Work Journal* 38, no. 4 (2010): 379–387; Ibrahim Kira et al., "The Effects of Trauma Types, Cumulative Trauma, and PTSD on IQ in Two Highly Traumatized Adolescent Groups," *Psychological Trauma: Theory, Research, Practice, and Policy* 4, no. 1 (2012): 128–139; Laura K. Murray et al., "Cognitive Behavioral Therapy for Symptoms of Trauma and Traumatic Grief in Refugee Youth," *Child and Adolescent Psychiatric Clinics of North America* 17, no. 3 (2008): 585–604; Rene Papadopoulos, "Refugees, Trauma and Adversity-Activated Development," *European Journal of Psychotherapy and Counselling* 9, no. 3 (2007): 301–312.
19 Kira et al., "The Effects of Trauma Types," 128.
20 Betancourt et al., "Trauma History and Psychopathology."
21 Papadopoulos, "Refugees, Trauma and Adversity-Activated Development."
22 Donald Kalsched, *The Inner World of Trauma: Archetypal Defenses of the Personal Spirit* (London and New York: Routledge, 1996).
23 Anne Alvarez, *The Thinking Heart: Three Levels of Psychoanalytic Therapy with Disturbed Children* (London and New York: Routledge, 2012).
24 C. G. Jung, "Psychological Factors Determining Human Behavior," 1937/1969, CW 8, para. 253.
25 Haydée Faimberg, "The Telescoping of Generations," *Contemporary Psychoanalysis* 24, no. 1 (1988): 99–118.
26 Samuel Kimbles, *Phantom Narratives: The Unseen Contribution of Culture to Psyche* (Lantham, MD: Rowman and Littlefield, 2014).
27 Alessandra Lemma, "The Many Faces of Lying," *International Journal of Psychoanalysis* 86, no. 3 (2005): 737–753.
28 Sverre Varvin, "Our Relations to Refugees: Between Compassion and Dehumanization," *The American Journal of Psychoanalysis* 77, no. 4 (2017): 359–377, 360.
29 Wilfred R. Bion, *Experiences in Groups* (London: Tavistock, 1961/1983).
30 Johan Norman and Björn Salomonsson, "'Weaving Thoughts': A Method for Presenting and Commenting Psychoanalytic Case Material in a Peer Group," *International Journal of Psychoanalysis* 86, no. 5 (2005): 1281–1298.
31 Ibid., 1281.

32 Andrew Samuels, "Political and Clinical Developments in Analytical Psychology, 1972–2014: Subjectivity, Equality and Diversity—Inside and Outside the Consulting Room," *Journal of Analytical Psychology* 59, no. 5 (2014): 654.
33 Marianna Leutzinger-Bohleber et al., "What Can Psychoanalysis Contribute to the Current Refugee Crisis?" *International Journal of Psychoanalysis* 97, no. 4 (2016): 1078.
34 Ibid., 1082.
35 Ibid., 1092.
36 Monica Luci, "Disintegration of the Self and the Regeneration of 'Psychic Skin' in the Treatment of Refugees," *Journal of Analytical Psychology* 62, no. 2 (2017): 227.

Chapter 3

Long Wandering

Long wand'ring way for you the pow'rs decree.
—Creusa's ghost speaking to Aeneas[1]

Summarizing The Aeneid is probably better left to educational websites that promise help to high school and college students who haven't finished reading their assignments. That said, I want to give something of an overview of the tale, because it offers a mythical version of migration and its perils. Virgil's epic obviously comes to us as part of the Western canon; therefore, it is somewhat debatable as to what extent its themes apply more globally. However, even with this limitation, The Aeneid reveals many elements that characterize migrants' journeys, from seeking refuge to being led far off course to eventually fighting for a right to remain. Creusa, Aeneas's wife who perishes in Troy before he leaves and then appears to him as a ghost as he is leaving, continues her statement above, "On land hard labours, and a length of sea."[2] Many migrants have traveled across vast stretches of land before dangerously crossing a body of water. Even today migrants from Africa and the Middle East cross the Mediterranean to reach Europe. The "boat people" who fled Vietnam in the late 1970s also made an arduous, terrifying journey.

There are many translations of The Aeneid. Robert Fitzgerald's is often recommended, as is John Dryden's; both adhere to the verse form of Virgil's epic.[3] Dryden, whose translation I refer to in this chapter, was a seventeenth-century English poet who became the first poet laureate of England. He translated the works of Virgil into English. William F. Jackson Knight created a prose translation that works around some of the difficulties a reader may encounter in reading verse.[4]

Virgil lived from 70 BCE until 19 CE. Many scholars consider The Aeneid to be an unfinished work because of its abrupt ending. Virgil wrote it in the decade following Cleopatra's defeat by Octavian in 30 BCE. Epic poems, including Homer's Iliad and Odyssey, are generally quite long, tell us about the adventures and mishaps of heroes, and describe humankind's

DOI: 10.4324/9781003119593-3

interactions with divine forces. The Aeneid, a Latin poem, conforms to various signifying rules of heroic conduct that emphasize showing self-control, avoiding excess, and being loyal, brave, and pious.

The story

The Aeneid is a lengthy, complex story about a mythical time before the founding of Rome, an event attributed directly to the heroism of Aeneas. Aeneas is a member of the royal house of Troy and the son of Anchises and Venus, a goddess (Aphrodite in Greek mythology). After Troy's defeat, Aeneas flees Troy with a band of survivors who, according to The Aeneid, eventually land in ancient Latium on the western Italian coast. Some classics scholars regard The Aeneid as a celebration of Octavian and his establishment of imperial Rome—the book was written during his rule. Following this reasoning, the character Aeneas was conceived to be analogous and flattering to Octavian, because he demonstrates cherished Roman values of self-discipline and fierce loyalty to family, homeland, and the gods.

Importantly, the founding of imperial Rome is echoed throughout the plot of The Aeneid, dating the city and the Romans far back in time to a mythological origin. An historical parallel is Octavian's success in transitioning Rome from a republic to a kind of monarchy. Octavian ruled Rome in one way or another from the year 43 BCE, when he was chosen as a consul, until his death in 14 CE. In 27 BCE, Octavian was given the title Imperator Caesar Augustus. He was referred to as princeps, or first citizen; and in 23 BCE, he secured an additional title (Imperial Proconsul) and was given the rights of tribune in perpetuity (without actually taking this post). Octavian, not wanting to be seen as a monarch or dictator, had to maneuver around a possibility of this perception by creating other vehicles for accumulating and exercising his considerable powers.[5]

The Aeneid contains twelve books. The first six deal with the Trojans' journeys after the fall of Troy in the late Bronze Age, about 1200 BCE. The second six books describe the war between the Trojans and native Italian tribes, including the Rutulians led by Turnus. The Aeneid begins in the middle of things (*in medias res* in Latin) with the Trojan fleet sailing toward Italy, also called Hesperia. Juno (Hera in Greek mythology) is the goddess most opposing the Trojans and obstructing them, because, long before, she lost the judgment of Paris, a Trojan prince, to Venus, Aeneas's mother. Aeneas thus has divine lineage and a divine opponent. The fleet is waylaid to Africa, where Aeneas meets Dido, the queen of Carthage, and tells her his story about the sack of Troy and his escape with his father, Anchises, and son, Ascanius. Dido is likewise a refugee who fled Tyre, a city along the shore of the Eastern Mediterranean, to escape her brother's tyranny. She tells Aeneas, "Myself distress'd, an exile, and unknown, /Debarr'd from Europe, and from Asia thrown, /In Libyan deserts wander thus alone."[6]

Because her experience as a migrant reflects his, she is capable of welcoming him after a strenuous voyage that tests a person with loneliness, despair, and alienation. She calls herself an exile, a word that conjures up a place where she once was at home, but can no longer call home. She confirms this feeling of being exiled later when telling him, "Like you, an alien in a land unknown, /I learn to pity woes so like my own."[7]

These first six books offer many accounts of the Trojans and how they were derailed to other locations, for example, to Thrace (Southeastern Europe), Delos and Crete (Greek islands), and eventually the island of Sicily, where Aeneas's father dies. These tumultuous wanderings depict the hardships and obstacles that migrants often face when seeking a new home, difficulties often requiring heroic efforts to overcome and persevere. This near universal or archetypal piece of The Aeneid helps us appreciate the incredibly long history of humankind's continuous adaptation to migration. A corollary is an acknowledgement of the not at all subtle passions that the topic of migration frequently arouses within receiving countries. Even in The Aeneid, Aeneas is not welcomed with open arms once he and his followers arrive in Italy.

In Carthage on the northern coast of Africa, Aeneas and Dido, weakened by Cupid's sneaky intervention, fall in love. When it appears Aeneas might stay in Carthage, Jupiter (Zeus) reminds him that his duty is elsewhere, so Aeneas leaves under cover of night. Betrayed by the man she trusted, Dido kills herself and curses Aeneas's family. Aeneas and the Trojans return to Sicily, where he organizes memorial games in honor of his father's death a year before. Meddling yet again, Juno sends the goddess Iris as a messenger disguised as an old woman to stir the Trojans' frustrations to a point of setting their fleet on fire:

> Now sev'n revolving years are wholly run,
> Since this improsp'rous voyage we begun;
> Since, toss'd from shores to shores, from lands to lands,
> Inhospitable rocks and barren sands,
> Wand'ring in exile thro' the stormy sea,
> We search in vain for flying Italy.[8]

The fleet is saved, although Aeneas agrees to build a town for the elderly and the women who want to stay in Sicily after seven years of wandering, a protracted migration indeed.

Aeneas then has a vision of his father who instructs him to make a journey into the underworld where he will learn about his own fate and that of his descendants. This underworld aspect of the story refers symbolically to the dangers, risks, unforeseen changes, and malleable hopes that migrants might experience in seeking new beginnings. In this situation, there are moments of facing darkness and uncertainty when opposing forces threaten to derail and destroy the journey. In the underworld, Aeneas hears a detailed prophecy from his father about Silvius, his first son to be born in Latium, and about his own heroic actions that will lead to the eventual founding of Rome.

The second half of The Aeneid chronicles a war that ensues after Aeneas and the Trojans reach Latium, a region in central western Italy, which includes Rome. Initially, the local king welcomes the Trojans, but soon, after another dollop of divine interference, war breaks out. This constant back-and-forth cycle of hope and disappointment mirrors the rising expectations and frequent collapse of them that many immigrants report when telling their own stories of migration and resettlement. This cycle occurs continuously throughout The Aeneid. Aeneas, craftily, seeks and finds local allies in his armed conflicts with the native tribes.

A reappearing father-son trope characterizes much of The Aeneid, as with Anchises and Aeneas, Aeneas and Ascanius, and then Aeneas and the son of a local king, a boy named Pallas, who agrees to fight with Aeneas. Earlier, Aeneas explains to Dido about when he carried his father, "And load my shoulders with a willing freight. /Whate'er befalls, your life shall be my care; /One death, or one deliv'rance, we will share. /My hand shall lead our little son..."[9] The three generations are thus connected in a symbolically potent image of their moving together as a family spanning a common lived time. Cultural transmission is further emphasized because Anchises carries with him the *penates*, the sacred relics of their local Trojan gods. Later on, Aeneas, aware of his fatherly obligation, functions as a surrogate father to Pallas, who is probably slightly older than Ascanius. Pallas is later killed by Turnus, an event that intensifies Aeneas's hate of him and fuels his determination to fight. After a short truce for Pallas's funeral, the war resumes. Ascanius is likely around eleven or twelve years old during this portion of the story. Speaking to him, Aeneas says,

> This day my hand thy tender age shall shield,
> And crown with honours of the conquer'd field:
> Thou, when thy riper years shall send thee forth
> To toils of war, be mindful of my worth;
> Assert thy birthright, and in arms be known,
> For Hector's nephew, and Aeneas' son.[10]

Aeneas invokes here a value system heavy on bravery, honor, and family, one he clearly wants his son to carry on with. He also reminds him of their Trojan heritage. In the Iliad, Hector was the eldest son of the Trojan king Priam.

Figure 3.1 Aeneas and his family fleeing Troy by Agostino Carracci, 1595 (This file is made available under the Creative Commons CC0 1.0 Universal Public Domain Dedication. This file was donated to Wikimedia Commons as part of a project by the Metropolitan Museum of Art.)

Turnus, king of the Rutulians, represents a man who lacks self-control, a hothead who violates essential Roman values. Turnus, though, sees himself as wholly justified in defending his territory against the migrants and pursuing his own claims, because he wants to marry King Latinus's daughter. However, King Latinus believes he should follow an oracle that his daughter is to marry a foreigner, that is, Aeneas. Turnus asserts that Aeneas's ongoing aggression is proof of what disorder he will ultimately create. Because he sees them as only disruptive to an established order, Turnus acts as a counterpoint to the position of accepting the new migrants into Latin society.

In Book X, a council of the gods convenes because of the unresolved human hostilities, which the divine factions are continuing to incite. Juno complains about Aeneas's apparent successes, whereas Venus (his mother) complains about the obstacles being put in his way. Juno vows to obstruct him and the Trojans because she finds their cause unworthy and unjust. She argues to Venus, "But yet is just and lawful for your line, /To drive their fields, and force with fraud to join; /Realms, not your own, among your clans divide."[11] Here, she expresses an anti-immigrant rationale as a basis for not allowing the Trojans to settle in Italy; they will occupy the land, steal, and conquer the natives. Contemporary politicians, like Trump, parrot her words, if not her eloquence, with similarly xenophobic warnings.

Addressing the council, Jupiter insists on an eventual compromise, and in Book XII, Juno finally agrees to desist provided that Aeneas and the Trojans *speak the native language and adopt local customs*. In other words, they assimilate to Latin society. Jupiter then pronounces:

> From ancient blood th' Ausonian [Italian] people sprung,
> Shall keep their name, their habit, and their tongue.
> The Trojans to their customs shall be tied:
> I will, myself, their common rites provide;
> The natives shall command, the foreigners subside.
> All shall be Latium; Troy without a name;
> And her lost sons forget from whence they came.[12]

Jupiter decides on what seems to be an ancient version of a melting pot. The newcomers must give up most of their traditions and blend into those of the receiving land. To counter Juno's xenophobic arguments, Jupiter relies on proclaiming assimilation, which accepts the migrants at a rather high cost, their own heritage. This sentiment rings eerily true to contemporary ears when political leaders profess not to be anti-immigrant as long as "they learn *our* language and follow *our* beliefs."

Further in Book XII, Aeneas is wounded during a battle, but he is healed through the assistance of his divine mother, Venus. He subsequently forces Turnus into single combat to decide the ultimate battle. This time, Turnus is wounded in the leg. On his knees, Turnus begs for his life, pleading for mercy, but when Aeneas sees that Turnus is wearing Pallas's sword belt, he becomes enraged and kills Turnus. The Aeneid ends here, and scholars have speculated about a thirteenth book describing Aeneas's marriage to King Latinus's daughter, Lavinia. Maffeo Vegio, a fifteenth-century Italian poet who wrote in Latin, composed a thirteenth book of The Aeneid with just that ending and also portrayed Aeneas's subsequent divinity.[13] Although the actual ending suggests a heroic outcome for the migrants who are fighting for a right to remain, it could also be seen as an invasion by outsiders, essentially making for a reality that a committed xenophobe might fear. Of note, Aeneas also loses self-control at the end of The Aeneid; he briefly contemplates showing mercy to Turnus, but is then blinded by his rage over Turnus's lack of respect for Pallas. Aeneas is often referred to as "pious Aeneas" because his character demonstrates a principal Roman value of *pietas*, or piety, namely reverence for the gods, country, and family.[14] Like all humans, however, he is flawed and does not consistently live up to these ideals.

Historical note

Aeneas's love affair with Dido is based on Virgil's reference to an earlier Greek epic, the Argonautika, specifically the romantic relationship between Jason and Medea.[15] Book IV of The Aeneid, when Dido falls passionately for Aeneas, owes much to Book III of the Argonautika, when Medea is charmed by Eros (Cupid) to fall for Jason.[16] Virgil wrote The Aeneid after Octavian had conquered Egypt. Octavian defeated Cleopatra, like Dido, another North African princess who had a Roman lover, Antony. Unlike Aeneas, Antony did not abandon Cleopatra for his own political glory. Cleopatra, called by Roman poet Horace "this monster sent by fate," was regarded as a dangerous foreign queen who could have destroyed the greatness that Rome stood for. It is in Virgil's *Aeneid* that Dido, as a North African queen, is linked to Cleopatra and, by extension, to Medea. Although I can't say with certainty that the character of Dido is completely based on Cleopatra, Virgil creates by allusion a connection that would have been evident to his educated contemporaries and to the political class. More conspicuously, all three women—Cleopatra, Medea, and Dido—were foreigners who represented exotic feminine otherness that posed a threat to masculine heroic order (both Greek and Roman).

Egyptologist Joyce Tyldesley notes, "As public enemy number one, Cleopatra was extremely useful to Octavian, who not unnaturally preferred to be remembered fighting misguided foreigners rather than decent fellow Romans."[17] Tyldesley comments on the parallels that exist between Cleopatra and Dido in The Aeneid and on the unflattering comparison drawn between the defeated Antony, believed to be a man "lesser than Aeneas," and victorious Octavian. Cleopatra VII, as the most famous Cleopatra was titled, was the last of the pharaohs. Descended from Ptolemy I, she was born in the winter around 69 BCE and died in 30 BCE. Her father was Ptolemy XII (known as Auletes), and her mother was unknown. At the height of her power, her kingdom stretched in North Africa from past Cyrene (eastern Libya) along the eastern shore of the Mediterranean to the south coast of Turkey. It included the islands of Cyprus and part of Crete.

Cleopatra met Antony, who served as triumvir (ruler) of Rome together with Octavian and Lepidus, in 41 BCE. He never married her; instead, when his wife Fulvia died, he married Octavian's half-sister Octavia for political reasons. About the same time, Cleopatra gave birth to their twins. Like Dido, Cleopatra committed suicide; the uncertain tale of her method of dying, allegedly by an asp's bite, further magnified her story as mythic history. More importantly, her death marked a clear divide in cultural history. Her capital, Alexandria, had represented the high point of Hellenistic culture. This cultural pivot accords with both the timing and theme of Virgil's *Aeneid*, as it depicts a foundation myth of Rome after the fall of Troy—but only after a near miss caused by the hero Aeneas's stay with another North African queen, Dido. At the heart of the stories about

Dido and Cleopatra are many superstitious beliefs that feminine wiles undermine men, leading to tragedy. Their fates also underscore a truth that certain cultures achieve hegemony mainly through violent expansion.

Perspectives on The Aeneid

Robert Fitzgerald, in a postscript to his translation, comments on the complex and unpredictable forces that emphasize how The Aeneid is really a story about a difficult migration and building a new home after resettlement. He notes the delicate balance between emotions of disappointment and hope that oscillate throughout the text, for example, when pitting extraordinary heroism against what seem to be insurmountable odds. "Mordantly and sadly it suggests what the effort may cost, how the effort may fail."[18] As a migration story, then, I believe that inevitably, there must be costs, failures, and much random luck, more than perhaps ever considered.

Elizabeth Lisot-Nelson, an art historian, remarks that hospitality and welcoming strangers were significant customs for ancient Greek and Roman cultures, but it often ended badly for the hosts.[19] This is one lesson that can be taken from The Aeneid—that Aeneas and the Trojans bring misfortune and violence almost wherever they land. However, they too were fleeing violence after the sack of Troy and losing the Trojan War. Citing postmigration theory, Lisot-Nelson explains that it posits that migration is a normal human activity characteristic of our history and irrespective of borders. She notes that violence often creates migratory trends; for instance, in countries that are destabilized because of war and domestic terrorism, many people will naturally seek opportunities to leave. Concurring with my rationale for using The Aeneid as a migration myth, she states, "Aeneas ... is an archetypal story of a refugee."[20] As an archetype, this story belongs to each of us and to all of us, because that is in the nature of archetypes.

Postmigration theory conceives of dismantling national labels that separate and oppress us. These so-called national identities are often imposed by mechanisms of power to divide human beings from one another. More likely, we are mosaics, not discrete identities given or handed to us; and these mosaics are, as Roger Bromley, a professor of cultural studies, writes, *bricolages*, a term from cultural anthropology that means improvised out of what is available, created out of various things.[21] Identity can denote fixity; instead Bromley proposes that we think in terms of interculturalism, implying our personalities and selves are "always under construction" in a fluid process.[22] This idea accords with more contemporary explanations of a psyche that consists of multiplicities, which defy essentialist labeling, a topic I discuss in Chapter 6. In such a theory, a mosaic of inner variations potentially makes us more uniquely individual than fixed identities can capture. Hopefully, this mosaicism across a society would diminish bias and othering. Applied to the myth, it would be as if Aeneas were to arrive in

Latium, and there would be no war because his foreignness would be tolerable as only one sliver of him and his fellow Trojans. Obviously, this theory is a heavy lift into what could be a more promising future.

History shows that imagery from The Aeneid can and has been used to portray anti-immigrant sentiment. Consider John Enoch Powell's 1968 "Rivers of Blood" speech in Birmingham, United Kingdom. Powell was a classics scholar and Conservative politician in the United Kingdom, serving in Parliament for over thirty-five years and as Minister of Health from 1960 to 1963. He railed against immigration to the United Kingdom, warning that it would become "a horror" like in the United States. He opposed anti-discrimination legislation for immigrants, and a majority of the public supported him at the time. In his speech, he said, "Like the Roman, I seem to see the River Tiber foaming with much blood."[23] Robert Todd, another classicist, notes that Enoch Powell made an error in attributing this quote to "the Roman," instead of to the Sibyl who is speaking with Aeneas in Book VI and telling him about the war ahead of him, in which she predicts that the Tiber is "rolling with a purple flood."[24] Enoch Powell further neglected to mention that Aeneas and the Trojans, the purported ancestors of the Romans, were refugees themselves. He misused this quote to incite anti-immigrant feelings among the populace by implying that street violence could only be avoided by restricting immigration because immigrants were a visible threat, as in Virgil's metaphor of a river foaming with blood.

Barbara Cassin, a French philologist, in her 2016 book about nostalgia, has a chapter in which she discusses The Aeneid.[25] There, she observes that when Aeneas leaves behind women and the elderly in Sicily, he establishes a situation in which the young Trojan men will have to mate with natives to produce their own children. She explains an irony in The Aeneid—that the founder of Troy, named Dardanus, was supposedly from Italy, so Aeneas's voyage is a homecoming of sorts as he travels in reverse. Thus, Aeneas is returning to the land where his ancestors originated, and in that sense, he embodies that we are all exiles, for he is a foreigner but from "here," that is, Italy. As Cassin writes, "Migrations, immigrations, conquests—no part of humanity has remained in its place of origin."[26] There is in this recognition a sense that our feelings of not belonging reach back nostalgically for a point of origin that should explain something fundamental about ourselves, if only we could figure that out!

Thinking about the implications of this myth for psychotherapy, Martha Bragin mentions The Aeneid when writing about her clinical work with adolescents who are refugees. She believes that a refugee's personal narrative has to incorporate this person's history from the time premigration; as much as adolescents might crave a new beginning, a fresh start without trappings of the past, they excise their past and deny it at risk to their emotional life.[27] She notes that exposure to trauma and violence can cause significant harm to a young person's capacities for symbolizing and making meaning, which, especially in adolescence, are important tasks for linking past to present. Aeneas, as an example of remembrance, tells his story to Dido in great detail and with attention to where things in the story twisted and turned. We create such stories because they enable empathy, open space for deeper exchanges, and recall the past. Stories make real the lived mosaics of our existence, mosaics that defy linear reasoning and are full of irrational happenings.

Archetypal elements of The Aeneid for migration experiences

The Aeneid has many archetypal aspects, and, as archetypes have innumerable variants, there are too many to describe. Still, it is important to consider which of them stand out as illustrative of migration and resettlement. Clearly, heroism is central, and although immigrants and refugees are not necessarily heroes, they often undertake journeys with heroic ordeals and unusual tests of strength. A patient once told me how tiring it had been to wait years for her visa to be approved to come study in the United States and how she spent that time working hard and saving as much money as she could. "Most of the time, I was tired to my bones." Such perseverance is not only about realizing a desire or implementing a plan; it is also fundamentally about effort, persistence, and working for a better life. A hero's journey is rarely straightforward but full of detours and obstacles, and this is tiring.

How does someone keep at it? A motivation to continue when the odds are daunting speaks to the heroic in our psyche, the part of us that assumes challenges and fights not to give up or yield. Not mere stubbornness, this tenacity frequently has to be flexible in dealing with different kinds of adversity. As with Aeneas, it requires adapting to various roles, unpredictable circumstances, and encounters with random events that can determine where we end up. In its simplest form, everyday heroism can mean sticking to a task when we also have to bend to accommodate the unforeseen. The complexities of immigration demand this combination of iron and aluminum, hard and malleable, firmness and flexibility, traits often seen in heroes when they improvise to meet the moment.

The tension of coping with differences appears throughout The Aeneid, and it too mirrors a piece of the immigrant experience. Aeneas is often welcomed but then rebuffed. He is the Trojan seeking to be Roman (Latin) to start a new life for himself. In this myth, differences are not handled well. As an ancient myth, The Aeneid contains a duality that is both characteristic and insistent in the story. Either Aeneas is Trojan *or* he becomes Latin; he cannot be both, which reflects a modern understanding of incorporating various incongruent aspects of experience into who we are and how we present to the world.

Yet, a problem with differences follows Aeneas and leads to the climactic conflict with native Italian tribes. Immigrants report many aspects of this unavoidable dilemma around differences in telling their stories of coming to the United States. Their accents, their skin colors, their languages, their names, their social interactions, their perceptions, their goals, their aspirations, their religions, their habits, their preferences, their foods, their clothing, their travels—that's only a short list of the ways of being that undergo an uneasy process of reconsideration and reevaluation when immigrating. Intolerance of differences often leads to social othering as well as an insistence on conforming to the values of the receiving country. As with the divine compromise at the end of The Aeneid, there still are plenty of areas in the United States that stress assimilation rather than a mutual exchange between groups. That stance perpetuates a kind of cultural violence—ours is better than yours, take it or leave it. In psychotherapy and analysis, it is essential to make a safe space for speaking about differences and understanding what is unknown, especially by the analyst or psychotherapist. A therapeutic attitude necessitates approaching our immigrant patients not only with acceptance, but also with an admission that we simply do not know enough about them or their backgrounds.

Tribalism surfaces repeatedly in The Aeneid as a familiar social enclosure that contains Aeneas and the Trojans as well as those they meet along their way. When threatened, they usually retreat. Tribalism is an archetypal social safety net. For contemporary readers of The Aeneid, it is almost uncanny to see how the myth's use of tribalism resonates deeply with how social and political beliefs are nowadays expressed in the United States to divide the country into tribal areas. As a result, we have proponents of a more closed country who advocate—like Enoch Powell in 1968 in the United Kingdom—restricting immigration and closing our borders, perhaps because they are unconsciously under the influence of a Junoesque archetype; recall that she consistently opposes Aeneas and the Trojans in their migration.

As another small scale example, tribalism is well known in analytic culture. Jungians, Freudians, Kleinians, and so forth—these have become descriptors for our safe enclosures, especially when we feel threatened, something that happens far too often and prevents us from talking across our tribes. This excessive localism makes conflicts harder to approach, to discuss, and to resolve, and it magnifies theoretical differences when we know to the contrary that analysis as a healing tradition emphasizes making links, building connections, and being available to what is seemingly other.

Intergroup conflicts, stemming from tribal affiliations and localist appeals, are resolved in The Aeneid through aggression and violence. Refugees, especially, experience violent intergroup conflicts in their homelands, and migration may be their only hope for finding a safer life for themselves and their families. A patient who came to the United States from a dictatorship in South America once told me, "Americans have no clue about what it's like to live in fear of the government. When I hear people protest here about government interference in their lives, I think, really? You want to know what that is like?"

He went on to describe how one day his family awoke to discover that the apartment next door to theirs was empty—the couple living there, who had been political activists, were just gone with no explanation. This patient was voicing several aspects of what I have just described—differences in perspective (around trust in government), tribalism (activists are rooted out), and intergroup conflict that results in violence.

Gender in The Aeneid is binary and reinforced through the duality of how characters appear and act. Aware of this, I note that the father-son theme in The Aeneid reminds us that migrants try to carry their culture forward. Anchises, Aeneas's father, carries the *penates*, which are all that remain as artifacts of Trojan culture. He wants to ensure they travel with them to their new homeland, as reminders of Trojan culture and religion and as connectors to their mutual past. Cultural transmission is a part of nearly every immigrant's journey. Of course, how they choose to express their heritage culture varies greatly. The father-son relationships in The Aeneid represent an enduring connection across generations, one linking a common history to an unshared future, since the elders often do not make it for long. When they do, they frequently cannot manage within the new homeland in the same ways as their children and grandchildren do. It is crucial, however, to consider the profound depth for what gets transmitted psychologically and unconsciously. For example, intergenerational trauma can be brought along to the receiving country from the heritage country. This trauma can complicate not only the children's adjustment, but also the grandchildren's. Haydee Faimberg, a French psychoanalyst, describes this "telescoping" effect that stretches unconsciously across generations in ways that appear perplexing and unexplainable.[28] This is often the psychological terrain of family secrets, and most immigrants have considerable experiences with them.

Finally, I believe that Aeneas's side trip in the tale into the underworld is not simply to add mythic drama. Rather, it constitutes an important element in a migration story. The underworld can be understood as a place of darkness. It conjures up the multitude of dangers that have been unanticipated by an immigrant as well as the unimagined consequences of their immigration. A young man whose family had immigrated to the US from Southeast Asia said to me during a session, "My parents never expected there'd be so much crime where they had their store. The first time they got robbed, I think they just were in shock for months." He explained that they were ashamed about the robbery and never considered getting any help for themselves because they viewed themselves as being at fault. This kind of underworld experience turns us on our heads because it seems so senseless and is emotionally very painful.

Aeneas luckily learns in his underworld sojourn a bit about his future. This is a comforting aspect of the underworld when it symbolizes the unconscious and when it implies dreaming and the containing functions of the psyche. Although there may be no real prophecy coming as a precognition, there are meaningful and significant dreams that immigrants have which help guide them through their resettlement experiences and into their new lives in strange places. The underworld is not just about unseen dangers—it is also about unknown possibilities.

Notes

1 Virgil, *Aeneid,* trans. John Dryden (Project Gutenberg E-Book #228, 2008), 153. Hereafter references to Dryden's translation of *Aeneid* will appear as Dryden and page number.
2 Dryden, 154.
3 Robert Fitzgerald, trans., *Aeneid by Virgil* (New York: Vintage Books, 1990).
4 W. F. Jackson Knight, trans., *The Aeneid by Virgil* (London: Penguin, 1958).
5 Anthony Everitt, *The Life of Rome's First Emperor: Augustus* (New York: Random House, 2006).
6 Dryden, 43–44.
7 Dryden, 68.
8 Dryden, 350.
9 Dryden, 147–148.
10 Dryden, 917.
11 Dryden, 695.
12 Dryden, 957.
13 Maffeo Vegio, *Libri Xii Aeneidox Svpplementvm Maphaei Vegii,* http://www.thelatinlibrary.com/vegius.html
14 Susanna Braund, *Virgil's Aeneid,* podcast, 2007, Stanford on iTunes, https://podcasts.apple.com/us/podcast/virgils-aeneid/id384233916
15 Robert Tyminski, "The Medea Complex—Myth and Modern Manifestation," *Jung Journal: Culture & Psyche* 8, no. 1 (2014), 28–40.
16 Braund, *Virgil's Aeneid.*
17 Joyce Tyldesley, *Cleopatra: Last Queen of Egypt* (New York: Basic Books, 2008), 206.
18 Fitzgerald, *The Aeneid by Virgil,* 405.
19 Elizabeth A. Lisot-Nelson, "Refugees of War: Federico Barocci's Aeneas Fleeing Troy, Classical Antecedents to Contemporary Issues," *Journal of Art History* 89, no. 1 (2020): 35–56.
20 Ibid., 49.
21 Wikipedia, s.v. "Bricolage," https://en.wikipedia.org/wiki/Bricolage
22 Roger Bromley, "A Bricolage of Identifications: Storying Postmigrant Belonging," *Journal of Aesthetics & Culture* 9, no. 2 (2017): 37.
23 Robert Todd, "John Enoch Powell and Vergil: Aeneid 6.86–87: A Supplementary Note," *Vergilius* 45 (1999): 73.
24 Dryden, 571.
25 Barbara Cassin, "Aeneas: From Nostalgia to Exile," in *Nostalgia: When Are We Ever at Home?* (New York: Fordham University Press, 2016).
26 Ibid., 39.
27 Martha Bragin, "Memory, Myth, and Meaning: Understanding and Treating Adolescents Experiencing Forced Migration," *Journal of Infant, Child, and Adolescent Psychotherapy* 18, no. 4 (2019): 319–329.
28 Haydee Faimberg, "The Telescoping of Generations," *Contemporary Psychoanalysis* 24, no. 1 (1988): 99–118.

Chapter 4

Careful about the Forest

No harm shall happen to you.

—Old woman speaking to Hansel and Gretel[1]

In Chapter 2, I discussed my experience consulting to a program in Berlin that resettled unaccompanied refugee minors from the Middle East. Here, I expand on interactions I had with adolescent refugees in this program at the Frei Center.[2] I asked a Syrian boy, with whom I spoke at greater length, if he could tell me a version of his story. I explained that I would disguise his identity, and his reaction was to smile and eagerly agree. He was pleased that I wanted to tell others about his experience.

I met ten adolescents housed through the Frei Center. They received social services and educational counseling from the staff. They were expected to take language classes, enroll in school or a vocational activity, and attend weekly meetings with staff to discuss their goals in Germany, including resolving their legal status. Most of the current clients were male refugees from Syria and Afghanistan ranging in age from sixteen to eighteen. I had longer conversations with three clients. They invited me to their celebration of Eid-al-Fitr, the breaking of the Ramadan fast. I helped them prepare food and cook in the kitchen at Center's main location.

Breaking the fast

It is early evening when I enter a crowded kitchen. As I take a place at the table, an eighteen-year-old young man from Syria sits next to me. I'll call him Nasir. After we introduce ourselves, he asks me in English if I can show him how to chop vegetables. He shrugs, saying, "I'm not good at cooking." I show him how to hold a knife so he can chop zucchini. He is introverted, perhaps because of a language issue. Later, he speaks with me more. He says that he rarely prepared food himself in Syria. I sense that he is nervous, is aware of me as another stranger, and uncertain whether I will be open with

DOI: 10.4324/9781003119593-4

him. Nasir wears a sports shirt, jeans, and running shoes, and he has a recent haircut, stylishly longer on top and shaved short on the sides.

Two young Afghanis also speak with me in the kitchen. They are more relaxed and extraverted than the others. A young man Abdul and a young woman Bashira are obviously a couple.[3] Bashira explains that she already finished secondary school in Afghanistan and studied accounting there. She is now looking for work in Berlin. She says that most of her education is recognized in Germany. I ask if she has a dream or goal for herself, and she replies that she eventually hopes to start a business. I ask what kind, and she says she would like to open a kindergarten because of a shortage of kindergarten spots for preschoolers in Berlin. Abdul jokes that she likes other people's children more than having any of her own. He hasn't been able to find work because he lacks documentation of his secondary school education in Afghanistan. He strikes me as quite a bit older than eighteen, and I wonder if his problem about lacking official documents is strategic— an intentional loss because his asylum claim might be handled less favorably if he is found to have been older than eighteen when he came to Germany.

The Afghanis I meet are generally more outgoing and expressive than the Syrians. One Syrian girl, Dina, hardly speaks at all. She seems painfully withdrawn. Another young Syrian man, Hassan, has recently become engaged to a German woman in another city. He is already wearing a wedding ring, although he says his engagement just occurred the prior weekend. He is a muscular man who appears to be in his mid-twenties. Hassan speaks little, quickly retreats to another room, and spends the evening looking at his phone. I wonder how his age might isolate him because he clearly does not appear at all adolescent. I speculate whether his engagement is to ensure another way to obtain a residency permit.

Nasir, meanwhile, begins to warm up and become talkative. He tells me that he likes Berlin because of the different people he's met here. I ask how it compares to Damascus where he is from. He replies that it is very different, saying "many kinds of people here" while spreading his arms wide apart. I ask about his school, and he answers that he is finishing tenth grade at a *Gesamtschule*, which is primarily a less academically oriented German high school. I ask if he lives near his school, and he says that he lives in the east of the city, but his school is located in the west of the city.

I realize that his apartment and school are not at all close, and I ask him how much time he spends on the subway and bus. He says at least two hours a day. As we talk, he looks at me with wide eyes that seem to plead for something, maybe just my continued interest. Nasir is a handsome young man, conveying at once both eagerness and shyness. He wants to connect with me but seems to feel awkward about wanting this. Once, he nearly cuts himself while chopping zucchini, and he asks if I can show him again how to better position the knife. I demonstrate that it is important to hold the blade slanted away from his fingers. He nods with appreciation and says in English, "It's not good if I cut me."

My interactions with Nasir remind me of the value of participating in a shared activity like cooking. Child and adolescent analysts know this especially well from play therapy and see its therapeutic effects.[4] Earlier in my career, at a day treatment program, parents and grandparents of the children who were clients repeatedly asked that we find times to cook together and have suppers as a community. They reported that they felt better about their connections with their children when we did these events. While cooking in the Center's kitchen in Berlin, there are enjoyable and playful moments as we wash, chop, and slice vegetables. I feel like an elder in their group, and it is heart-warming how they welcome me. Looking back, I wonder whether any of these young refugees might have felt something reciprocal toward me, such as seeing me as a father figure. I may have unconsciously represented both positive and shadow aspects of father, for example, someone benevolent and someone dangerous.

I ask Nasir whether he observes Ramadan, and he tells me that he fasted and emphasizes that this is not hard. Asserting an active masculine stance, he explains that he plays sports, mostly soccer, even during fasting, and he is proud that he does not get tired. He indicates that when he eats in the evening, he is not too hungry. During Ramadan, he usually stays up until 3 AM, sleeps for a few hours, and gets up at 6 AM—a time that makes sense given his long commute to get to school by 8.

Nasir is eighteen and has been in Germany for two years. He arrived during the main influx of refugees in 2015. I am careful not to ask him questions that might come across as intrusive or too personal. He tells me that he knows English, which he says helped him to learn German, although he repeatedly mentions that German is very difficult, "too many strange words." Later, he decides to sit next to me at the dinner table.

Some of the conversations in the kitchen center on questions I ask them. What is different about life in Germany? I mention that sometimes these differences can strike us as strange. Abdul quickly says, "Oh, *die Stempel*, the stamps." Everyone becomes animated. Several speak about the German fondness for officially stamped documents. Abdul explains that his papers are not valid because they have not been stamped. Ruefully, he says that others who came after him have gotten their stamps, and he adds with frustration that it seems random who gets them and who has to wait. I make a stamping motion with my hand and say, "This is part of German life," and they all laugh. The implication, however, is that without properly stamped documents, a person is adrift and unrecognized. Not quite a full person. Without papers, there are limitations on what they can do. For example, it is difficult, if not impossible, to acquire a mobile phone in their own names. Someone remarks, "No papers, nothing happens."

In a makeshift dining room, the meal is mostly quiet with episodic chitchat that the adults—many staff join this dinner—try to kindle. Much of the conversation goes through Bashira and Abdul, the two Afghanis. To myself, I wonder how many of them are thinking about their families on this religious holiday. There is a sense of sadness within the quiet. Nasir shares with me his impressions of German cuisine, which he says took getting used to. He says that the flavors ("sauerkraut, ugh!") and textures (thick breads full of grains) are very different from what he knew in Syria. As he tells me this, I think about the broad scope of adjustments facing a refugee or immigrant, things ranging from an intimidating, paternalistic bureaucracy to odd tasting foods unlike anything their mothers would have cooked. This makes me wonder about the fragility of psychic containment in such situations, especially when adolescents and children are separated from their parents.

After dinner, Nasir continues talking with me for about ninety minutes. He shifts into being more like a typical teenager, occasionally stretching out his body in careless ways, yawning now and then, and leaning forward excitedly to make a point. An art teacher from the program, a middle-aged man, sits with us and occasionally encourages Nasir to tell more.

A family's division

I learn that Nasir's older brother arrived in Germany before him. I ask Nasir why he decided to come to Germany, and he says that his decision was influenced by news reports that he and his family watched. The news indicated that there were possibilities for Syrians immigrating to Germany or Sweden, and that many Syrians had succeeded in doing so. When I ask about the war in Syria, Nasir says that there was no negative news coverage of the war on Syrian TV, and the government was always shown winning battles.

Nasir followed his brother and arrived in Germany at the start of summer in 2015. I ask whether he feels comfortable telling me about his journey, and he proceeds to carefully describe the entirety of it. He traveled during the spring, and the trek lasted about six weeks. The group he was with walked at night so they could remain under cover. There were considerable dangers of attacks by local police as well as from criminal gangs looking for refugees to take advantage of. Nasir traces their route on a large global map that hangs on the wall.

His group went by foot through Turkey to the Balkans. At first, there were about fifty of them, and they apparently did not know one another prior to this. Nasir recalls a short boat ride after sunrise, he thinks, crossing a river. He says that boats in the dark were dangerous and people drowned. I ask if he knows how to swim, and he says he does not. The group hiked through Macedonia to Serbia, and across Serbia to Hungary. They walked this whole way at night. As he outlines this route on the map, I see that it makes geographic sense, although, at times, Nasir questions himself about certain details.

I ask what it was like walking so much, and he says that it was boring, a good adolescent reply. Sometimes he was tired, although he adds that he feared falling asleep and becoming separated from the group. He explains that some did fall behind and they were lost. "At night, walking ... just black sometimes." Hearing about his journey, I feel unsettled at the sheer effort and emotional toll of it. Nasir's story strikes me as heroic and nightmarish.

Once they were in Hungary, human traffickers escorted what remained of the group into transport trucks to carry them through Austria and into Germany. I ask how it was being in the truck, and Nasir says there was no light and no fresh air where they huddled in the truck's cargo area. I tell him this sounds very rough, and he replies that he had no choice—it was "what I had to do." There is an occasional flicker in his eyes, almost a twitch, that conveys hints of a trauma that he has gone through. I notice this especially when he speaks about the possibilities of separation and being left behind by the group. I ask whether he could communicate at all with the traffickers, and he says that he could not and that they spoke a language he had never heard before. He remarks that the language sounded "like loud dogs" (barking) to him. To cope with these linguistic difficulties, he copied what others in his group did. I find his comments about not knowing this language compelling, as if he is describing a necessity to behave submissively while someone growls at him, not knowing what might happen next, and fearing for his life. This level of disorientation is probably familiar to many refugees as well as the feeling that submission might be the only way to get through something extremely threatening.

After arriving in Munich, Nasir took a bus to Berlin because his older brother was living in a town near there. In 2016, his mother came to Germany. They are still living apart. When he got to Germany, in June 2015, Nasir spoke no German. He still seems to rely as much on English as halting German to communicate. I am curious about what accommodations his German school might make to include a refugee group into its student population. I later learn that there is a wide variation in how schools provide language assistance, and that many schools do not have resources to offer any supplementary language instruction.

As we speak longer, I wonder about Nasir's father, who remains in Syria. I feel that I can tentatively ask him how often they speak and when his father might come to Germany. Nasir becomes visibly sad and slightly upset. I indicate that he does not have to answer if he prefers not to. However, he states that his father, who is a doctor but unemployed because of the war, is stranded in Syria. His father applied for a visa to leave, but since there was no German embassy open in Damascus, he had to get his visa papers in Beirut. This was—and remains—a dangerous journey, and often the border is closed because of the war. They speak by phone—Nasir's mobile phone is on the table the whole time we talk—a couple of times a week. Nasir describes where they lived in Damascus as having become a war zone because government troops and rebels fired at each other and at civilians.

He tells me that his neighborhood has been bombed by government planes. I ask Nasir whether he knows anyone who died in the war, again indicating that he does not have to tell me. I am aware that our conversation has become much more personal, and I am conscious of being sensitive to Nasir's emotional responses to what I ask him. Although there are a few times when he hesitates, he seems to genuinely appreciate my interest in him. He pauses, then says, "Yes, one person." Then a minute later, "Two people." He explains that they were both boys from his neighborhood. I choose not to pursue this emotionally charged topic of loss, and instead I ask how he now thinks about Syria. Nasir answers, "There is no future." I ask what would have happened to him if he were still living there, and he replies that he would have been drafted into the army. He explains that the government favors a few people but not the majority. Using English, he says that "connections" matter, and he describes that having ties to the ruling elite provides a person or family some protection.

"There is no future" is a statement often repeated by victims of trauma who feel that there is nothing positive ahead for them. This belief is particularly associated with childhood and adolescent trauma, and it is among one of the complicating factors in their treatment.[5] I ask Nasir what he hopes for his future in Germany. He replies that he wants to finish high school and then to start a technical training (*Berufsausbildung* in German) in the IT field. Students in Germany who follow this path usually do well and often find well-paying middle-income jobs. Nasir says that he also wants to obtain a permanent residency permit so that he can stay. He already knows some coding in HTML, and he is overly modest when telling me that he enjoys learning to code.

As we speak, I wonder about the cultural dimensions of our interacting. Nasir seems to find me approachable, but I realize that I introduced myself as from the United States, and I imagine that this might evoke unpleasant associations for him. I feel, too, that I see evidence of underlying trauma, for example, when Nasir does not claim much for himself, perhaps in case he might lose what he has already achieved at great cost. His holding back contrasts with how straightforward many adolescents his age can come across in making assertions about what they want and how they believe they can get it. At times, Nasir's eyes dart around, as those who have experienced trauma sometimes do, tensely scanning the environment and showing traces of emotional turmoil. I ask at several points whether he feels all right talking with me about these things, and he nods saying, "It's good." Occasionally, I feel a pit in my stomach, a somatic countertransference, and I wonder how this feeling resonates with whatever trauma has happened to Nasir.

Nasir continues to talk with me and his teacher, even after the other adolescents leave. He appears to like it that his teacher affectionately jokes with him and keeps encouraging him. He seems to regard his teacher as a trustworthy guide, and the positive feeling between them is apparent. They tell me that they are soon going on a camping trip to the Baltic coast. Each year, the entire program does something like this. His teacher recounts that last year they had to cut their trip short while staying in Brandenburg (the German state surrounding the city of Berlin), because local residents became openly hostile toward the teenage refugees. I ask, "Does this happen to you in Berlin too?"

Nasir confirms that this prejudice and overt antagonism also occurs in Berlin. Others in his group have experienced it as well. He does not want to tell me exact details, although he says that "drunks" often start hassling him or others with verbal insults, and "sometimes…," his voice trails off. I wonder about his reluctance to tell a fuller story. Perhaps he worries that he might offend his teacher with comments that reflect poorly on Germans. Nasir appears respectful toward staff, and this attitude may be a mix of gratitude and dependence. Dependence like this can have a shadow side when adolescents come to resent authorities and their rules. Nasir also may not want to tell me about a physical confrontation that recalls other traumatic memories, either from his journey or from Syria. It may be too much.

Nasir's survival strategy seems to be based on accommodating to his environment, learning to conform to what he perceives is expected of him. He portrays himself as determined to fit in as much as possible and to avoid situations that may compromise his life in Germany. I wonder whether he is speaking about a common tension that typifies a young refugee's dilemma of discovering how to define himself. How much conformity is required in this process? When does accommodation override significant aspects of personal history? Nasir makes clear that he does not want to attract extra attention to himself. I press him a little about that and he maintains that he is not bothered by taking this stance. He explains that his self-monitoring, which he calls "being careful," is a better option than what he left behind in Damascus, namely, living in fear of the war and its awful consequences. Nasir shakes my hand when we say goodbye and I thank him for telling me about his remarkable journey. I add that he has admirable strength in getting through all he has told me. He smiles nervously, not knowing how to accept my praise. His teacher affirms that Nasir is strong.

As Nasir is getting ready to leave, his teacher tells me about a new problem that these young refugees have encountered: proselytizing from the German branch of the Church of Scientology. Its members approach adolescents whom they believe to be refugees, and they offer them free room and board. They promise that they will "take care of" them. The refugees have no previous experience with this group, and a couple of them were fooled into accepting the offer before understanding that it was a trick. They are confused by this deception. Fortunately, they told the Center's staff when this happened. They did not realize, within their new cultural context, that they were being targeted for recruitment to Scientology. Staff have been educating the adolescents about Scientology and have cautioned them to be wary if approached. Like in the fairy tale about Hansel and Gretel, there remain many reasons to be suspicious of apparent kindness.

Cultural differences

One observation stood out during my brief time interacting with these adolescent refugees. There were obvious differences in how they expressed themselves. The Afghani adolescents did not strike me—and granted, this was a time-limited, subjective observation—as being as traumatized as the Syrian refugees. A notable contrast was evident in their stated plans for the future, with there being an open enthusiasm about it among some of the Afghanis. This was not the case among the young Syrians I met. Child psychiatrist Lenore Terr documented decades ago that childhood trauma often leads to a gloomy belief in a foreclosed future, one without viable options or much hope.[6] Experiences of trauma can permeate a victimized young person's psyche to such an extent that vitality, *Eros*, and agency feel out of reach. Libido is often trapped by the events of trauma and held in check afterward. When Nasir spoke to me about his desire to learn to code, for example, he did so with noticeable hesitation, as though he worried about even allowing himself to have this goal.

This contrast that I noticed between the Afghani and Syrian refugees might pertain to underlying differences associated with their reasons for migration. Being an economic migrant is a very different life experience than being a refugee fleeing a war zone.[7] As I was only briefly with these adolescent refugees, I do not have a fuller understanding of what contributed to the contrast that I observed among them. I was in no position to diagnose any of the adolescents whom I met at the Frei Center. However, my analytic self could not overlook, for example, the hypervigilance, the suspicion, and a sense of terror just below the surface of mundane interactions. For example, when we were making dinner in the kitchen, one of the adolescents accidentally dropped a metal pan on the floor causing a loud noise. Nasir and two other Syrians immediately sprang up from their seats before realizing it was just a pan. As he sat back down, Nasir told me that he did not like loud noises, and that this was why he avoided clubs and parties. Perhaps the relative quiet during our dinner was welcome. Nasir, like many of his peers, wanted "a normal life" in Germany. How does that quest for whatever a person calls "normal" intersect with trauma from war and dislocation? What emerges internally as a young person starts to consider his experiences of moving and resettling during this process?

The hero's journey

Germany has a history of being a land of reconstruction, with tremendous costs and labor, following World War II and again after reunification in

1990. Many newer young refugees might know little about this history or about the tragic events of the two world wars that Germany waged. A young man like Nasir is involved in a form of personal reconstruction—no simple task, and one that involves its own kinds of costs and labor. Along his journey, he showed admirable strength and persistence. He made me think about a hero's journey, like a modern-day Aeneas or Odysseus looking for home. Whereas Odysseus's tale is of a prolonged homecoming, Aeneas's story describes an immigrant's account after a terrible war devastated his home.[8] As I mention in Chapter 3, a complication for Aeneas is that so much violence is woven into his nature, that it follows him wherever he lands. He is a warrior who never stops fighting and probably could not reconstruct a sense of self without it. He is like many modern-day warrior-soldiers who struggle mightily upon their return home from war.

Monica Luci, who has written compellingly about refugees, also discusses the hero's journey as a representation of their psychic transformation. She comments that the mythical hero "offers productive reflections on the experience and possible psychological development of refugees."[9] Luci explores this idea in terms of the extreme hardships and dangers that refugees often have to confront and endure. She explains that the loss of culture, as part of both collective consciousness and collective unconsciousness, can mean not only mourning and depression, but also humiliation and betrayal for the psyche. Such difficult affects burden a refugee's individuation in a new country. Risks that are linked to the hero archetype are inflation as well as the shadow of the hero, the former reinforcing omnipotence and the latter martyrdom.[10] Possession by either of those tendencies infuses a psyche with archetypal energies that increase splitting and intolerance when a person identifies with one of them.

As refugees settling in Germany, most of the Syrian male adolescents will have to reorient themselves to Western European concepts about gender equality, tolerance about differing sexual orientations, and the importance of mutuality in male-female relationships. This re-learning about a dissimilar cultural attitude is neither quick nor trouble-free because it can challenge psychological constructs regarding masculinity and femininity that have been shaped early in development. In Cologne, Hamburg, and other German cities, the sexual assault of hundreds of women on New Year's Eve 2016 shocked Germans because many of the attackers were recently arrived refugees, and many Germans experienced these violent events as evidence of profound cultural incompatibility.[11] There are many explanations for what happened then, although I wonder exactly how do young men who are refugees begin the task of reconstructing their masculine ideologies that they carry inside them from their home countries? I explore in another book some of these problems at revising self-concepts, problems that lead to heightened alienation when an internal definition of maleness is challenged and a boy or man cannot adapt.[12] An adult male patient, who had immigrated as an adolescent to the United States from a Middle Eastern country, once said to me, "My ideas about being a man—it's like they never made the move after I'd arrived here." This description articulates a gap between cultural expectations and societal norms that can create a troubling split in a person's self-image.

For a young man like Nasir, clues about additional cultural struggle were implicit in his reluctance to speak in more detail about "the drunks" who had hassled him. Possibly, he did not want to offend the German staff at the Center. However, earlier in the kitchen, Nasir and others readily joked about German "stamps," essentially having fun over German fondness for them. Nasir's reluctance to talk about the "drunks" may have been related to a fear that the violence he knew at home could follow him into his new environment and that there were still people around him who would behave violently and cruelly. His psychological reconstruction of a self-image as an immigrant in Germany would be tested by such interactions that strike at the core of being a young man, standing up for himself, and having a need for safety as well as a desire to fit in.

The story about the refugees' unpleasant trip from the previous year to Brandenburg underscores the widespread social power of expressed biases that contribute to feeling marginalized. Psychologically speaking, marginalization weakens a capacity for feeling centered with a resilient ego related to the Self from which to speak and act with a degree of confidence. The report about the proselytizing Scientologists further illustrates social interactions that are deceiving and confuse an adolescent who is potentially lost somewhere between needing to fit in and having a fear of marginalization. The plot of being deceived by the kindness of strangers is well known in myths and fairytales. One such German tale is "Hansel and Gretel," about two children who are exiled to a forest by their parents.[13] This theme of exile reflects what Nasir and others have faced in leaving Syria, a land where a cruel father-as-dictator was, and still is, killing many of his children. The Scientologists, however, appear like the old woman in the tale, apparently kind, but really a witch in disguise who offers the abandoned children the goodies of room and board. As the reader likely knows, her true intent is to kill and eat the children, which is a symbolic action for destroying what makes them unique and concretely incorporating them—like what happens in a cult.

Suffering abandonment and being exiled from home usually create psychological vulnerabilities, and when confronted with them, naturally enough, someone might seek whatever appears safe. Disorientation and longing for safety can cloud an ability to discern what is actually dangerous. Lost in a forest, like in a foreign land, a person might trade for what seems reassuring to avoid alternatives that look too demanding or threatening. I sensed Nasir's confusion about this when he covered up his feelings about the "drunks," whose wildness might have reminded him that he was still in a forest. For someone like him, opting for conformity comes with big psychological costs, especially if it means that the new culture devours the old.

The long reach of father

Speaking with Nasir, his visible sadness about his father's situation was hard to overlook. All the adolescents in the program at the Frei Center were separated from their parents. Nasir's mother lived in another part of Germany, and he gave no sign of wanting to join her. Staff explained that his attitude was not unusual because he enjoyed considerable freedom while being apart from closer parental supervision. If and when his father arrived, Nasir might lose an autonomy that had become part of how he now saw himself. Thus, his father was both missed and regarded ambivalently as someone who could impinge on Nasir's developing self-image of who he is in this new country. Staff explained that in almost all of the Syrian families they have worked with, they have found that the father has the power to decide what everyone else in the family does and does not do.

The arrival of a father in Germany was usually accompanied by intense and unexpected conflict with the sons who have recently adopted European attitudes of clearer independence from parental authority. These sons valued their new freedoms and did not want to return to the family dynamic of their homeland. Many of them who have lived in Germany for some time have become rebellious and directly rejected their father's authority. Moreover, these young men have preceded their fathers in arriving at a safe destination and adjusting to it. They have learned many important and necessary things that their fathers would not yet know, literally surpassing the father's position in a move that diminishes his central authority. This juxtaposition creates situations that effectively reverse the family's pre-existing power dynamic because the sons have gained a deeper understanding of German culture and society and its day-to-day workings, all of which would be comparatively strange and unfamiliar for their more recently immigrated fathers.

Renos Papadopoulos and Nikos Gionakis discuss the lack of research into the plight of refugee fathers.[14] Focusing on fathers' resilience in the face of whatever trauma they have experienced, these authors find that a synergistic approach can promote healing of trauma and reinforce inherent strengths that fathers have developed. "The role of the father is central in maintaining the functionality of the family as the most supportive system, especially during times of adversity."[15] Their holistic family-systems perspective emphasizes the father as essential for a family finding its way in new and foreign surroundings. They discuss what happens to fathers dealing with grief and loss when members of a family have died during their migration. By comparison, the adolescents at the Frei Center confronted different features of family breakdown, chiefly because they immigrated alone as unaccompanied minors. As a result, many of them showed signs of having shifted prematurely into quasi-adult independence further straining their distant family connections. Papadopoulos and Gionakis cite numerous risks that refugee families encounter, such as "allowing new realities, new identities, and new imbalances to create destructive divisions within the family."[16] Fathers who are refugees have to deal with multiple losses in employment, autonomy, property, authority, and other functions of their role within families. Working with refugee families, Papadopoulos and Gionakis propose a therapeutic stance that deconstructs a tendency to polarize refugee fathers as either damaged-victimized or resilient-omnipotent.

The intensity of mourning an absent father while growing into early manhood can be quite problematic.[17] For Nasir and his father, there was a logistical reality of physical alienation keeping him and his father apart. From what the staff at the Frei Center explained from their experiences of refugee fathers and their sons, Nasir might also face psychological alienation from his father, especially if he were eventually able to join his family in Germany. In the meantime, Nasir was trying to hold onto the father he knew, while becoming a young man in his absence.

Luigi Zoja, in his book about fathers, discusses the Trojan War, providing an analytic interpretation of the male figures Hector and Aeneas.[18] Zoja suggests that, although each is different, Hector and Aeneas represent a type of dedicated, heroic father who claims fatherhood as a duty to his children and to his elders. This duty includes a respect for the significance of generational passage. Furthermore, this ideal, protective father wants the best for his sons, even as this desire admits that his own star must eventually fade. Such a desirable father allows for feelings of competition and envy as inevitable aspects within a father-son dynamic, but he has enough intuition or consciousness to contain his reactions when they might threaten his son's aspirations and ambitions. Zoja, in discussing these Trojan male characters, notes that Hector lifts his son, Astyanax, above himself in a symbolic gesture of presenting his son for the future and superseding himself, and that Aeneas also carries his father, Anchises, during their flight.[19] He sees these actions as representing "vertical" generational bonds that fathers transmit to their sons as messages about shouldering burdens and facing their own futures head on: "The image of Aeneas in flight with his father and his son is the central link in the chain of fathers that held society together."[20]

As I describe in Chapter 3, Aeneas's story includes three generations immigrating together (although Anchises, his father, dies on the way). Aeneas's immigration story is, therefore, quite different from what a boy like Nasir has experienced in leaving his father behind in a desperate war-torn situation. When Nasir said that there was "no future" in Syria, perhaps he also alluded to his separation from his father. It was unclear whether his father would be able to come to Germany. Nasir's father was not physically present to metaphorically lift him into his new future. Keeping these separate realities in mind would tax any adolescent with difficult feelings, such as guilt, remorse, and anger, making his transition into adulthood fraught with untold conflicts.

Father as carrier of a spiritual impulse

A rather different father-son story in The Aeneid concerns Laocoön and his two sons.[21] He is the priest who attempts to warn the Trojans about the ruse of the wooden horse. The horse hides the Greek soldiers who will later escape and sack the city. To stop Laocoön from uncovering the Greeks, Minerva (Athena) sends a giant sea serpent to strangle him and his two sons. A famous classical sculpture of this scene by Agesander and Polydorus is located at the Vatican. Here, I mention this story not only because it contrasts with Aeneas, who represents warrior culture, but also because it shows a paternal carrier of the spiritual lineage of the Trojans being attacked and destroyed. Based on my observations of the adolescents at the Frei Center, this other role of a father as representing a spiritual attitude did not seem especially relevant for them. The staff indicated that few of the clients seemed genuinely religious. When I asked Nasir if he prayed outside of Ramadan, he shrugged and said, "Sometimes."

Laocoön's fate can be understood as symbolizing certain cultural elements that died for the Trojans when they fled after their defeat—for example, something of their own unique spiritual tradition was lost. Considering Nasir's situation and that of his Syrian peers in this light, I wonder how a Muslim boy separated from his father would begin to make sense of the cultural traditions belonging to an overwhelmingly Christian country with an especially violent and genocidal history around religious differences. At a minimum, there was a sociocultural irony in the proselytizing of devout Scientologists who appeared to be trying to take advantage of an absence of paternal guidance that might have otherwise held onto these adolescents' spiritual traditions, keeping them alive in a family. I can imagine that a physically present Muslim father would protect and shield his family from such masquerading intrusions and deceptions that try to undermine the religious life of his family. Further, such a father might himself seek connections with Muslim spiritual communities and cultural organizations to preserve the values and beliefs of the family's religious background. Without these efforts, a young Muslim refugee could become further alienated from his heritage as well as confused by whatever presentations of Christianity he encounters.

Interventions, coping, and resilience

When researching material for this chapter, I discovered Renos Papadopoulos's informative edited book about refugees, *Therapeutic Care for Refugees: No Place Like Home*.[22] I wish I had read it before I went to Berlin. Celia Jaes Falicov, in her foreword, writes, "To build bridges of human connectedness between strangers in language and in values about health and mental health, gender discourses, styles of emotional communication and other aspects of relational life, is the daunting task of all cross-cultural work."[23] A multitude of potential stumbling blocks, biases, and misunderstandings around culture, race, gender, sexuality, language, and ethnicity can easily occur.

When work with refugees incorporates psychotherapeutic principles, Papadopoulos terms it *therapeutic care*. He discusses intense psychic disruptions happening due to the loss of a home, which is typically a place that contains and organizes us at multiple levels, for instance, psyche, family, culture. Symbolically, a home is also like a psyche with its different rooms and levels, points of entry and exit, windows to the outside, and contents of what is inside. "Homecoming nostalgia" implies a search to return to the familiar in our environment and in our psyches.[24] The word *nostalgia* comes from Greek and means an ache for being home, to return home, and it arises with homesickness when what is unfamiliar overwhelms us.

Papadopoulos emphasizes that not all refugees are traumatized. He explains that trauma means wound, and many wounds activate self-healing capacities in us.[25] He believes it is vital that those working with refugees avoid mislabeling them as traumatized just because they have been through "devastating events," when usually, there are different phases to their journeys and not all of those will be devastating or arduous.[26] Other contributors to this book discuss paradoxical situations that arise when working with refugees. For example, Valerie Sinason comments, "Working with the actual pain of external reality is not popular."[27] She speaks to professional biases that tend to overlook and even downplay the lived realities of suffering as opposed to fantasies and internal beliefs about them. Psychotherapists and analysts might inadvertently show such biases when they engage either directly by treating refugees or indirectly by providing consultation to those who do. Speaking to a need for an expanded therapeutic framework, Maureen Fox writes, "The burden of the psychological pain suffered by refugees is enormous and its survival requires considerable resilience to tap into whatever personal, social and agency support may be on offer."[28] She reminds us that interdisciplinary therapeutic teams are often necessary to help refugees who are unable to mobilize their inner resources, and this can include case management as well as practical assistance with daily living tasks.

A more recent book, *Mental Health Practice with Immigrant and Refugee Youth: A Socioecological Framework*, which is written by two psychologists and a social worker from the Refugee Trauma and Resilience Center at Boston Children's Hospital, sketches a picture of concentric circles to illustrate a social ecology for supporting refugees and immigrants.[29] These include family, school, neighborhood, society, and culture. This book's authors name four core stressors often emerging during resettlement: (1) trauma exposure, (2) resettlement stress, (3) acculturative stress, and (4) isolation.[30] Additionally, they use the idea of intersectionality to understand the various social and identity categories that refugee and immigrant youth belong to. *Intersectionality* "refers to the way in which we all are the product of multiple, interacting social and cultural identities."[31] *Resettlement stress* pertains to actual resource problems that refugees and immigrants have with financial support, healthcare, and employment. I discuss trauma exposure and acculturative stress in Chapter 1 of this book.

Elaborating on resettlement stress, the authors of *Mental Health Practice with Immigrant and Refugee Youth* mention that for immigrants and refugees, lack of trust in authorities and suspicions about government agencies hinder their access to mental health care.[32] Refugees and immigrants might not believe assertions about confidentiality and instead think that psychotherapists are acting on behalf of the government. This observation is consistent with what the staff at the Frei Center articulated as a main reason why the adolescents in their care often refused referral for psychotherapy. Citing additional research, these authors note that full proficiency in learning the English language frequently can take eight or more years and is made more difficult for those who have had their schooling interrupted by migration.[33] As English is considered a Germanic language, I would infer that learning German for Syrian and Afghani youth could be similarly difficult unless, of course, they had already acquired some English or German at school in their home countries.[34] A unique problem for younger children who migrate is that they might not become fully proficient in any language especially when they have not done so in their native languages. Besides resisting mental health support and facing language obstacles, refugee and immigrant youth are particularly hard to assess with psychological tools because there is a lack of any standardized tests for this purpose, and even when translations can be used, they have not been validated on the appropriate reference populations.[35]

The Economist reports that there are mixed results for the migrants Germany took in recently.[36] On August 31, 2015, Angela Merkel famously declared, "*Wir schaffen das*," meaning "We can handle it [or do it]."[37] She invited Middle Eastern refugees stuck elsewhere in Europe to come to Germany, and over a million did so. This humanitarian gesture was generous and full of good intentions. *The Economist* notes, however, that although more than 60 percent of these refugees found employment, "barely half" work in skilled jobs, whereas more than 80 percent of them did in their home countries.[38] This article mentions the disillusionment of some refugees, especially in contending with a dense German bureaucracy, and notes that many failed asylum seekers are struggling to stay in Germany. A poll of Germans found that a majority thought the country should not take in any more refugees.

Even trying to grasp a bit of understanding about the plight of refugees from the war in Syria is depressing and haunting, to say the least, because so many of their experiences have been incomprehensible. Feras Fayyad's documentary film *Last Men in Aleppo* portrays the relentless horror that people in Syria have suffered.[39] This film shows the heroic activities of the White Helmets, a volunteer civil defense brigade that tried to rescue victims of bombings from collapsed houses and fallen buildings in Aleppo. Over 250,000 people were stranded in Aleppo when Russia began a bombing campaign in 2015. In many scenes, babies and children are dug from the rubble, some screaming, bleeding, and terrified but alive, others sapped and dead. A main character, Khaled, persists and says, "It's our duty. We're in this together." A boy saved by another volunteer, Mahmoud, keeps asking him later during a visit, "How did you get me out?" because it seems he cannot believe that he survived. Moments of hope in the documentary include a rainbow during a ceasefire, goldfish that Khaled buys and puts into a fountain basin he and his friends have cleaned out, and celebration of a local wedding.

The dark brutality of Assad and his Russian allies, however, is never far away in the film. Fayyad was himself imprisoned and severely tortured by members of the Syrian regime's military. As I write this, he is in hiding in Europe and has testified at the first worldwide trial of state torture in Syria.[40] The trial is taking place in Koblenz, Germany, with two Syrian military men accused of torture.[41] Torture is defined in the Istanbul Protocol, a manual for investigating and documenting torture, as "severe pain or suffering ... intentionally inflicted on a person for such purposes as obtaining ... a confession, punishing him ... or intimidating or coercing him ... with the consent or acquiescence of a public official...."[42]

When I heard Fayyad speak at a workshop on human rights, he said about his work in film, "Humans tell the story, not the camera." He emphasized the importance of telling these agonizing stories, including his own, and of our hearing them, because they show the world some of the darkest parts of human experience that would likely be otherwise ignored. The act of telling their stories helps survivors to overcome their isolation and suffering.

Considering these various perspectives, I wonder about the psychosocial challenges for the young refugees I met as they try to adapt to their new country, which has had, and continues to have, a troubled relationship with marginalized groups and which still harbors authoritarian expressions of xenophobia and anti-Semitism.[43] The degree of their success at individuating in this context will depend in large part on what happens with their *identity formation*, a concept that I will evaluate more in Chapter 6. Salman Akhtar, a psychoanalyst born in India who practices and teaches in the United States, comments on the difference between "living" and "living in someplace" as representative of the strain that many immigrants feel upon resettling.[44] Whereas "living" assumes a felt continuity and flow with a person's environment and society, "living in someplace" refers to a very different experience when a person is, instead, aware of gaps in these relationships. Psychologically, those gaps can lead to discomfort, distress, and anxiety over dislocation. Akhtar has found that immigrants adapt through various means, such as *repudiation* (the real changes in circumstances are considered minimal to nonexistent), *return* (planning on going back), *replication* (re-creating a homeland here), *reunion* (longing and nostalgia for an idealized homeland), and *reparation* (identification with treasured aspects of homeland).[45] I wonder which of these patterns becomes dominant within a young refugee's psyche and eventually shapes how they understand themselves.

Repudiation suggests problematic splitting of the self from before the move and after it. The trauma of war and violence can reinforce psychic splits and reliance on dissociation to avoid emotional pain. Return implies leading an "as if" existence, tentative and on hold, and not ready to put down any roots. Replication denies the effects of real changes and perpetuates a melancholic stance of trying vainly to preserve the past and live in it. Reunion defers real developmental opportunities by forsaking what presents itself here and now, and instead clinging to a utopian fantasy of a future elsewhere. Reparation offers some sign of a depressive position, namely, showing a combination of gratitude for where an immigrant comes from and what they have gone through during their journey, and mourning their losses along this path. A grieving process often allows refugees to let go of the past and make it more secure internally as memory. Keeping treasured memories of a homeland alive as inner resources in late adolescence and early adulthood can help a person who has migrated to a new place answer questions such as "Where did I come from?" and "How does that live on in me now?"

Researchers from Germany found that marginalization poses a central obstacle for adolescent refugees, and that unaccompanied minors, who are frequently older adolescents upon migration, show increased PTSD symptoms.[46] To aim for better psychosocial outcomes, they emphasize the importance of forming connections to new people and communities where they now live. Essentially, they recommend a grieving process that helps an immigrant to move on psychologically. Sometimes, this is not possible. For example, Lenore Terr states that psychotherapeutic intervention for children and adolescents with complex trauma is much more difficult: "The child's story, as far as it is known, even if fragmented, is the story that the clinician will work with."[47] Obviously, psychotherapy with traumatized refugee youth will be vastly different from what a clinician does with non-traumatized patients, and therapeutic expectations have to be adjusted about slowly piecing together personal narratives that evolve bit by bit.

I experienced impressive resilience in Nasir and the other youth whom I met at the Frei Center. A lot of what happens in adolescence is a result of trial and error. An ability to shed what has not worked and to bounce back is crucial for rebalancing needs for education, sexuality, intimacy, spirituality, and friendship. Containment in this process, those external concentric circles mentioned earlier, comes through the meaningful actions of parents and other important adults who can lift—somewhat analogously to Aeneas or Hector—a discouraged or dispirited young person and present them an orientation to the future. Psychosocial adjustment doesn't only imply showing heroism or fighting for a place. When it includes a spiritual dimension, a young person's life experience is enriched and made soulful. I believe it is important along an immigrant's path for them to remain open to a spiritual dimension, a spiritual link with their heritage. That is what Laocoön and his sons stand for.

Of course, there are many kinds of fathering, most of which are not mythical like that of Hector, Aeneas, or Laocoön. While I was helping prepare dinner in the Center's kitchen, as I chopped vegetables, I had a memory of my father showing me how to remove the husk from an ear of corn. This mundane, down-to-earth fathering passes along something implicit that is tied to traditions, skills, and a shared heritage. Nasir seemed to be finding some of this fatherly concern in his relationship with his art teacher by learning from him, and I hope that this eased his adjustment to Germany, especially since he was separated from his father.

Notes

1 The Brothers Grimm, "Hansel and Gretel," *Grimms' Fairy Tales,* trans. Edgar Taylor and Marian Edwardes (Project Gutenberg, E-Book #2591), 197.
2 Based on Robert Tyminski, "Just Black Sometimes, Part 2: Reflections on an Adolescent's Journey," *Journal of Analytical Psychology* 64, no. 3 (2019): 386–405.
3 Not their actual names.
4 Phyllis M. Cohen and Albert J. Solnit, "Play and Therapeutic Action," *Psychoanalytic Study of the Child* 48, no. 1 (1993): 49–63; Linda C. Mayes and Donald J. Cohen, "Playing and Therapeutic Action in Child Analysis," *International Journal of Psychoanalysis* 74, no. 6 (1993): 1235–1244.
5 Lenore C. Terr, "Children of Chowchilla: A Study of Psychic Trauma," *Psychoanalytic Study of the Child* 34, no. 1 (1979): 547–623; Kathleen Kostelny, Nancy Dubrow, and James Garbarino, *Children in Danger: Coping with the Consequences of Community Violence* (San Francisco, CA: Jossey-Bass, 1992); Daniel J. Siegel, *The Developing Mind: Toward a Neurobiology of Interpersonal Experience* (New York and London: Guilford Press, 1999); Bessel van der Kolk, *The Body Keeps the Score: Brain, Mind, and Body in the Healing of Trauma* (New York: Penguin, 2014).
6 Terr, "Children of Chowchilla."
7 This chapter was written many months before the fall of Afghanistan to the Taliban; it is based on events from 2017.
8 Robert Fagles, trans., *Homer: The Odyssey* (London & New York: Penguin, 1996). See notes from Chapter 3 for references to translations of *The Aeneid.*
9 Monica Luci, "Inner and Outer Travels: Analytical Psychology and the Treatment of Refugees," *Quadrant* 46, no. 2 (2016): 35–55.
10 Ibid., 49.
11 Rick Noack, "2,000 Men 'Sexually Assaulted 1,200 Women' at Cologne New Year's Eve Party," *The Independent,* July 11, 2016, https://www.independent.co.uk/news/world/europe/cologne-new-year-s-eve-mass-sex-attacks-leaked-document-a7130476.html

12 Robert Tyminski, *Male Alienation at the Crossroads of Identity, Culture and Cyberspace* (London: Routledge, 2019).

13 Grimms Fairy Tales, "Hansel and Gretel."

14 Renos K. Papadopoulos and Nikos Gionakis, "The Neglected Complexities of Refugee Fathers." *Psychotherapy and Politics International* 16, no. 1 (2018): https://doi.org/10.1002/ppi.1438

15 Ibid., 4.

16 Ibid., 4.

17 Tyminski, *Male Alienation at the Crossroads*.

18 Luigi Zoja, *The Father: Historical, Psychological and Cultural Perspectives* (Hove & New York: Brunner-Routledge, 2001).

19 Ibid., 87, 142.

20 Ibid., 142.

21 Virgil, *The Aeneid*, trans. John Dryden (Project Gutenberg E-Book #228, 2008), Book 2, 124–149.

22 Renos K. Papadopoulos, *Therapeutic Care for Refugees: No Place Like Home* (London: Karnac, 2002).

23 Ibid., xvii.

24 Ibid., 24.

25 Ibid., 32.

26 Ibid., 157.

27 Valerie Sinason, "Killing Time: Work with Refugees," in *Therapeutic Care for Refugees*, ed. Renos K. Papadopoulos (London: Karnac, 2002), 136.

28 Maureen Fox, "Finding a Way Through: From Mindlessness to Minding," in *Therapeutic Care for Refugees*, ed. Renos K. Papadopoulos (London: Karnac, 2002), 110.

29 B. Heidi Ellis, Saida M. Abdi, and Jeffrey P. Winer, *Mental Health Practice with Immigrant and Refugee Youth: A Socioecological Framework* (Washington, DC, American Psychological Association, 2020).

30 Ibid., 15.

31 Ibid., 27.

32 Ibid., 39.

33 Ibid., 44.

34 William G. Moulton and Anthony F. Buccini, "Germanic Languages," *Encyclopædia Britannica*, February 23, 2020, https://www.britannica.com/topic/Germanic-languages

35 Ellis, Abdi, and Winer, *Mental Health Practice with Immigrant and Refugee Youth*, 72.

36 "Germany's Refugee Influx: Did They Handle It?" *The Economist*, August 29, 2020, 39–40.

37 von Mathis Feldhoff, "Fünf Jahre 'Wir schaffen das'—Ein Satz für das Geschichtsbuch," *zdf Heute*, August 29, 2020, https://www.zdf.de/nachrichten/politik/wir-schaffen-das-merkel-100.html

38 "Germany's Refugee Influx," *The Economist*, 39.

39 *Last Men in Aleppo*, directed by Feras Fayyad (Grasshopper Films, 2017).

40 European Center for Constitutional and Human Rights (ECCHR), "First Criminal Trial Worldwide on Torture in Syria before a German Court," https://www.ecchr.eu/en/case/first-criminal-trial-worldwide-on-torture-in-syria-before-a-german-court/

41 "Syrian Victims of Torture Testify in German Court," *DW*, https://www.dw.com/en/syrian-victims-of-torture-testify-in-german-court/a-53699921

42 United Nations High Commissioner for Human Rights (UNHCHR), *Istanbul Protocol: Manual on the Effective Investigation and Documentation of Torture and Other Cruel, Inhuman or Degrading Treatment or Punishment*, No. 8/Rev. 1 (New York and Geneva: United Nations, 2004), 1, https://www.ohchr.org/Documents/Publications/training8rev1en.pdf

43 Derek Scally, "German Outrage over High-Profile Anti-semitic Attacks," *The Irish Times*, April 21, 2018, https://www.irishtimes.com/news/world/europe/german-outrage-over-high-profile-anti-semitic-attacks-1.3468681

44 Salman Akhtar, *Immigration and Acculturation: Mourning, Adaptation and the Next Generation* (New York, Jason Aronson, 2011).

45 Ibid., 9–17.

46 Linda P. Juang et al., "Using Attachment and Relational Perspectives to Understand Adaptation and Resilience among Immigrant and Refugee Youth," *American Psychologist* 73, no. 6 (2018): 803.

47 Lenore C. Terr, "Treating Childhood Trauma," *Child & Adolescent Psychiatry Clinics* 22, no. 1 (2013): 57, http://dx/doi.org/10.1016/j.chc.2012.08.003

Chapter 5

Ad Astra

As Aeneas recounts an earlier part of their voyage, he mentions a brief landing at Chaonia in Epirus, an area of the northwestern mainland of Greece. There, he and his followers meet one of Priam's sons, Helenus, and Hector's widow, Andromachë. Survivors of the Trojan war who were brought to Greece against their will, they now rule a kingdom. Seeing Aeneas, Andromachë asks him about Ascanius: "What hopes are promis'd from his blooming years?"[1] It is the primary question that many migrants face when thinking about the fate of their children in a new country.

Aeneas's son Ascanius is present throughout The Aeneid. Aeneas describes their escape from the burning city of Troy, when Ascanius would have likely been a child of around four or five. By the time the Trojans reach Italy in the last part of Virgil's epic, about eight years have passed, and Ascanius would now be around twelve or thirteen.[2] His uncle is Hector of Iliad fame. In the course of The Aeneid, Ascanius develops, learns to ride horseback and to hunt. He witnesses battles and later kills a Rutulian before being admonished by a disguised Apollo to leave the battlefield because Ascanius must survive to become the ancestor of the Julian line that will rule Rome. Ascanius represents an archetype of a male youth who is oriented toward a promising future. Louis Feldman, a classics scholar, writes, "The divinely-chosen Ascanius has a great mission to perform… It was Virgil who introduced into the epic the fighting and history-making *puer* as an important type."[3]

In Latin, *puer* means boy or child. As an archetypal symbol, *puer* can designate many remarkable qualities including, as Jung notes, "wonder-child, divine child, born, and brought up in quite extraordinary circumstances" and not a human child.[4] Ascanius fits this category as an example of a boy with divine heritage—his paternal grandmother was Venus (Aphrodite)—and with a potential to accomplish exceptional things in the mortal world. As such, he transcends the limitations of earthly reality because he symbolizes what could be, what could happen, and what could ensue. Ascanius thus reflects a hope, perhaps unconscious, often present in immigrants and refugees, which their families will aspire to realize, because of sons and daughters who have a capacity for something outstanding. This

DOI: 10.4324/9781003119593-5

hope fuels dreams, ambitions, and plans for achieving a better life. It is not something to be dismissed or taken for granted based on whether these possibilities can be actualized according to some plan because, instead, its magic for motivation comes from imagining them.

Jung thought the child archetype conveyed human wholeness, a worthy goal that is so often beyond our reach, but one that still moves us: "The 'child' [archetype] is all that is abandoned and exposed and divinely powerful: the insignificant dubious beginning, and the triumphal end."[5] In the context of The Aeneid, a small boy flees a defeated and burning city, beginning a voyage that endures for years. Whatever magic his destiny contains is constantly challenged by threats, detours, and fighting. He could have died, as did other boys in The Aeneid. Instead, he makes it to Italy, older but still a youth, and becomes in Roman ideology about ancestry the ultimate forbearer, more than even his father Aeneas. His triumph, of course, is mythic, not what really happened, although amazing consequences unfold often enough in actual life. Almost 44 percent of Fortune 500 companies were founded by immigrants or their children, quite a statement about pursuing hope and making it something real.[6]

The fragility of the child archetype is also illustrated, by way of contrast, in The Aeneid. Two other boys die in battle. Lausus, the son of the Etruscan king Mezentius who fights against the Trojans, dies trying to save his father from Aeneas. Aeneas regrets killing Lausus because he sees the boy's loyalty to his father. Recall that *pietas* or piety, in this case *filial piety*, was an honorable virtue in The Aeneid and in Roman society. As I explain in Chapter 3, Pallas, the son of King Evander, who is allied with the Trojans, also dies in battle after accompanying Aeneas. Aeneas regards his responsibility toward Pallas as paternal and thus of great importance. His fate serves as a dramatic parallel to Lausus's; Pallas is killed by Turnus, Aeneas's main rival, who takes his sword belt as booty. Aeneas is enraged over losing Pallas because he was protecting the boy like a son, and later, at the end, his rage motivates him to kill Turnus. The deaths of Lausus, Pallas, and Euryalus, another youth, demonstrate that young men are mortal and vulnerable in ways that cannot be predicted. This contrast with Ascanius's destiny makes not only their deaths even more moving, but also his survival more compelling for representing a positive orientation toward the future.

Case example—not knowing

Arturo, a Latino man in his early thirties, came to see me because of a recent HIV positive diagnosis. He had seroconverted and was depressed at this news. He told me that he was an only child who grew up in Texas with a single mother. He never knew his father. Arturo had moved to the San Francisco Bay Area five years before and worked in retail for a department store. His mother had died ten years ago from a massive heart attack. At his first visit, Arturo was casually dressed, talkative, and friendly. He was upset about his HIV status and worried about dying prematurely like his mother.

As we got acquainted, I learned that Arturo had been very close to his mother. He called himself "a mama's boy," and he explained to me in Spanish this is *niño de mama.* He added that he was teased throughout elementary and high school for being effeminate and was often called *marica,* or sissy. His father was a man in Mexico whom he had never met or spoken to. Arturo never came out to his mother although he realized he was gay when he was nine and had a crush on another boy. After she died, he began going more to the gym to life weights, becoming muscular. He became tearful whenever he mentioned her, and I thought about his grief at losing her and never knowing his father. Perhaps, I wondered, his muscularity was both protection from this grief and a search for a masculine ideal that he had never known.

After working together for a few months, Arturo came in one day and said, "I have to tell you something. It's been on my mind since we met, and I haven't known how to bring it up. It's a little embarrassing." I commented that he must be anxious holding on to something like this and not knowing how to tell me. He agreed and continued, "My dark side has a name. It's actually like a personality that I can use."

RT: What do you call him?
Arturo: Rico. Rico Suave.
RT: What does his name mean?
Arturo: It's kind of a joke, really. *Rico* is rich, and *suave* is gentle or soft. But Rico Suave is like a player.
RT: A player?
Arturo: Yeah, a player. You know, someone who fools around for the heck of it, who gets excited about sex just to have sex, and it doesn't matter. No strings attached.
RT: I see. How do you feel when you're Rico?
Arturo: Powerful, exciting, sometimes even campy. You know, Latino guys and the whole macho thing. It's like I can play at being extreme and see who's going to fall for it. You'd be surprised how many guys do.
RT: I'm thinking that you just told me about Rico and said you hesitated until now. Do you think Rico was checking me out to see if I might be a man who'd fall for him?
Arturo: (Laughs) *Posiblemente* (in Spanish). I'm a little worried about what you'll think about me and probably him too.
RT: Did you intend to use Spanish right then?
Arturo: Did I? (Pauses) It slipped out, I guess.

I thought it was important that Arturo used Spanish with me in this unconscious way, and it reminded me of the dualities that exist in all of us.

Arturo described many in his life: mother/father, Arturo/Rico, English/ Spanish, ego/dark side, Texas/Mexico, sissy/muscular, HIV–/HIV+. His using Spanish might also have expressed his sexual feeling toward me and a wish that I would fall for Rico's charms. Would I be seduced by the "player"? What kind of man was I compared to an absent father and the cultural trappings of Mexican machismo?

Soon after this session, I asked Arturo whether he was aware of any other split parts in his life, especially anything from his childhood. He replied,

> It's funny you should ask that because I've been thinking about what happened my freshman year of high school. There was this huge secret my mother was keeping, and it all spilled out when my classmates and I were supposed to cross the border for a day trip to Juárez [Mexico].

I asked him what had happened. Arturo explained that his mother told him he could not go on this field trip. At first, she simply insisted she needed him to come home from school early that day, but he saw through her ruse. He continued to protest, and finally, she told him the truth: they were not citizens; they were illegal; and if he was discovered at the border, then he could be detained or even deported to Mexico. He was shocked to learn this; he thought he had been born in the United States. However, his mother recounted that he had been born in Mexico, and she brought him along when she crossed illegally. They had lived at first with her uncle until she found work as a seamstress in a clothing factory. She never had a driver's license, which explained why she had taken buses to and from work and around town to shop. He had never thought about this when he was younger, but when she told him as a high school freshman, he felt pieces of their lives falling into place. He remembered once asking her whether they could visit their Mexican relatives, and she told him that it was not possible because these relatives had disowned her. He was confused hearing her say this because they exchanged cards, letters, and even presents at Christmas, so how had they disowned her?

As Arturo spoke, he alternated between sadness, guilt, and anger. He did not want to speak badly about his mother, yet he felt this deception hung over his entire childhood. He did not go on the field trip to Juárez and began to wonder how he would get a driver's license or later, a job, if he did not have documents. His mother apparently "borrowed" a cousin's social security number in order to work herself. Arturo now said he understood why the two of them had lived in comparative isolation, because his mother needed to protect their identities. I asked him what he remembered about being in high school as a teenager with this recognition about him and his mother and their status in the United States.

Arturo said that "it was a little nightmare." I inquired whether he had had nightmares then, and he said, "Yes, they started around that time. They were versions of someone coming and taking me away from her. She'd be crying and I'd be screaming, and I'd wake up sweating. These are violent memories." When he was a sophomore in high school, he was in a car that an older friend was driving when they got into an accident with a truck. The police came, and Arturo recalled "blanking out." He remembered that no one was seriously hurt, but that he and his friend were taken to the hospital with cuts and bruises. He recalled staring at a form in the emergency room and not knowing what to write on it. Would he get into trouble if he used his real name and address? He pretended to be too woozy to be able to complete it, and a nurse told him never mind. When his uncle and mother arrived at the hospital, the first thing they asked upon seeing him was "Did you fill out any forms?" He told them no, and his mother looked relieved. He was angry that they had not first asked how he was.

In 1986, Congress passed and President Reagan signed the Immigration Reform and Control Act. This law granted temporary legal status to illegal residents who entered the United States before 1982 and once they had this status, they could apply for permanent residency and a Green Card.[7] Approximately 2.7 million illegal residents were given legal status under this law.[8] Near the end of his junior year of high school, Arturo's mother and uncle informed him that they had a special surprise—his mother had applied for legal status and it had been granted. Arturo remembered going to a government building in their city with his mother and uncle where he and his mother filled out paperwork and soon obtained legal residency. He explained to me that right afterward, he went to get his driver's permit.

In the following months of his psychotherapy, Arturo tried to bridge what he came to understand as the divides in his life. He tracked down and wrote to his father in Mexico. He remained unsure about whether he wanted to see him, but it seemed like a step in the right direction to healing a deep wound around paternal absence in his psyche. Rico Suave held less of a grip on Arturo as he spoke more about this character. After a session in which he blamed Rico for contracting HIV, Arturo reported this dream:

> I walk into bedroom and see a boy sleeping in the bed. He's about ten, thin and gangly like I was. He's holding a stuffie. I slept with those until I was thirteen. Morning light is coming through the blinds. I hear the boy moaning because he's having a bad dream. I go over to his bed and sit on the edge. I reach over and pat him on the back and he settles down.

He looked moved as he told me the dream, and I asked him how he felt. Arturo answered, "It's sad how alone I used to feel. All that loneliness in me, all those years living with a big secret no one told me."

Thinking about his dream, I replied, "Yes, you suffered from many secrets as a boy. And now as a man, you are looking for truth about yourself. Sometimes, the dawn brings relief." Arturo smiled at me. "I think Rico was a creation of mine to cope with all the things I felt I never knew. He was a man of secrets to cover up the existence of secrets. Maybe I can let go of him now." I agreed with Arturo that his insight about Rico was valuable and that having some distance from Rico might allow him to take better care of himself.

This period of Arturo's psychotherapy illustrates the divisive aspects of an immigrant story in which a child's potential is hidden from him because of real constraints imposed by the government, by his family, and by his own differences growing up as a gay boy in an unsupportive environment. Arturo's dream is about him locating that potential—in morning light—to reconnect with a capacity to know what he needs and how to find it. The multiple secrets—his father, his origins, his legal status in the United States, his mother's history—all encapsulated Arturo as a man not yet able to know himself. The creation of Rico Suave was a symbolic expression of his search for masculinity, for a father, and for a male partner who could know Arturo. His personal story shows the psychological burdens of an immigrant growing up unsure of who he is or who he can be.

Children and differences

How do the burdens such as the ones Arturo carried turn up and manifest for children who come to a new country as immigrants? Questions such as "How am I seen?" and "What do I see?" are salient here. They point toward visible differences that can be bridged mostly, partly, or not at all. What occurs when children become aware of differences in culture, ethnicity, race, religion, sexual orientation, and language? And how does their social environment support, stigmatize, and suppress this awareness?

Bias develops early in childhood. *Explicit bias* is conscious stereotyping, holding prejudice, and engaging in discriminatory behaviors. It emerges between the ages of three to six and declines between the ages of seven to twelve when children usually learn that openly showing bias is problematic and undesired among peers and at their schools.[9] *Implicit bias* is unconscious stereotyping, having prejudice, and engaging in discriminatory behaviors. It too begins around age three when children demonstrate preferences for wealthier and higher status racial groups. Miao Qian et al. studied Chinese children and found that although explicit bias declined after age ten, anti-Black implicit biases persisted.[10] Jennifer Rennels and Judith Langlois, using picture boards of Black children and white children, likewise reported that children's biases based on perceived attractiveness were especially strong for girls, even exceeding, in some instances, those for race.[11]

Implicit biases appear more stable throughout childhood than explicit ones. Antonya Gonzalez, Jennifer Steele, and Andrew Baron looked at whether implicit bias can be reduced through positive educational interventions that expose them to counterstereotype examples.[12] They found that older children of about ten years do reduce their implicit biases through this intervention but that younger children do not.[13] According to the authors, this occurs because of older children's increased cognitive skills and flexibility, whereas younger children do not always use race as a primary category in reasoning tasks. Older children use race more measurably and thus may be more open to this sort of intervention.

Similar research around perceptions of pain with incidents like burning one's tongue and stubbing one's toe also found racial biases in children. Rebecca Dore et al. reported that by age ten, white children judged Black people to experience less pain in these situations than white people would.[14] Noting that this bias emerged as a trend by age seven and was not detectable at age five, they speculated that this bias was explicit rather than implicit because it did not remain stable across age groupings. Their research shows a difficulty among white children about empathizing with Black children when they cannot appreciate their pain.

Racism can be defined by behaviors, laws, and procedures that establish advantages for a privileged group and that exclude and deprive having these advantages to minority groups.[15] Examining the personal experiences of African American boys, Vanessa Nyborg and John Curry found that exposure to racial biases damaged their psychological well-being. These children, with an average age of twelve and a half, showed a correlation between experiences of racism and more internalizing symptoms like somatic complaints, depression, anxiety, and withdrawal. Their self-concept was lower, and they reported higher levels of hopelessness.[16] This study is important for illustrating that the detrimental effects of racism can impinge on healthier psychological development in profound ways.

Children learn about differences within their families, spanning a continuum from embracing them to tolerating them to rejecting them. Parents provide direct and indirect, conscious and unconscious, information and behavioral patterns about where on this continuum a family is situated. Jenna Kelley Zucker and Meagan Patterson examined the racial socialization practices among white American parents with children aged eight to twelve.[17] They reported that these parents were unlikely to address or discuss racial issues openly with their children and less than one-third of parents encouraged their children to bring these up within the family. Further, they found that less biased parents and families were more likely to have color-conscious attitudes about society, in other words, that skin color mattered, racial discrimination existed, and egalitarian beliefs helped with acceptance of one another. Color-blind attitudes, on the other hand, tended toward avoidance of discussing racial differences. "Racial socialization practices are meant to inform children of the role of race in society and in their own lives," and these practices sort into categories of cultural socialization, egalitarianism, preparation for bias, and mistrust of others.[18] Their findings underscored the dramatic challenges for children learning to admit to explicit and implicit biases as well as learning about diversity as an enriching social dynamic.

Although much of this research centers around racial differences, it nonetheless documents the emergence of explicit and implicit biases in early childhood. These biases extend potentially toward any outgroup, including immigrants and their many differences, which can of course include race. Although explicit biases appear to diminish by early adolescence, implicit biases become steadier and more difficult to address. Family socialization patterns appear to reinforce American attitudes of denial that differences matter and to convey extreme and even paranoid anxieties about engaging with them. Clearly, immigrant children have to navigate this rocky terrain as they acclimate and adjust to life in the United States. Many of them will suffer, and many of them will demonstrate remarkable resilience, persistence, and courage, qualities that make immigration so vital and necessary for our future.

Case example—colonized

When I met Miguel, I was struck by his crisp and neat appearance. He was a dark-skinned Latino man in his thirties who worked at a law firm, though not as an attorney. His hair was carefully styled, his suit looked new, his tie smoothly angled, and his shirt unwrinkled even though we met later in the day; nothing was out of place. He formally but very lightly shook my hand. Miguel seemed like a person who put a lot of effort into his appearance and into coming across as cool. He was looking for a psychotherapist who would see him more than once weekly for what he described as "being in the dumps." As he repeated these words in our first session, his lip curled like he detested what he had just said. He spoke in a quiet, almost monotone voice and showed little expression of feeling. He told me how important his job was, adding that he was proud of his educational and professional achievements.

As we talked, I asked Miguel to tell me more about his personal life. He stared at me and replied, "Oh, that," and again I noted the curl of his lip. Miguel was gay and lived with his partner. They had been together for two years. He described how his partner, Bob, looked—that he was more artistic than Miguel about how he dressed, for instance, wearing socks that were odd—and where he worked, though he said nothing about their relationship. I felt confused by Miguel's way of talking. I wondered whether my questions made him uncomfortable, though I had not asked him that many. Miguel wanted therapy more frequently, but I could not tell what else he might want.

I saw him two days later, and again, I noticed how polished he looked while I was self-conscious that I wore khakis, a wrinkled shirt, and a loosened tie. I realized, however, that Miguel barely registered me, and this too confused me. I wondered how a man who dressed so carefully would not see the contrast between us, but I also understood that this was only our second session. I asked whether anything had stayed with him from our first meeting, and he slowly, almost methodically shook his head no. He began telling me more about a problem he had at work. After listening for a few minutes, I asked Miguel how this problem made him feel. He frowned and then replied, "Oh, that." I encouraged him to say how he felt, to see whether he could, and he thought for a good two minutes or longer in silence. Then, he said flatly, "I guess perturbed."

I have not often heard *perturbed* used to describe a feeling, and I thought that it was an unusual choice to make his feelings seem bland or neutral. Perhaps Miguel's whole persona was dense and designed to push away anything having to do with feelings. As we were just getting to know another, I did not say anything to Miguel. He asked if we could meet three times weekly, and I said that it was possible, although it would help me to understand him if he could say what he hoped to get from me, even if just a vague hope. For the first time he smiled ever so slightly. "I think I'm an enigma and people seem put off by that." This was a somewhat curious answer, and when I asked for further thoughts about it, Miguel told me he was not sure what else to say to me.

Shortly after this, we began meeting three times a week. Miguel was always five minutes early for his appointment. He sat in the waiting area reading a men's style magazine on most days. He unvaryingly had on an elegant tie and wore a smart suit. During these early sessions, I explained that it would be helpful for me to know about his background, his family, and how he had grown up. Predictably, he responded, "Oh, that." As I was hearing "oh, that" more frequently, I then felt comfortable saying that I wondered what he meant when he used that phrase because it often seemed unclear and even confusing at times. He smirked, "An enigma needs a code. That's part of my code when I don't know what to say to a person." I indicated that I would like to learn some about his code, and by doing so, I thought we would be able to communicate more deeply. This remark was not well received because I failed to consider his defensive need for the code. Later, I modified what I had said about learning his code by remarking that codes were important for protecting special information and providing security. Miguel nodded. "That's very true."

About three months into Miguel's treatment, I was on the way to my office, and I stopped in a coffee shop and ordered a takeaway cup of tea. As I was affixing the lid, I squeezed too hard, and the tea exploded from the cup onto the counter, my shirt, my tie, and my hands. I cleaned up as best I could and went to my office. I took off my tie, and noticed a large brown tea stain on my shirt. There was nothing to do about that. I saw a child patient who asked me about what had happened, and we had a lively discussion about accidents that he had skateboarding. My next patient was Miguel. I greeted him in the waiting area and we went into my office and sat down. We sat in silence for nearly five minutes, which was unusual. He kept looking at me and averting his eyes as if he could not believe what he saw.

RT: You look like you're seeing something about me that makes you uncomfortable.

Miguel: (Shrugs) Perhaps. (Another pause) Well, if you must know, you look... (pauses again)... I don't know.

RT: You can tell me.

Miguel: Messy, you look messy. That stain.

RT: Yes, I look different to you today and that is perhaps upsetting.

Miguel: No, not that. I am not upset. You ought to keep a spare shirt here. That's what I do. You have to be ready for things like that. If you're not ready, well, then you can end up looking...

RT: Just messy?

Miguel: Untidy. You look messy and untidy. (He rubs his hands on his pants to smooth out creases from when he sat down.)

We sit in silence for another five minutes. Miguel continues to look at me and then glances away quickly.

RT: Could you say how my being messy and untidy makes you feel right now?

Miguel: (Shrugs and pauses for a while) I guess perturbed.

RT: Perturbed, that's an interesting word. I wonder if feeling that, as you see me being messy and untidy, reminds you of anything, anything at all from your past? Because often these kinds of feelings reach back at moments belonging to our story.

Miguel: (Nods and thinks for a minute) It does. I am a bit surprised. I just had this memory come to me, something I haven't thought about in years.

RT: Can you share it with me?

Miguel went on to describe that when he was in first grade, six years old, he had spilled chocolate milk all over his school uniform. The teacher scolded him for fidgeting and making a mess. She told him that he would have to walk around for the rest of school day with a big stain on his uniform and that this should teach him a lesson. Miguel's voice got softer as he told me about his school memory. I encouraged him to keep going, and he said that he had attended a religious school in Utah, where the teachers were strict and often made examples of what they saw as poor or bad behaviors in the children. He recalled wearing his chocolate-stained uniform and being made fun of by other children who teased that the color of the stain matched the color of his skin. They called him "cocoa." Miguel could not quite say that he had felt ashamed, but he described these details well enough to convey that he had.

Over the following weeks, Miguel explained more about his family and his origin story. His parents were from a town in a Central American country and had lived there when they married. They met missionaries from the Church of Jesus Christ of Latter-day Saints (LDS, also known as Mormons) and both of them had converted. Through the church sponsoring them for resettlement, they had an opportunity to move to the United States. At the time of their move, Miguel was just an infant. They settled in a town in Utah and were the only visible minority in the community. His parents became very active in the church and remained devout as Miguel grew into adulthood. Although he described instances of standing out because of his skin color and doing whatever he could to avoid attention, he did not describe many feelings, leaving me to infer them. Occasionally, I would say things like "sounds quite rough" or "that seems very hurtful." Miguel tolerated these comments with a small nod. I began to think that he had been traumatized over his difference, and he had developed a wish to hide what he considered was a stain so he would not be humiliated like that again. His skin color became, for him, a stain about his origins, and he came to believe his differences were unacceptable. In high school, there was a school play with a Black character, and the drama teacher cast Miguel in that role without even asking for his consent. When he complained about his experiences of discrimination to his parents, they told him to pray about it. Their consolation came only in the form of assuring him that they had done the right thing by leaving a country descending into war. A hopeful sign emerging in his analysis was when he started more frequently using words like *irritated, annoyed, sad,* and *embarrassed,* instead of *oh, that; perturbed;* and *being in the dumps.*

About two years into Miguel's work with me, another kind of synchronicity occurred that opened up further exploration for him. I had been away during August for three weeks, and when I returned to the office I was wearing a wedding band on my left hand. I wondered what Miguel might say about it. At first, he seemed not to notice it at all. Then, one day I discerned a familiar pattern as he looked at my hand and quickly averted his eyes. Other patients had noticed the ring and shared their reactions with me, but not Miguel. I waited for a couple of weeks because I realized the separation of my vacation had been disruptive for him, and I felt it important to get him back into a safer place of therapeutic holding.

On that day, Miguel sat on the couch sequentially drumming the fingers of his left hand on the armrest. This was new, and I commented that I had not noticed him ever moving his hands like this. He gave me an icy look that went quickly to my left hand before he turned away.

RT: I suspect you're having a feeling about something you see on me.
Miguel: Oh, what makes you say that?
RT: As you drum with the fingers of your left hand, I thought I saw you look at my left hand. Perhaps you noticed something different and aren't sure what to do with it?

Miguel:	(He's silent for a minute.) Maybe.
RT:	Miguel, it is all right to say what you see here. I'd like to know.
Miguel:	(Sighs) That … that ring. (Seems flustered)
RT:	Yes, you see it, and you don't know what to do with what you see because maybe you're worried how I will react.
Miguel:	(Nods) Are you, you know … um, … (His voice trails off.)
RT:	I think we can handle what you want to say.
Miguel:	(Sighs) Are you … married?

I encouraged Miguel to keep talking about what went through his mind when he saw the ring on my finger. He explained that he had assumed that I was gay, and that now, it did not make sense to him because "gays can't get married" (which was true at that time in the United States). Miguel had not told me much about his being gay—I didn't know how he had come out to his family and what his experiences as a gay man had been. What little I knew of his partner, Bob, were mostly complaints about sloppiness, carelessness, and overspending. Miguel became desperately anxious, doubting himself and feeling himself "a fool." He recalled that the person who had referred him to me had said that I was a gay man, but now, Miguel wondered whether he had made that up. Much of his self-criticism here was homophobic. I noted that he was beating himself up because he thought he had made a mistake about my being gay. After several sessions of trying to understand why this situation made him so desperately anxious, I made a decision that I realize other analysts and therapists would not have made. Previously, Miguel had expressed that he felt his father used religion as a shield to distance himself, and I felt I was on the cusp of enacting a similar pattern with him now, my "religion" then being linked to a belief about analytic neutrality. Taking more of a side, I commented that it was possible for gay people to show their commitment and love by wearing a ring that symbolized togetherness, if not a legal tie.

After I said this, Miguel sank into the couch, and for the first time, he cried. He told me that he was "mad at" me for not saying this a week before because he would have been spared his doubts if I had. I agreed that I could have handled it better, and I asked if his hurt about it resonated with something else in his life? Still angry, he rebuffed my curiosity, but in a following session, he revealed that when he came out to his parents after finishing college, they acted as if he had never told them. He said that he even began to think that he had "hallucinated that conversation" because his parents deftly pretended it had never happened. This experience of reality becoming unreal seemed to get at a core of Miguel's experience of himself. He was a boy who came to the United States as an infant and, as he grew up, was colonized by a combination of rigid religious beliefs, family denial about the strains of immigration, and exclusionary biases over perceived differences within his social milieu.

I suggest that Miguel's sense of being intruded upon, what I am calling *colonizing*, extended into his adult life when he put most of his psychological energies into his persona at the expense of his deeper Self. This was another colonization that certainly enabled him fitting in and conforming, but hid other parts of who he was—like being gay, an immigrant, Central American, darker skinned, and no longer religious. Miguel left the church after coming out to his parents because he found there was no room in it for a gay man like himself. The colonizing forces in his life included the church as well as the homogenously distilled values of the small town where he had grown up. An immigrant child in Miguel's place had and has no choice about such matters. As an adult, however, a process of decolonization can bring about healing for what has been crushed and buried during earlier development. This process was not easy for Miguel, but the more he could claim that something was real and not imagined, the more his psyche appeared to open to other possibilities for accepting who he was.

When differences are punished

Many immigrants have lived along the continuum that I have described here—from an open-arms welcome to relative tolerance to expressed hostility—and when American society suddenly shifts along this continuum, the results can be cruel and inhumane. John Okada's novel *No-No Boy*, first published in 1957, vividly describes such circumstances for Japanese Americans who were horrifically interned by our government in desert concentration camps in the United States during World War II.[19] Over 110,000 suffered this fate.[20] No-no boys were a group of young men who refused to answer yes to two questions on a loyalty questionnaire required by the War Department. One question was about a willingness to serve in the US military, and the other was to swear allegiance to the US while for-swearing allegiance to Japan.[21] Those answering no were guilty of draft evasion and over 300 were sent to prison.[22]

Ichiro Yamada is the main character of Okada's book. He is *nisei*, meaning born in America of parents who immigrated from Japan. Taking place in 1946 Seattle, the story has Ichiro, a no-no boy, arriving home after two years in prison for draft evasion and two years before that, having been in an internment camp. Ichiro's parents own a small grocery store, and his younger brother Taro sees himself as more fully American and does not share Ichiro's conflicts around who he is. Ichiro's mother remains loyal to Japan, refusing to accept that Japan has lost the war. Much of the plot revolves around their conflicted relationship with themes of love, devotion, and huge differences in perspective.

Because of Ichiro's experiences in the camp and in prison, he rightly doubts his place in the United States.

> Was it possible that he … and all the other American-born, American-educated Japanese who had renounced their American-ness in a frightening moment of madness had done so irretrievably? Was there no hope of redemption? He was still a citizen.[23]

Ichiro is understandably disoriented about his place in American society, and he has to contend mostly by himself with complicated emotions of anger, disillusionment, bitterness, sadness, shame, and anxiety, especially about his future. Questioning his own sanity, he wonders whether his having stood up for himself will result in continued discrimination and a life on the margins. There are echoes of this dilemma around exclusion and belonging in Arturo's and Miguel's stories too.

Ichiro connects with a school friend, Kenji, who fought for the United States, badly injured a leg, and is dealing with the painful consequences of that wound. Okada writes that they are "two extremes" because one was "more American than most Americans" by enlisting and fighting, whereas the other was "neither Japanese nor American" because he did not take the route of assuming his birth nationality as a given for defining himself.[24] This dichotomy about what identity means to a person reflects a strand of immigrant experience when someone does not feel they fit in seamlessly with mainstream American society, and certainly, that pull to belong even when it overrides elements of self would have been greater and the risks of stepping outside it that much more threatening in the United States during the mid-twentieth century. Nonetheless, this social force to bend toward homogeneity remains part of American life, as seen in recent years with the rise of white nationalism. We can also see it in Arturo's confusion and fear when he discovered that he and his mother were undocumented. Likewise, Miguel's shame over the chocolate stain that resonated with his skin color shows how disturbing childhood experiences of not belonging because of visible differences can linger painfully into adulthood.

Affirming that notion, Ichiro tells a fellow inmate in prison that it was "tough … for kids of immigrants because parents and kids were so different and they never really got to know each other."[25] He comments here on the divide that can emerge in families when immigrant parents hold a competing set of expectations and values from those that their children frequently internalize from their peers, teachers, and other native-born adults. In many ways, this familial tension is central to Ichiro's decision to answer no and no to the two questions that result in his imprisonment. Loyalty to parental values can come at a cost for immigrant children when it is diametrically opposed to what the native society demands.

Later, after having driven with Kenji to a hospital for treatment of his worsening pain, Ichiro wonders about the topsy-turviness of inside and outside that characterizes so much of life in the United States, a revolving door within American society around inclusion and exclusion that makes people dizzy wondering where they will end up. He thinks that

> maybe the answer is that there is no in. Maybe the whole damned country is pushing and shoving and screaming to get someplace that doesn't exist, because they don't know that the outside could be inside if only they would stop all this pushing and shoving and screaming....[26]

How insightful, and how poignant that this still describes contemporary American society. Ichiro realizes that the lines used to distinguish inside from outside are artificial. They exist to alienate us for false reasons because the compartments they draw, the borders they outline, all largely exist in our minds to separate us from one another. *No-No Boy* is worth revisiting today, and not just for high school and college students. It is a powerful statement about some of the darkest sides of being an immigrant to the United States.

Transference and countertransference

I am white. I am a gay man. My grandparents, as I mention in Chapter 1, were immigrants. My husband is an immigrant from Israel. I have a doctoral degree in mental health, and I also have a master's degree in business administration (MBA). I could go on, but the point is that patients know some of these things about me, and perhaps several of them. They will react to me as being different based on perhaps only one or two of these characteristics, or they will probably imagine me in their unique ways to be whoever they need me to be despite what they know.

When I bring up differences in psychotherapy or analysis, I usually find myself wondering how I am perceived and how those perceptions might make a patient feel. Which fantasies about the two of us are important to them? Which feelings seem more like projections? Which have elements of truth in them? What have their experiences of difference been? How do we make sense of one another in this process of understanding who we are in analysis? Most importantly, how can these interactions become painful and enact earlier wounds when we cross and do not connect?

Many months into his treatment, I noticed Arturo staring at my name on the door before he came into a session. After he had settled in, I thought it opportune to ask him about it.

RT: I noticed you were looking at my name coming in today.
Arturo: Yeah. What kind of a name is that? I've never seen a name like that before. I mean growing up in Texas most foreign names were Hispanic.
RT: I wonder if you have any ideas about it?

Arturo: Hmm. It's one of those places in Europe that was in the news about ten years ago. There was a war there. (He thinks for a bit.) Yugoslavia? Was your family from there?

As we talked more, Arturo explained that he imagined my parents had escaped from Communism and come to the United States before I was born because I did not have an accent. I asked him what he made of this idea that they had fled, and he replied that he did not know much history, but he thought Communism had meant citizens were poor and lacked freedom. I commented that his idea seemed to mean that my parents might have been looking for a better life for their children, and he nodded. I wondered whether that felt similar to how he understood what his mother had done in coming to the United States. He said she had always told him how hard life had been in Mexico for her, that her family had little money when she was growing up, and that there were better jobs in the United States. As I thought about what Arturo was telling me, I saw what I thought was his attempt to find a bridge between us around immigration experiences.

I was, however, aware of our ethnic and racial differences; and in a session following this one, I brought that up with him. He responded that he had originally requested a referral to a Latino therapist but had been informed there was a long waiting list. I asked how he felt meeting me and seeing that I was white. He was rather open in saying that it was disappointing and that I also looked too young and that caused him concern that I was inexperienced. He joked, "I mean you're not exactly Doogie Howser, but it made me think about that TV show when I first met you." Doogie Howser was a character in an American television show, played by Neil Patrick Harris, who acted the role of a teenage doctor. Arturo explained that he had thought a Latino therapist would get the cultural pieces of his life much more quickly. He said that his initial disappointment went away about our ethnic difference, although he continued to have doubts about my age and experience. I wondered whether this were not a kind of displacement, meaning that it might have felt easier to focus on my age rather than my being white. I do not think I pursued this enough at the time, and looking back, I wish that I had. Arturo might have felt uncomfortable with how I addressed our differences, and his fantasy about my Yugoslavian background seemed more associated with his trying to locate a way in which we shared something in common around immigration from troubled circumstances.

Early in Miguel's treatment, whenever I brought up the topic of his reactions to our being different, he would become annoyed with me. Even after his recalling the memory about the spilled chocolate milk, when I thought an opening might present itself for discussing our racial difference, he resisted, angrily telling me, "Oh, please, not that again!" I wondered about my failure to address it in a way that would have made Miguel feel safe. Clearly, I was not doing that, and I did not grasp why at the time.

Only after the discussion about the wedding ring I was wearing did I have a clearer understanding of how terrified Miguel had been about how different I might have seemed to him in a way that felt very threatening. He had voiced a terror that I was, at first, mis-attuned to, and only later, after I commented that the ring did not imply I was not gay, did I begin to see that Miguel felt the differences he had struggled with were powerfully negative, discriminating, and soul depleting. He had grown up in a family that pretended differences did not matter, and here I had been trying to encourage him into feeling safer with me by bringing up what was for him a dangerous subject!

Thankfully, after the ring incident, we were able to circle back to the topic of our racial difference, although this time, it was Miguel who brought it up. He had applied for a promotion at work and received it. He then overheard two coworkers in a break room saying, however, that he had been chosen because of the company's diversity needs, and this had upset him. I waited, and Miguel said that he had been angry with me too for focusing on this subject in therapy because he felt I was implying he did not know how to handle it. In other words, I brought it up to help him with a weakness. I listened, and he continued to expand on how he had worked his entire life in situations where he was surrounded by white people and that he knew how to conduct himself so as not to make them feel uncomfortable. I said, "Oh, you were taking care of them." He raised an eyebrow and said that it had been a stab in the back when he heard the coworkers saying that he was promoted because of his race.

As Miguel spoke more about the blatant prejudice at his workplace, I listened and learned. I understood, albeit slowly, that my bringing up differences with him had felt to him like yet another white person asking him to take care of them by talking about what I had believed important. What I learned was that he had felt this way almost his entire life. He had experienced such terrifying incidents around difference as a child, in his family, in his schools, and in the LDS church, that he came to believe that differences were brought up to shame people and that the people doing the shaming instead needed to be taken care of, to be protected from their own discomfort at talking about it. I am grateful that Miguel put up with my clumsy attempts to address differences and that he showed me other ways I could be conscious and attentive to many unseen burdens in this process, such as taking care of those who have more power or privilege.

Sic itur ad astra

In Book IX of The Aeneid, Apollo says this in Latin to Ascanius: that his future will be bright and "thus goes one to the stars."[27] Basically, Apollo promises Ascanius immortality through his descendants, fame, and a gateway to the heavens. Symbolically, this promise motivates many immigrant parents as an expression of their desire that their children will live better lives than they themselves have had. Arturo mentioned that his mother referred to this as a main reason for coming to the United States, staying even though undocumented, and living many years with that secret. This promise also illustrates elements of Jung's idea about the child archetype: troubled origins, hidden talents, and eventual success.

In Miguel's history, his parents literally looked to the heavens by converting to a foreign religion that became their vehicle for immigrating to the United States. Although Miguel was very successful, he was plagued by the shadow aspects of the child archetype, namely, chronic self-doubts, perfectionism, and inflexibility. Many of these can likewise be seen in the character of Ichiro from *No-No Boy*. However, his story unfolds within the frame of an historical injustice that forced upon him a ludicrous choice. Ichiro's comments about the divisions between immigrant parents and their children show that the stars that parents see may not be the ones that their children look at.

"To the stars" is a hopeful message for immigrants and their children. Immigrant parents are frequently leaving behind poverty, like Arturo's mother, or widespread civil unrest, like Miguel's parents. Naturally enough, they seek safety for their families and their children. Stars are visible objects that sparkle within the night sky, and they have been referred to throughout history, not only in astronomy, exploration, and navigation, but also in astrology, art, and literature. They are what Jung termed "scintillas" that represent, among other things, sparks of the soul.[28] He also described them as bits of consciousness waiting to be claimed from the darkness of unconsciousness. Stars or scintillas thus symbolize potentially central guiding principles, which could be reflections of spiritual beliefs, psychological attitudes, generational aspirations, or ideological frameworks. Yet despite these different forms, they remain compelling for guiding us. Many immigrants will look to them for orientation, meaning, and succor as they raise their children in new places. Their children will over time become a new generation that reaches for what once might have seemed unreachable.

Notes

1 Virgil, The Aeneid, trans. John Dryden (Project Gutenberg E-Book #228, 2008), p. 156. Hereafter references to Dryden's translation of The Aeneid will appear as Dryden and page number.
2 Louis H. Feldman, "The character of Ascanius in Virgil's 'Aeneid,'" *The Classical Journal* 48, no. 8 (1953): 303–313.
3 Ibid., 310.
4 C. G. Jung, "The Psychology of the Child Archetype," *The Archetypes and the Collective Unconscious* 9i (1940), *The Collected Works of C. G. Jung* (Princeton: Princeton University Press, 1959), ¶273n. Hereafter, references to Jung's *Collected Works* will appear as Jung, title, date, and volume number in the *Collected Works* (CW).
5 Ibid., para. 300.

6 "Almost 44 Percent of All U.S. Fortune 500 Companies in 2018 Were Founded by Immigrants or Their Children, New Research Shows," New American Economy, October 10, 2018, https://www.newamericaneconomy.org/press-release/almost-44-percent-u-s-fortune-500-companies-2018-founded-immigrants-children-new-research-shows/

7 "Immigration Reform and Control Act of 1986," Ballotpedia, https://ballotpedia.org/Immigration_Reform_and_Control_Act_of_1986.

8 Ibid.

9 Miao K. Qian et al., "Differential Developmental Courses of Implicit and Explicit Biases for Different Other-Race Classes," *Developmental Psychology* 55, no. 7 (2019): 1440–1452.

10 Ibid.

11 Jennifer L. Rennels and Judith H. Langlois, "Children's Attractiveness, Gender, and Race Biases: A Comparison of Their Strength and Generality," *Child Development* 85, no. 4 (2014): 1401–1418.

12 Antonya M. Gonzalez, Jennifer R. Steele, and Andrew S. Baron, "Reducing Children's Implicit Racial Bias through Exposure to Positive Out-Group Exemplars," *Child Development* 88, no. 1 (2017): 123–130.

13 Ibid., 128.

14 Rebecca A. Dore et al. "Children's Racial Bias in Perceptions of Others' Pain," *British Journal of Developmental Psychology* 32, no. 2 (2014): 227.

15 Vanessa M. Nyborg and John F. Curry, "The Impact of Perceived Racism: Psychological Symptoms among African-American Boys," *Journal of Clinical Child and Adolescent Psychology* 32, no. 2 (2003): 259.

16 Ibid., 264.

17 Jenna Kelley Zucker and Meagan M. Patterson, "Racial Socialization among White American Parents: Relations to Racial Diversity, Racial Identity, and School Diversity," *Journal of Family Issues* 39, no. 16 (2018): 3903–3930.

18 Ibid., 3905.

19 John Okada, *No-No Boy* (Seattle: University of Washington Press, 2014).

20 Ruth Ozeki, Foreword to *No-No Boy* by John Okada (Seattle: University of Washington Press, 2014), x.

21 Ibid.

22 Annie Nakao, "A Unique Tale of WWII Resistance: Japanese American Internees Refused Draft," *San Francisco Chronicle,* October 26, 2001, https://www.sfgate.com/news/article/A-unique-tale-of-WWII-resistance-Japanese-2865725.php

23 Okada, *No-No Boy*, 47.

24 Ibid., 68.

25 Ibid., 125.

26 Ibid., 143.

27 Dryden, 995–996.

28 C. G. Jung, "On the Nature of the Psyche" (1947), *Structure and Dynamics of the Psyche,* CW 8, para. 388.

Chapter 6

Is Identity a Fiction?

Why is it that people in power think they get to tell me who I am? They don't know me.
17-year-old immigrant to the U.S.

This question of whether identity is a fiction has been on my mind more as I have watched the United States absurdly descend into polarized camps that barely acknowledge one another. Even wearing a face mask or not during a pandemic signifies which group a person belongs to. The reality of who we are is not a new consideration; for example, it was a theme in Calderón de la Barca's Spanish Golden Age drama *La Vida Es Sueño* (*Life Is a Dream,* 1635). That play explores how far we can go to keep illusions and dreams alive while ignoring other aspects of "reality."[1] This tendency raises doubts about the stability of anyone's identity. For instance, what do we mean when we say, "I am ..." followed by a list of personality traits, demographic variables such as race and gender, a profession, educational level, an indicator of where we are from on a map, and a reference to ethnic background, to name some of the common elements often used when defining ourselves as a person? Depth psychologists would not claim that anyone is just an amalgamation of these statements because so many of them evolve and change across a lifespan. Such mutability belies a constant definition of who we are and, to some extent, seems more akin to what happens in our dreams—like in Calderón's title. Yet, if we really were more like characters in a dream, then statements of identity become salient for how emphatically and insistently—or rigidly—we make them. To put it another way, with what surety would we claim a character in one of our dreams has something like a fully developed identity? Most dream characters are actors on an internal stage, transient actors at that, whose evanescence causes us to investigate what they mean and, usually, to be uncertain about any lasting conclusions. In addition, most of us have had the waking experience of asking ourselves, "Am I dreaming this or not?" At those times, we typically are incredulous about what is happening in perceived reality. This dreamlike aspect of waking life occurs during synchronicities, dejá vus, powerful intuitions that shake us, spiritual awakenings, and

DOI: 10.4324/9781003119593-6

encounters with the uncanny. When facing dramatic inner uncertainties, we might look for what instead appears in outer reality to be steady, firm, definitive, and constant to orient us, even when these things themselves might be fictions, including statements such as "I am ..." this or that.

In this chapter, I examine various forces impinging on identity in light of what I call *perimeters* that are related to race, nationality, culture, sexuality, religion, political affiliation, language, and analogous terms that box us into a category.[2] Perimeters are both external demarcations of reality (such as societal regulations, laws, and national boundaries) and internal representations that we take from our experiences of them. Perimeters constitute a paradox about what we absorb from outside and subsequently believe to have made our own. For most of us, this is as if outer spatial lines wiggle inside us to then complete psychological puzzles about who we are, what makes us different, and where we belong. For example, borders with walls are external perimeters that affect how those on each side think of themselves and of those on the other side. In this chapter, I will discuss an example of how a wall functions psychologically as a perimeter. Analytically speaking, there is an irony, of course, in using too much outer reality to build an internal self-concept. In doing that we risk losing the creativity of relating with our own unconscious to make fuzzier determinations about who we believe we are. However, most developmental models of human psychology support internalization of reality as an evolving and central task for cognitive, social, and emotional growth. Exploring this idea about perimeters, I will address the continued relevance of identity as a useful psychological concept, given its tendency to become static, not only in our own minds but also within contemporary social and political discourses. Statements about identity can be especially complicated for immigrants. This discussion of perimeters is an attempt, like a work in progress, to describe something that is relevant for contemporary psychotherapists and analysts, and as such, I take a little liberty in not pinning it down too exactly.

Looking at this idea of perimeters, I believe that, in addition to concepts of identity, it is important to look at constructs of self, persona, and reality to see how they relate to it. A few short definitions will help to clarify my reasoning here. *Identity* is understood analytically to be "a sense of one's continuous being as an entity distinguishable from all others."[3] Notice the emphasis on *stability* and *uniqueness,* features that imply identity is central to a person's psyche, like the roots of a plant. *Self,* in Jungian terms, is an archetype of "unity and totality," and it constitutes "an integrating factor" that provides inner guidance for psychological growth and individuation.[4] Self in this context is not equivalent to ego, persona, or identity, because it is much more than any of them and mysteriously so. *Persona* is an individualized social mask that we each present to society "designed on the one hand to make a definite impression upon others, and, on the other, to conceal the true nature of the individual."[5] The dual nature of persona is protective and egocentric and refers to attributes related to status and power. Defining *reality* is certainly beyond my scope, but to offer a concise explanation, I think of reality in terms of how it is often taught in developmental psychology as based on perceptions of external things, not usually in dispute, that derive from collective evidence and consensual meanings. A definition from Wikipedia explains, "Reality is the sum or aggregate of all that is real or existent, as opposed to that which is only imaginary."[6] The *reality principle* in psychoanalysis emphasizes an ability to assess the operations of the external world and to differentiate it from an internal one. These definitions are all terms that still inform analytic theory and training. Before delving into their relationship to the idea of perimeters, though, I turn to an important, recent discussion about identity.

Figure 6.1 Detail of the remains of the Berlin Wall, Berlin, Germany. Segments of the wall left as a reminder of events leading up to the fall of the wall in November 1989. A lamppost can be seen through a gap in the wall (Photo: Lois GoBe, Shutterstock).

Kwame Anthony Appiah, a professor of philosophy and law at New York University, questions the firmness of identity in a recent book with a title that proposes much of it is founded on lies: *Lies That Bind: Rethinking Identity.*[7] Although he does not give reference to Jung, Appiah defines identities similarly to Jung's persona mainly because of identities' social underpinnings. He describes this social element as "objective" while also considering a "subjective" position.[8] He believes the objective part relates to labels and stereotypes, and he views the subjective as based on our perceptions of who we appear to be to others—for example, do we agree with what they see of us or not? Appiah notes that *intersectionality*, a conception of self that is not defined solely by one thing, means we all have multiple strands of identity that vary—and intersect—over the course of our lives. Illustrating the psychological malleability of identity, he cites the Robbers Cave experiment, which compared the social dynamics of two groups of eleven-year-old boys at nearby campsites.[9] Initially, the two groups did not know about one another. When the existence of a neighboring camp was revealed to them, the groups became competitive, named themselves, and challenged each other in contests of strength. This experiment is often cited to explain group dynamics that turn into *us-them* hostilities because identity is used to alienate groups from one another. Consciousness of "others" in this experiment created social bonds that organized each group around fight and domination. Prior to this awareness, each group functioned more cooperatively and playfully. This experiment is a warning about how identity can be commandeered for purposes of aggression and that it can form in the most temporary of ways—a bit like a dream.

Appiah examines different sources of identity that we rely on such as religion, country, color, class, and culture. He points out many contradictions within each of them. For example, countries have often had moveable boundaries that displaced other groups while insisting on a claim of shared ancestry. A key point is that the dominant group "cares" about having "that supposed shared ancestry in common."[10] He looks at historical examples of how boundaries change; for instance, during the early twentieth century, Central and Eastern Europe were parts of the Russian, Austro-Hungarian, and Ottoman Empires. After the World War I and World War II, millions of people moved, new countries appeared, and borders were redrawn. National identities did not stay frozen in time; they evolved. Appiah argues that identity as such is highly changeable and not static. To claim otherwise is a fudge—or lie—to assert a common bond that belies historical facts. "When the state gazes at us … it invariably fixes and rigidifies a phenomenon that is neither fixed nor rigid."[11] Appiah calls this the "Medusa Syndrome," and it is characterized by a powerful entity, such as a government, inflexibly defining how a person is officially recognized, similar to how the mythical Medusa petrified those who looked at her. Significantly, this relies on an external authority to issue opinions or statements, often orthodox, about personhood. As analysts and therapists, we recognize that something like this also occurs in families, for example, when parents narcissistically use their children to mold them into who they need them to be.

Appiah believes three conditions apply to labeling identity: 1) labels with rules for their application, 2) labels that subsequently define behaviors, and 3) labels that dictate social perceptions.[12] An example of the first might be the use of physical natal anatomy to assign gender as masculine or feminine. An illustration of the second is a young boy's avoiding doll play after hearing that boys don't usually play with dolls but girls do. And an example of the third is an adult buying a three-year-old boy a truck for his birthday because of a social assumption about what three-year-old boys supposedly like to play with. These different labels incorporate objective and subjective dimensions of experience, with the subjective referring to how a person *assumes* the label's meanings and imposition (that is, the boy avoiding dolls).

Labels can backfire. Appiah understands Donald Trump's populist appeal as a rebellion against perceived elites who, rightly or wrongly, are thought to have labeled rural and working-class whites in condescending and dismissive ways. I often think that Trump is a collective manifestation of an archetypal middle finger aimed at those whose labeling makes many people feel disempowered, alienated, and forgotten. Trump understood that many Americans felt unappreciated and devalued, and he told them he saw them for who they are—that their identity mattered. Appiah writes,

> There is a liberal fantasy in which identities are merely chosen, so we are all free to be what we choose to be. But identities without demands would be useless to us. Identities work only because, once they get their grip on us, they command us, speaking to us as an inner voice; and because others, seeing who they think we are, call on us, too ... you cannot simply refuse them [identities].[13]

Appiah articulates an important notion about the interplay of objective and subjective elements of identity when what is outside crosses what is inside, even if that is unwanted. I wish, however, that he had read Jung, because he describes not so much identity, but rather what Jung would have called an *identity complex* that can possess us and make us a bit mad. Still, Appiah does explain that what we call *identity* is not at all simple and is, in so many ways, based on what we absorb, often unconsciously, from our environments.

I read Appiah's book after writing a talk that looked at identity as it relates to immigration.[14] While working on that paper, I found myself wondering about the slippery qualities for how the term *identity* is often used as if it has become a referential shorthand for segmenting us into categories that are quite the opposite of individuality. How does psychology based on individuation handle newer, more fluid meanings of identity? Is identity still useful as a developmental idea? I began to consider a polarization that sometimes arises around discussions of identity, and as I pondered walls, boundaries, and demarcations, I came upon the word *perimeter* because it provides a spatial sense of existing either inside or outside an area of experience. *Perimeter* is defined as a border, an outer boundary, a line marking an area, and a fortified position at that line.[15] It derives from the Greek *perimetron* meaning a linear measure around something, its external dimensions. Perimeters, like skin, characterize an interface between outer and inner, although they also delineate separate categories that exist both outside and inside ourselves. For example, *citizen* and *noncitizen* constitute external definitions coming from a legal system that can be internalized as psychological experiences about belonging and not belonging, being included and not included. But what happens when we refuse, challenge, and cross these perimeters because we do not accept what they tell us about who we are?

A psychology of crossing perimeters poses an interesting challenge because it should be able to meaningfully address characteristics such as gender, sex, class, race, nationality, religion, sexual orientation, and ethnicity. Perimeters can be viewed as spatial representations for what Appiah calls "labels." We use them to separate as well as to determine identities. I believe, though, that perimeters are more than just labels because they expose a trick about identity, perhaps a similar trick that Appiah refers to in the title of his book; like lies that bind, perimeters obscure something truer by instead insisting on dividing up human experience. These perimeters reside both outside and inside us to create an order, perhaps an order that is fundamentally inhuman. Outside us, there might be a state that defines us as a noncitizen, whereas inside us, there exists a feeling we have about not fully belonging to this society because we are denied rights, access, and recognition. Although denial of those things is certainly real, the outer perimeter itself is constructed around imposing an artificial division on humanity. Failing to recognize this characteristic, we might concretize our inner perimeters into an identity that then does not have much room to grow. The safety of sticking to what is familiar and known within a particular set of perimeters might preclude adventuring beyond and learning about what does not fit the scheme of identity as it has been previously defined. I believe the crossing of perimeters enables psychological growth, whereas the use of them solely to define identity is anti-growth.

In the next sections, I examine perimeters that we now encounter more commonly as inhabitants of an interconnected globalized world in which modern trends continue to supplant rigid traditions and older value systems. These perimeters frequently pertain to race, national borders, wars, gender, and sexuality. I hope to offer a deeper look at the psychological factors emerging from them. The perimeters that I comment on derive from external categories used to define personhood without regard for who a person actually is. Some of them might appear conceptual, however, they are usually traceable to elements within our physical existence that we perceive as definite things belonging to reality, even when that conclusion might not be completely accurate. An example is an adult's assumption that a child is heterosexual. The physical notion in play here is grounded in a belief that a man and a woman constitute a couple through its physical representation. Heterosexuality (man + woman = couple) underpins this assumption to form a perimeter regarding sexual orientation. Likewise, religion seems at first glance to belong mainly to an ideational, spiritual realm of beliefs and ideas. Consider, however, its many physical manifestations such as churches, temples, sacred texts, icons (statues, paintings), modes of dress, rituals of its clergy. These can concretize a belief system into a field of tangible perimeters that separate believer from nonbeliever.

Example of how perimeters obstruct

In Chapter 4, I describe preparing a meal to break the Ramadan feast with adolescent refugees from a program in Berlin. Abdul was especially vocal then about *die Stempel*—the stamps—that are necessary on many documents in Germany, stamps that he had not yet obtained. Hearing him say this, I knew immediately what he meant. I had lived in Germany years earlier, and I recalled times my papers were taken, eyed carefully, and officially stamped, because without a stamp, I wouldn't have been able to do something important like get my residence permit. In that kitchen, I heard how school transcripts aren't valid without stamps. Many felt stuck, because they could not prove their age, and without proof, their asylum claims would fail. Several told me that they had lost their passports and other papers during their journeys to Germany. Missing documents are part of many immigrant tales.

In Germany, without an official stamped ID, even getting a cell phone is difficult. Beneath a trickster-like mirth about stamps, I detected their anger and anxiety at the enforcement of a legal perimeter that left them feeling powerless and excluded. There was further confusion at what seemed to them a cultural rigidity in the bureaucratic insistence on official stamps and seals. This appeared to me as another perimeter about external norms that have to be respected within German society and probably contributed to their inner sense of exclusion. It is hard not to consider German history here—during the Third Reich, various stamps meant a death sentence, including the horrific tattoos on those sent to concentration camps.

I believe that these young men and women were speaking to their own anxiety about being labeled as outsiders because they had not sufficiently met the criteria for crossing a perceived perimeter to insider status. They noted how artificial and insubstantial this perimeter seemed—that it placed more value on stamped documents than on their own stories. It was as if their individuality was subsumed under a fixation on rules, procedures, and papers. This Kafkaesque reality is not particular to Germany; many refugees and immigrants to the United States undergo similarly dehumanizing trials and worse—like the cruel family separations of parents and children and forced detainment under traumatizing conditions. The main factor for refugees or immigrants, virtually anywhere, is the regulation of various perimeters, not just physical borders, but also the proper documents to define who has standing as a person—who matters.

This process of obtaining stamped documents seems far removed from anything to do with psychological identity, and in this case, it would simply be better to say that the identifying documents do not—and probably never—tell an individual story about who someone actually is. In this sense, identity is more pertinent to a discussion about power and stigmatizing those who are viewed as others. This situation characterizes a social reality in which a person without stamped papers or documents is essentially considered less than a person. It derives from a concretized understanding of perimeters that is not psychological. The power of the state, any state, sets an individual into legal and social categories that override individuality. A definition of identity derived from this process can be used to discriminate against a person. These hard perimeters are typically upheld as inviolable in order to separate between "us" and "them." Looking at it analytically, a focus on using perimeters in this manner is paranoid, closed, and anti-growth. It is emblematic of a nightmare for those caught in it.

Many of the adolescent refugees whom I met in Berlin appeared to want to conform to their new surroundings by learning German and adopting Western adolescent attitudes, especially independence from family. They desired to find a way inside. As I observed them speaking about this, I wondered about a tension between adaptation and conformity. When does a desire to fit in begin to squash who one is? What sacrifices are made in hope of becoming a person living inside? Piaget coined the term *accommodation* to describe the cognitive changes that happen when new information is absorbed and modifies what has already been developed.[16] Piaget believed accommodation occurs when preexisting cognitive schema must change to update a person's ability to handle information in new ways. Accommodation can also revise perceptual biases that might otherwise lead to misunderstandings about social interactions. The story in Chapter 4 about the proselytizing Scientologists is an example of when accommodation has not yet happened to warn an immigrant about dangerous consequences. Although accommodation re-edits our understanding about such things, the cultural components can still be vexing. If too much emphasis is placed on conformity in an attempt to accommodate, then valuable autobiographical traits and quirks could get lost to the detriment of individuality. Cultural perimeters are a critical factor in unconsciously shaping the outcome of this process.

Personal example of crossing a cultural perimeter

In the spring of 1980, I enrolled in medical school in Berlin. For a year-and-a-half, I completed coursework that medical students do at the beginning of their training, and I worked in several of the city hospitals to learn about first steps in patient care. It was both challenging and stimulating, and this time showed me aspects of German culture and of myself that I had not known before. I gave up on my idea of being a writer and, instead, tried to learn about the human body, disease, medicine, and mortality. For the most part, I found these opportunities exciting, and I tried as best I could to quell an unease I felt whenever I came up against cultural perimeters, particularly the way bureaucracy worked in Germany and a recurrent hostility my peers felt toward the United States about various "isms": militarism, consumerism, materialism, imperialism, capitalism, superficialism. I often felt ashamed of what my nationality represented to my peers.

I lived with my German boyfriend, who was a social work student, in Neukölln, a part of the city that was run down and dilapidated, *kaput* in good German. We lived a few blocks from the Berlin Wall in an apartment with no hot water and no shower or tub.[17] Looking back, we did not feel deprived because so many lived similarly. I made my own Piagetian accommodations as I adjusted to a lifestyle quite different from how I had grown up. Sometimes, though, I felt weary, and for comfort, I would walk along the canal near us. In spring, it was lovely; in winter, foreboding. The Wall was always visible at just a short distance.

Figure 6.2 From a viewing platform in West Berlin looking over the Wall at Dead Man's Strip and East Berlin (Photo courtesy of the author).

The Wall contributed to a heavy sense of nearby doom, and many young people, myself included, were preoccupied with ideas that nuclear war could end life as we knew it. The doomsday clock was a familiar symbol. The Wall was not only a military perimeter, but also an ideological, cultural, economic, and historical one. It separated more than the actual people, and it is true that many died trying to get across it. I recall an early morning when I heard machine-gun fire, and later that day, I learned that East Germans had been shot trying to climb the Wall near us. It is strange to me now that I hardly considered the psychological perimeters of what the Wall might have meant then. That may have been because I was consciously trying to conform in my own way, and since my German friends accepted it, I made an effort to do so.

First-year medical students take a year-long course in human anatomy, which includes a lab to dissect a cadaver. In this lab, I worked with five other German students. It became oddly intimate, perhaps because of what was happening—the gradual taking apart and exploration of someone's body, which been donated for such a purpose, really a remarkable gift at the end of a life. I still remember the other five students: Günther, Eva-Lisa, Beate, Katrin, and Rolf. We learned quickly who among us was squeamish, who got nauseated, who was clumsy, who studied hard, and who was lazy.

After the lab, the six of us would often go for a drink. One afternoon, while we were sitting in a café, the conversation turned to the upcoming oral exams and speculation about how strict our instructor would be about the Latin terms for the various body parts. We were expected to know both the German word and the corresponding Latin one. For example, the shin bone would be *Schienbein* in German and *Corpus tibiae* in Latin. Most struggled with Latin, although we had taken a required class in Latin medical terminology.

One of our group, *which was all German except for me,* said about our instructor, "She'll want the Latin too. *We Germans* are just that *pingelig.*" The word *pingelig* does not have an easy translation; it refers to a trait that is exacting, exaggerated, and precise. I remember asking my friend if she had meant all of us when she said, "We Germans," and without hesitation, she replied, "Of course." Perhaps this was a momentary slip of the tongue, but it revealed something unsettling to me.

On the subway home, I realized her comment had made me uncomfortable because I was assumed to be inside a perimeter, and I was not especially pleased about that. I had become part of "we Germans" and, to me, in a way that overlooked my story and who I was. I wondered how I had come to this moment. Had I accommodated so much that I fit in seamlessly with my German fellow students and that some of them might even perceive me as German? I was certain that I didn't want to be seen as *pingelig*, and I felt at best ambivalent about the idea that I could be seen as German. On the one hand, it seemed to compliment my language skills as well as my social ones, yet on the other, it looked as if I had lost something essential about myself, my American-ness. Not only did I appear to be inside of a perimeter related to speaking German well, but also inside of one about acting German and capable of being *pingelig*.

This dissonance contributed to a developing desire to leave Berlin. Recall that Salman Akhtar, a psychoanalyst who immigrated to the United States from India, writes about the distinction between living and "living in some-place."[18] He believes that an idea of living, without needing to name a place, means we are comfortable enough where we are to feel continuous with our environment. In this situation, identity does not feel so much in question. "Living in someplace," however, communicates a different experience in which a gap feels present, and this gap implies a lack of connection with the society, the environment, and our location in it. I would add to his formulation the concept of perimeters. I suggest that "living" means a barely noticeable awareness of perimeters and their potential to exclude us. "Living in someplace" implies a definite consciousness of perimeters as obstacles, being unsure of our position in regard to them, and often believing that we remain outside. Living in someplace means we are anxious about perimeters. The spatial dimension of perimeters emphasizes their symbolic power to separate, divide, and ostracize, as well as to include and assimilate. An irony in my story is that once I noticed I was included, I suddenly did not want to be. Crossing perimeters is not necessarily a conscious choice.

Although I had unconsciously crossed some cultural perimeters, I recognize that my gradual awareness of my differences proved helpful because it allowed me to move my life in other directions. Crossing perimeters, or upending them, shows up in clinical practice in many ways when, for example, adolescents rebel against the labels their parents have for them. Other times, adolescents cross perimeters of gender and sexuality as they explore who they are. I think they are offering us important information about the concretization of gender and sexuality, even nowadays when psychologists understand the social construction beneath both. On the other hand, immigrants contend with legally constructed perimeters that are often bewildering. Sometimes immigrants find that these perimeters are burdens that cannot be overcome.

Example of turbulence at many perimeters

Ursula was an Austrian woman in her early forties who phoned me asking to start psychotherapy for her depression following a miscarriage. She was married to a British man who worked in banking and had been transferred the year before to an office in San Francisco. She explained that this had been her third miscarriage, and she worried about time running out for her to become pregnant because of her age. With her visa, she was only able to work part-time and had given up a career as a designer to join her husband. In our first meetings, we spoke at length about her sadness over the latest miscarriage and her fears about not being able to have a child. She was fairly reserved but appeared to welcome my encouragement to talk more. Ursula had had one brief course of therapy after an earlier depression in Austria, and she had found it helpful. She wanted to use her health insurance to cover her treatment with me, and we agreed to work together on handling the administrative pieces for that.

Ursula grew up in a small city in Austria. Her family was affluent and ran their own business. She had an older sister who had almost died in a climbing accident when Ursula was ten. She described her parents as bickering a lot because of disagreements about their business, with clear and troubling memories of her father shouting. She reported many dreams about threatening birds like vultures and hawks, car accidents, and dead people who had been murdered. She was fascinated by organized crime syndicates and read many novels and nonfiction books about them. I asked her whether there was anything from her family that she associated with this interest, and she was offended. She said her parents were "upstanding, good people."

Ursula was extremely frustrated by what she described as "being in prison" in San Francisco—friendless, without family nearby, subject to work restrictions, and struggling over her fertility treatments. The insurance company that covered her healthcare through her husband's employment only provided three rounds of fertility treatments, after which they would have to pay for it themselves. They had already used two. Ursula felt this was unfair and explained it would be different in Europe because they had never had to pay for healthcare and would not have had to pay anything if they still lived there.

A few months into her therapy, her insurance suddenly stopped paying for her sessions with me. I contacted both the billing office and the clinical authorization office several times to clear up what I could about their clerical errors, coding mistakes, a missing authorization, and lost claims. I realized that I was shouldering considerable extra time to do this for Ursula, and I decided to bring it to her attention because we had originally arranged to work together to sort through any insurance problems that might arise. Frequently, psychotherapists in the United States report very high dissatisfaction in dealing with insurance claims for their patients because of the administrative time burdens involved.

RT:　　I realize we've been talking a lot about losses, yet I want to alert you to something. There has been another problem with the insurance company.

Ursula:　What now? (Annoyed)

RT:　　I get that this is frustrating, but they said that your husband's company changed some of the benefits and he has a new policy.

Ursula:　(Stares at me icily) So?

RT: When I phoned them last week, the rep told me that you would have to update his information with them because he has a new policy number.

Ursula: (Sighs) These American insurance companies only want profits! It's ridiculous. What am I supposed to do?

RT: Yes, it really is different for you. I think if you call them with the new policy number, that would help.

Ursula: I never had problems like this [in Austria]. I'll never understand how these companies operate here. It's all big business, everywhere in this country. It's criminal. At home, we know doctors look out for us and we never have to take care of … these details, these silly clerical things.

RT: I hear how frustrating this experience is for you, and that you are angry too about feeling uncared for. Maybe it makes you feel uncertain about me because of this, whether I'm a caring doctor. I also recall that we agreed to work together on it when we started.

Ursula: Yes, I remember. (She seems less irritable now.)

Ursula went on to say that she wished her husband had never taken the job in San Francisco and that she wanted to return to Austria. She complained that American ways were too extreme, too hard to get used to. After this session, I thought she would call the insurance company, but instead, she brought me a copy of her husband's new policy number and asked me to call them during her session. I felt ambivalent but recognized that this was her communicating a wish that we tackle this together. Although it was unusual, I decided to call with her present, and she was able to clarify the policy changes with them. I realized she might have been afraid of doing this alone.

This brief example is complicated. It highlights when perimeters become persecutory, hard to penetrate, and oppressive. For Ursula, she felt like an outsider, powerless, and threatened by American big business that cared nothing for her suffering with either the miscarriage or depression. Her powerful negative transference put me into a difficult position of managing certain of these perimeters for her so she did not feel overwhelmed. I believe that her focus on the insurance company was a symbolic stand-in, displacing her anger about her shouting father, American values that she disapproved of, her visa issues, and her potential infertility. The insurance company became a huge barrier, fortified and impenetrable, that she could react against with rage. There were levels of familial, cultural, legal, and personal and procreative or biological perimeters operative in this symbol. Ursula's resettlement and ac-culturative stresses were compounded by isolation and lack of a community. She felt all alone, struggled to see that she had any power in her situation, felt victimized, and used her perceptions of various perimeters to project some of her shadow problems onto them. For instance, her criticism of American business appeared to represent an unconscious link to her fascination with organized crime. In trying to address Ursula's aggression, I often treaded a careful line between empathizing with her emotional pain and reminding her that she had a voice too and we could think about where she might make changes if she wanted. I often felt pressured, defensive, and powerless to speak to the many issues she brought into her sessions because I felt she often regarded me as someone simply guarding the barrier. Months later, after becoming pregnant, Ursula and her husband moved back to Europe.

Example of cruelty at the perimeter

Jenny Erpenbeck's novel *Go, Went, Gone* depicts a contemporary problem in Germany and most of Europe about dealing with refugees.[19] The operative, significant legal perimeter is the Dublin regulation of European Union law that allows a country to submit a take-back request for asylum applicants believed to have entered another country *before* the one in which they are applying for asylum.[20] Take-back requests mean refugees must return to that country where they first entered the EU; this is practically interpreted, however, to mean the country that first documented or identified a refugee or irregular border-crosser by fingerprinting them and entering their fingerprints into an EU database.[21] Refugees who have applied for asylum can thus be sent back to that first EU country without being heard or listened to in the country where they currently live.

The novel centers on Richard, a widower and retired classics scholar, formerly East German, who befriends a group of African asylum seekers. They have occupied a public square in central Berlin before being rehoused elsewhere, and it is there that he starts to interview them. In a striking parallel, Richard's mother had fled with him from Silesia after WWII, when 12 to 14 million ethnic Germans were expelled from Central and Eastern Europe. Richard thus has a refugee history of his own, and he has witnessed the collapse of East Germany and its absorption into the Federal Republic, when another perimeter fell dramatically.

Richard's journey in getting to know the refugees takes the reader into their lives and the trauma they have experienced, and his increased understanding evokes empathy for the suffering caused by their displacement.[22] He wonders, "Must living in peace … inevitably result in refusing to share it with those seeking refuge, defending it so aggressively that it looks almost like war?"[23] Richard speaks to an archetypal aspect of displacement as a human experience across time, stemming from a natural impulse to search for safety, and he cannot understand the unwillingness to accept this. This novel addresses the artificiality of perimeters that change historically, as in Richard's case when his mother fled and later the Wall fell, and ones that create impossible legal hoops to prevent asylum cases from being adjudicated, as with the African men Richard comes to know. The Dublin regulations, real enough, are thus no better than what the Trump

administration had done in the United States to strangle the inflow of refugees. Both function to identify refugees as undesirable and unwelcome by
erecting perimeters designed to keep them out.

Identity as fiction

Like Appiah, I now wonder to what extent identities are not much more
than presumptions, performative acts that we publicly decide to engage in.
Instead, what if they are like rain clouds—or dreams—that come and go,
release condensation, and evaporate? If so, what are the implications? We
might feel pulled to choose material perimeters to define ourselves because
of their ready availability, although we become more concrete when doing
this, both in Piagetian (developmental) and Jungian (analytic) senses, than
we might admit.[24] This would imply our identities are perhaps more
fictional than we acknowledge. Unlike Appiah, though, I don't believe these
fictions to necessarily be lies, but rather constructions—literally to mark
perimeters—that we make our own to simplify explaining ourselves both to
ourselves and to others. Fiction usually bears relation to truth, as most
authors would attest, but the authoring of who we are is oversimplified
when we rely too much on perimeters. I am reminded that many obituaries
are purposely written before a person actually dies, as if crossing that perimeter between life and death signifies a loss of vital details about who they
once were. Perhaps, there is anxiety that an obituary written after a person's
death might open a door to other fictions about what their life was.

Jung gave us a useful term that allows us to think about the fictions we
show one another: *persona*. His idea of a social mask that we wear certainly
underpins an aspect of what we call identity, especially in the context of our
relationships with social environments.

> Individuality reveals itself primarily in the particular selection of those
> elements of the collective psyche which constitute the persona. These
> components ... are not individual but collective. It is only their
> combination, or the selection of a group already combined in a pattern,
> that is individual. Thus we have an individual nucleus which is covered
> by the personal mask.[25]

An idea of perimeters is implicit in what Jung wrote because the collective
does define the "elements" or "components" that are inside and outside what
a society desires, accepts, rejects, is repelled by, and so on—and all of these
are established, more or less, by socially consensual lines, borders, and
markings, in other words, perimeters. Perhaps we cling to them in moments
when we cannot bear living an ambiguous dream of existence. In many
ways, persona represents our complicated and negotiated relations to the
perimeters of our lives, many of which involve degrees of compromise. Jung

believed, however, that whatever was unique to persona rested in the combination of elements chosen to craft it—there was nothing he found compelling in those elements by themselves because they depended on collective assent. Jung did not equate persona with identity.

Jung wrote about identity, however, in a disparaging manner that could possibly have been the result of a translation issue.

> I use the term identity to denote a psychological conformity. It is always … unconscious … characteristic of the primitive mentality and the real foundation of participation mystique … responsible for the naïve assumption that the psychology of one man is like that of another, that the same motives occur everywhere ….[26]

The only positive thing he wrote in this context was that identity allowed for important social groups to form, based on shared characteristics, and therefore to make contributions to collective life. I was surprised reading this, although it makes sense for two reasons. One is that he wished to differentiate his ideas from Freudian developmental theories that center around various identifications with parents; and second, that the German word *Identität* often connotes *Gleichheit,* which in English is *sameness.* For Jung, identity meant a *lack* of individuality, which is ironic, given how nowadays identity is frequently claimed as a *banner* of individuality.

Alane Sauder MacGuire hypothesizes a connection between persona and soul.[27] She situates the latter within the Self and describes how persona can show vitality about who we are when it is associated with soul. When not, it is usually false, degraded, and ego-driven. "The persona is a cover and a conduit for our identity. But the persona should not obscure identity. And one rigid persona cannot fit all the circumstances of life."[28] Her emphasis on persona is helpful as a contrast to what we traditionally call identity because it recognizes that we do sometimes need masks, which would appear to be about acting out various fictions. However, I would argue that she did not need to assert anything about identity unless she meant identity was a collection of personas. If so, then identity is very close to being a compilation of socially useful fictions.

Erik Erikson provided a psychoanalytic rationale for identity during the 1960s and 1970s when rebellion characterized many youth movements in the Western world. Erikson's ideas are still occasionally referenced because he is seen as having given psychologists a term that supposedly describes the perceived self as it is lived with others. In *Identity: Youth and Crisis,* he wrote:

> An optimal sense of identity … is experienced merely as a sense of psychosocial well-being. Its most obvious concomitants are a feeling of being at home in one's body, a sense of "knowing where one is going," and an inner assuredness of anticipated recognition from those who count.[29]

His reasoning partly mirrors Akhtar's distinction between living and "living in someplace." Erikson emphasized that optimal identity led to feeling oriented and continuous with one's surroundings, much like Akhtar's "living." Erikson's idea about optimal identity conveyed wholesomeness and acceptance, both of self and from important social institutions. Here, perimeters were not threatening, although Erikson was less interested in articulating what composes an identity than in noting attributes of a healthy one. A criticism I have of Erikson is that his writing invoked many perimeters that were explicitly normative for the mainstream, that was bounded by what wider society deemed acceptable, and that seemingly recommended adaptation to more conventional values.

Erikson asked, "Is the sense of identity conscious?"[30] His answer was that sometimes it was much too conscious when it presented as self-consciousness or affectation. Turning identity into theatrical display occurs when any of us pushes what a perimeter is supposed to mean in order to satirize it. This is partly what drag does in regard to sexuality and gender. Erikson mentioned *negative identity* occurring when a person adopted an identity that was viewed as transgressive and risky. Here, I argue an alternative is that choosing to live outside a perimeter can be a positive developmental impulse, something moving toward individuation, not away from it. I believe that Erikson's definition of *optimal identity* referred primarily to existing safely inside the comfort of our perimeters, whereas his concept of negative identity meant being outside them. I don't believe, however, that being an outsider is necessarily unhealthy, suboptimal, or disturbed. In my view, these are dated aspects of Erikson's theory.

Erikson's question about whether identity was conscious speaks to doubts about what we mean by the term *identity:* What are we attempting to describe? Is it relevant today? Similarly, Jung, too, found that persona was illusory. "Fundamentally the persona is nothing real: it is a compromise between individual and society as to what a person [man] should appear to be."[31] Jung indicated that the term *persona,* a cover or mask for each person, was nothing more than an intersubjective agreement, one negotiated chiefly on appearances. I wonder to what extent those appearances might be concretized by perimeters that define whether we are part of something or not. I believe we might use claims of "identity" to help us manage dreamlike qualities of who we are, and that we might, at times, prefer tangible perimeters to verify both personas and statements of identity to assert more certainty than is truly the case.

Simon, a teenage boy, recently said to me, "Why do I have to be straight, gay, or bi? Why can't I just be me whoever I'm with at the moment?" He voiced an awareness of perimeters that felt wrong to him, and I did not have a feeling that he was simply confused or unconscious of something conflicted in himself. Today's adolescents more and more show me the limitations of the word *identity* as I was taught it. Someone like Simon might want to live without the constraints of perimeters; he might instead prefer to feel free crossing them in the spirit of growth and exploration. He wants simply *to be* rather than *be something*.

Further considerations

Are psychological definitions of identity still useful for thinking about actual clinical work? Are they outdated for conceptualizing who a person is? Are we moving into a different *zeitgeist* in thinking of self as relatively fluid, along the lines of "sometimes, we might be everyone and sometimes, we might be no one"? In analysis and psychotherapy, as well as in other fields, identity is now routinely deconstructed to provide space for a rather different appraisal of a person's subjectivity, and consequently, objective categories have become less authoritative. When those categories intersect, it is their crossings that make them more interesting, not less so.

Complicating identity's changing place as a significant psychological term, the word *identity* has been co-opted, and to some extent corrupted, by media-driven political discourse to divide and polarize us. *Blue* and *red* are colors, but they are also defined by their physical wavelengths on the light spectrum, which characterizes a measurable scientific perimeter. That bit of science counts for little, at a time when the colors are used to map geographic areas into red and blue. How often do we hear either "they live in a blue bubble" or "they live in a red bubble" to mean not only separation but also incompatibility and isolation? This is another example of equating a type of perimeter with an element of collective identity. A more hopeful crossing of these perimeters occurs when the color *purple* shows up in political discussions, a blending of blue and red to create a mixed representation. In this example, a physical characteristic (color, wavelength of light) can be reduced to a concrete perception (red or blue) of division, unless one recalls that colors also mix and blend, which is a more flexible way of reminding us of what we share in common.

Like with contemporary adolescents, working with immigrants and refugees has shown me that I have to revise how I think about what I previously learned to call *identity*. Ursula saw in the US fixed perimeters that were foreboding and made her long to return to safer ground where she would not feel identified as foreign. The African men in Erpenbeck's *Go, Went, Gone* were identified by EU law as people to "take-back" in order to protect countries from having to listen to them and their stories. The adolescent refugees I met in Berlin desperately wanted to belong but were acutely aware they did not yet, because of how they were identified—their papers lacked the right stamps. In these examples, social, national, and legal terms identify a person without regard to who they are or what their stories might be.

Many immigrants, like many young people, would prefer not to feel bound by rigidities of self-definition that depend on insider-outsider distinctions and that rely on just respecting perimeters. Their desire to be simply who they are shows us a downside when perimeters like labels split us externally and internally, and they would rather not carry this burden. Perimeters perform this splitting function under the guise of identity. Many immigrants and refugees affirm instead that their growth occurs by crossing perimeters, by pursuing the intersections and resisting hardened determinations of identity. Considering all this, I now wonder whether

- What we call identity never really remains fixed across a lifespan and varies remarkably during a slice of it.
- Perimeters, both external and internal, are the actual markers for identity, and if so, they are inconsistent and erroneous ones, particularly when they concretize human experiences.
- We often turn to them when we hope to steady ourselves and when life's ambiguities are unbearable.
- Existence inside a perimeter pulls psychologically and socially for conformity and division while offering the apparent safety of group affiliation.
- The use of perimeters primarily to define us is nonsymbolic and contributes to decreasing our sense of self.
- A perimeter-enforced state of mind is anti-growth.
- *Identity* should be scrapped as a psychological term—it nowadays belongs more to epidemiology, sociology, economics, and political science than to depth psychology.

The adolescent refugees I met in 2017 described many struggles with trying to cross perimeters, which segregated them legally, culturally, socially, educationally, and economically. These various perimeters also blocked them. This was eye-opening for me, and yet I was struck by how similar they seemed to adolescents anywhere—mocking authority, vigorous in their opinions, posturing to impress, desiring an exciting future, and, importantly, vulnerable in many, many ways. I wondered how they would adapt to German society, and I found myself thinking that this would *not be easy*. I doubt that few of them would ever find themselves, like me, in a situation of being defined as "we Germans." That is not to say that I was cleverer or more adept than they are, but rather that I had several advantages, such as coming to Germany to study, not fearing for my safety and that of my family in my homeland, and not experiencing devastating circumstances during my journey there. Many of the young refugees saw the multitude of perimeters keeping them out and they longed to be inside. They are still uncertain whether they will find themselves inside or outside where they want to be. I slipped through, somewhat unaware, and woke up one day to realize I had to go because I was inside a place where I didn't really want to be. This was a dreamlike part of my time in Germany. In it, I was able to experiment with who I wanted to be so that I could cross many perimeters and be surprised by what I learned. I hope the same holds true for those adolescent refugees I met in Berlin.

At the end of Act Two in Calderón's *Life Is a Dream,* the protagonist, Prince Segismundo, suggests that we all are basically creatures of our dreams, which define us until the moment we wake up.[32] Four hundred years ago, an idea was expressed that a person's identity is dreamlike and not particularly reliable or constant. Even the perimeter between reality and dreams was thought in this play to be arbitrary. I think immigrants today, wherever they settle, are teaching us again that these borders, these labels, these perimeters are arbitrary, often imposed on one's psyche. They want the right to dream, not to be told a fixed meaning. They want to explore the ambiguous places, cross into them, and move on only when they choose to.

Notes

1 Roy Campbell, trans., "Calderón de la Barca. Life Is a Dream," in *The Classic Theatre, Volume III: Six Spanish Plays,* edited by Eric Bentley (New York: Doubleday Anchor, 1959). The Golden Age of Spanish theater refers to works mostly from the seventeenth century. Pedro Calderón de la Barca was a leading author along with Lope de Vega and Miguel de Cervantes. Many plays were written with three acts, rather than five, and dealt with political themes and philosophical allegory.

2 Based on Robert Tyminski, "Is Identity a Fiction," *Jung Journal: Culture & Psyche* 14, no. 2 (2020): 30–48.

3 Charles Rycroft, *A Critical Dictionary of Psychoanalysis* (Totowa, NJ: Littlefield, Adams, 1973), 68.

4 Anthony Storr, *The Essential Jung* (Princeton: Princeton University Press, 1983), 20.

5 Ibid., 94.

6 Wikipedia, "Reality," https://en.m.wikipedia.org/wiki/Reality

7 Kwame Anthony Appiah, *Lies That Bind: Rethinking Identity* (New York: Liveright, 2018).

8 Ibid., 18.

9 Muzafer Sherif, O. J. Harvey, B. Jack White, William R. Hood, and Carolyn W. Sherif, *Intergroup Conflict and Cooperation: The Robbers Cave Experiment* (Norman, OK: University Book Exchange, 1961).

10 Appiah, *Lies That Bind,* 76.

11 Ibid., 97.

12 Ibid., 141.

13 Ibid., 217–218.

14 Robert Tyminski, "Crossing Perimeters: Dilemmas of Immigrants with Identity" (Holding Paradox [Conference theme], February 28 to March 3, 2019, Santa Cruz, CA).

15 Webster's Unabridged Dictionary, 1997, s.v. "perimeters."

16 Jean Piaget, *Origins of Intelligence in the Child* (London: Routledge & Kegan Paul, 1936).

17 The Berlin Wall was built in 1961 and divided the city into East and West until 1989.

18 Salman Akhtar, *Immigration and Acculturation: Mourning, Adaptation and the Next Generation* (New York: Jason Aronson, 2011).

19 Jenny Erpenbeck, *Go, Went, Gone,* trans. Susan Bernofsky (New York: New Directions, 2017).

20 EN - Dublin III Regulation, Regulation (EC) No. 604/2013 (June 26, 2013) (recast Dublin II Regulation, Article 23, Asylum Law Database, https://www.asylumlawdatabase.

eu/en/content/en-dublin-iii-regulation-regulation-ec-no-6042013-26-june-2013-recast-dublin-ii-regulation#toc_255

21 The database is called EURODAC for *European Dactyloscopy*.

22 Brangwen Stone, "Trauma, Postmemory, and Empathy: The Migrant Crisis and the German Past in Jenny Erpenbeck's *Gehen, ging, gegangen* [*Go, Went, Gone*]," *Humanities* 6, no. 4, 88 (2017). https://doi.org/10.3390/h6040088

23 Erperbeck, *Go, Went, Gone*, 241.

24 For Piaget, concrete operations are characteristic of children from ages seven to eleven when children can begin to use logical rules but only when they are applied to physical objects; they cannot yet think abstractly. For Jungian analysts, concrete thinking would refer to a similar two-dimensional processing that is not yet symbolic or transcendent of literal reality.

25 C. G. Jung, "The Structure of the Unconscious" (1916) *Two Essays on Analytical Psychology*, vol. 7, *The Collected Works of C. G. Jung* (Princeton: Princeton University Press, 1953), para. 504. Hereafter, references to Jung's *Collected Works* will appear as Jung, title, date, and volume number in the *Collected Works* (CW).

26 C. G. Jung, *Psychological Types* (1921/1971), CW 6, paragraphs 741–742.

27 Alane Sauder MacGuire, "Embodying the Soul: Toward a Rescuing and Retaining of Persona," *Jung Journal: Culture & Psyche* 11, no. 4 (2017): 45–80.

28 Ibid., 49.

29 Erik Erikson, *Identity: Youth and Crisis* (New York: W. W. Norton & Co, 1968), 165.

30 Ibid.

31 C. G. Jung, "The Relations between the Ego and the Unconscious" (1928), *Two Essays on Analytical Psychology* (1953), CW 7, para. 246.

32 Campbell, "Calderón de la Barca. Life Is a Dream," 455.

Chapter 7

Pandemic

[People] even poison'd themselves before-hand, for fear of the Poison of the Infection,
and prepar'd their Bodies for the Plague, instead of preserving them against it.
Daniel Defoe[1]

In 1665, the Great Plague of London, an epidemic of bubonic plague, swept through England. Daniel Defoe published his work about it in 1722. It is estimated that more than 20 percent of the population, or 100,000 people, died from the plague.[2] Although considered historical fiction because of the narrator's imagined eyewitness descriptions, the book contains extensive research. Defoe included many London street details and contemporary records such as weekly bills of mortality listing deaths. The plague likely arrived from the fleas infesting rats on trading ships and spread rapidly owing to the poor hygiene standards of the time. Infection resulted in

> those spots they called the tokens... really gangrene spots, or mortified flesh in small knobs as broad as a little silver penny, and hard as a piece of callus or horn; so that, when the disease was come up to that length, there was nothing could follow but certain death.[3]

Defoe documents not only the ignorance about the plague, but also the population's willful denial, escape by the wealthier to rural estates, charlatans peddling fake cures, and local governments' attempts at containment. Presciently, we see many of these same human behaviors in regard to the SARS-COVID-2, or COVID-19, pandemic.

How will the pandemic affect immigration in various countries? *The Economist* reports that it has "frozen global migration," and notes that in the United States, Donald Trump associated immigrants with "germs," and he suspended visas for those coming to work in the United States.[4] His xenophobia was only surpassed by his mismanagement of the coronavirus pandemic within the United States. Yet almost every country has issued orders and regulations to restrict travel, and millions of migrants are either

DOI: 10.4324/9781003119593-7

stranded or facing deportation. Defoe might be surprised to recognize many similarities between today and what he wrote about almost three hundred years ago, such as false promises (promoting the anti-malarial drug hydroxychloroquine and claiming in March 2020 that a vaccine would soon be available before any rigorous study and testing) and denialism (believing facial masks and social distancing are not necessary).

John Barry, who wrote about the 1918 flu pandemic in *The Great Influenza: The Epic Story of the Deadliest Plague in History*, notes that the misnamed "Spanish flu"—mainly because it was freely and openly reported on in Spain and censored elsewhere—infected about a quarter of the American population and killed between 50 and 100 million people worldwide.[5] Both the 1918 flu virus and COVID-19 are zoonotic viruses that jump from animals to humans, and both infect many organs, not just the lungs. However, Barry remarks that the 1918 virus was more virulent. Oddly, little has been written about it, even in the decade following that pandemic—perhaps because it merged into the collective trauma associated with World War I and, in itself, was almost too disturbing to differentiate from that.

Other zoonotic viruses include Ebola, MERS, SARS, and Marburg. Bats are a natural reservoir of these viruses, including coronaviruses like COVID-19. The Great Plague, however, was caused by a bacteria, *Yersinia pestis*, and it spread across Europe between the fourteenth and seventeenth centuries. Carried by fleas traveling on rats and other animals, the plague had a mortality rate of 50 percent, and around a third of the European population died from it.[6] John Merrick also notes that plagues of smallpox, influenza, and chickenpox decimated the Aztecs and contributed to their defeat by the otherwise outnumbered Spanish forces.[7]

Emmanuel Le Roy Ladurie, a French historian, published in the 1970s a theory about the unification of the globe by disease.[8] With a mix of hindsight and foresight, he laid out the effects of globalization on disease transmission and mentioned air travel as particularly salient in this regard. For a contemporary reader as a potential warning about COVID-19, Ladurie writes, "If there has to be a plague, better the bubonic than the pulmonary."[9] Merrick remarks that in the 1970s zoonotic infections were just emerging and that Ladurie's essay now reads as "a kind of prophecy."[10] Worldwide trading by ship and by plane is another condition of globalization that unifies us and makes disease transmission easier. Early sprouts of global trading in the fourteenth and fifteenth centuries helped to spread the bubonic plague from Central Asia via the Silk Road and Black Sea to Western Europe.

There are three public health models for the spread of disease.[11] One is *germ theory*, the most common view among the general public, which proposes that infections are caused by various microbes. A second is that disease is spread by *human behaviors*, which can be controlled, although this interferes with personal choices. This model is controversial in the United

States where the guidance to wear a mask is seen among some as an infringement upon personal liberty. A third model is *ecological* and looks at environmental factors in public health; this model is more abstract in that it includes economic, social, and historical factors as well as collective belief systems that all interact to produce a picture of a country's public health.

Effects on immigration

In the United States, the Trump administration used the COVID-19 pandemic as a political opportunity to enact further restrictions on travel to the United States, visa limitations, and caps on new immigration. Bypassing Congress, these restrictions were enacted through presidential executive orders that cited public health protections while also requiring that applicants file their documentation only through online platforms.[12] For instance, the United States instituted entry restrictions for citizens from much of Europe, China, Iran, and stopped nonessential travel from Canada and Mexico. Deportation of detainees often followed their confinement in unsafe facilities where many have contracted the coronavirus. Guatemala's health minister stated that on one flight of deportees from the United States over 50 percent of them tested positive.[13] More than 5,000 people have tested positive in US immigration detention centers, and authorities have refused to comply with a judge's order to release all immigrant children in Immigration and Customs Enforcement (ICE) custody.[14] More than twenty people died in 2020 while in ICE custody.[15] Currently, there are over 25,000 people in ICE custody, and largely, they cannot socially distance from one another. Under Trump (and until 2021), some sources reported that guards who were working under contract for ICE were not being required to wear masks even when they were in contact with detainees, and children often were not provided with soap or toothbrushes.[16] As of early 2021, standard precautions against COVID-19, including masking, are now being enforced by ICE.[17] Further, since April 2021, the Department of Homeland Security, of which ICE is a part, is promoting vaccinations to prevent COVID-19 among its workforce.[18] Although the Biden administration is striving to reduce the numbers in detention, these recent changes drive home how the evolving political situation capriciously controls what can be life-or-death decisions for detained immigrants to the United States.

Because of COVID-19 rules, asylum seekers have routinely been denied their rights; the Trump administration proposed a new rule to bar entry and deport anyone with any infectious disease, anyone with symptoms of disease, and anyone coming from a country where a disease is prevalent. In addition, the Trump administration refused new applications for the Deferred Action for Childhood Arrivals (DACA) program, which affects over 50,000 young people who came to the US as children and have now just turned fifteen, the age at which they can apply for status under DACA.

On his first day in office, President Biden issued an executive order restoring the DACA program, yet until Congress passes a bill protecting DACA, their status is subject to political fluctuations; as of 2021, new applications for DACA are being accepted, although a judge in Texas ruled the program unlawful in July 2021, but allowed DACA to continue through the appeals process.[19] Another Trump administrative maneuver was to curtail funding for the US Citizenship and Immigration Services effectively creating a huge backlog that has slowed processing for new immigrants. Patients and supervisees who I know have reported that these frustrating delays and waiting times have extended indefinitely their uncertainty about their future in the United States. A telling contrast is Canada, which recently set a target of admitting 400,000 immigrants yearly until 2023.[20]

A further executive action by the Trump administration to limit immigration came in the form of a public charge rule that restricted noncitizens from entering the United States based on a determination of whether they are likely to need public support of any kind, including healthcare. This public charge statute has always been a part of US immigration law, rarely applied, until the Trump administration implemented a new form of it. This rule is currently being litigated and has been blocked temporarily during the COVID-19 pandemic. However, the effects of these orders have been chilling among noncitizens who now are afraid to enroll for public benefits, including Medicaid coverage, which would provide for medical care.[21] Medha Makhlouf and Jasmine Sandhu noted, "The new rule's disregard of public health consequences weakens our fight against the COVID-19 pandemic by discouraging noncitizens from accessing (1) health care treatment of COVID-19 symptoms, and (2) public benefits that enable compliance with social distancing."[22] They concluded this rule will have led to a greater prevalence of COVID-19 in the United States and that "cruelty is the point."[23] The intended purpose was to demonstrate how difficult life can be for immigrants to the United States to discourage them from even trying to come here. For those already here, such as agricultural workers who tend to be immigrants from Mexico, Central America, and the Caribbean, life is already plenty hard, and the $2.2 trillion economic relief bill passed in 2020 neither covers the approximately 50 percent of them who are undocumented immigrants nor does it give them any of the added healthcare protections covered in the act.[24]

Social and psychological implications

There has been some early research about COVID-19, mental health, and biases. Quarantine has long been understood as a psychologically stressful experience because of its isolation, stigma, and uncertainty about recovery from a disease. In a literature review of twenty-four papers on this topic, Samantha Brooks et al. found common factors, chiefly negative, of posttraumatic stress disorder, confusion, and anger.[25] The word *quarantine* comes from Italian and refers to the forty days that ships were anchored before being allowed to dock in Venice during the twelfth century to prevent the spread of leprosy and, in later times, the bubonic plague. The main principle is separation and restriction of movement to reduce the risk of spreading an infection to other people. Brooks et al. noted that various studies have looked at the SARS, MERS, Ebola, and H1N1 epidemics and commonly cited stressors include the duration of quarantine, infection fears, boredom, inadequate supplies, bad information, financial losses, and stigma. These psychological effects can arise months or years later.[26] Steps to minimize isolation are important, such as disseminating accurate information, access to mobile phones and Wi-Fi networks, and responsible social media that labels posts about false information.

COVID-19 can be especially hard on refugee and immigrant youth. Tarik Endale, Nicole St. Jean, and Dina Birman, documenting the experiences of a child trauma program in Chicago, mentioned that social distancing measures can decrease the psychological well-being of refugee and immigrant youth who may lack access to adequate technology to adapt to the need for separation.[27] Shelter-in-place orders can lead to feeling more isolated and excluded from important peer socialization processes. Missing school and regular social events mean that children and adolescents are being deprived of normative developmental opportunities that are critical for their growth.

Meiqi Xin et al. conducted a large study in China during the mandatory quarantines in February 2020, and they reported an increase in psychological problems during this time.[28] In particular, they noted a rising prevalence of depression, self-harming behaviors, suicidal ideations, and emotional distress when quarantined people were compared to those not in quarantine.[29] They attributed much of these changes to the perception of discrimination among those who were compelled to be in quarantine.

Chris Sibley et al. examined the effect of lockdown in New Zealand on attitudes toward the government and psychological well-being.[30] They commented that pandemic research generally has found that greater trust in the government is strongly associated with acceptance of public health recommendations. In post-lockdown New Zealand, this led to more trust in science and somewhat lower tendencies to gravitate toward conspiracy beliefs about the pandemic. However, they found mixed support for vaccinations, although they emphasized that the overall picture in New Zealand is one of resilience with "minimal short-term detrimental effects on physical health and subjective well-being."[31] This hopeful report, which may be something of an outlier, runs counter to what many other Western countries seem to be going through with their own polarized responses to the COVID pandemic that has led to protests against public health measures.

COVID Stress Syndrome has been identified to document the enormous toll that the pandemic is taking on mental health. Studies show that there have been global increases in the prevalence and severity of depression and anxiety as well as rises in PTSD and substance abuse.[32] There has also been a rise in the incidence of family violence, which is particularly dangerous to women and children during lockdowns and shelter-in-place orders.[33] The COVID Stress Scales, consisting of thirty-six items, show five categories of impact on mental health: (1) fear of contamination, (2) fear of socio-economic consequences, (3) checking and compulsive behaviors, (4) xeno-phobia, and (5) traumatic stress symptoms such as nightmares.[34] The authors noted, "Our findings suggest that the psychological footprint of COVID-19 is likely to be more substantial than the medical footprint."[35] They reported increased alcohol and recreational drug use as a coping strategy for isolation, and they suggested that psychoeducational techniques to address personal anxieties about COVID-19 might also help to reduce xenophobic attitudes.

The Plague

Albert Camus, who won the Nobel Prize in Literature in 1957, wrote *The Plague* in 1947. It takes place in the Algerian town of Oran. Although it would be simplistic to say this book is oracular, it nonetheless incisively captures the human dimensions of facing a plague epidemic. Dr. Bernard Rieux is the narrator, although that is only revealed near the end of the book. Over the course of nearly a year, Camus describes how the main characters and the residents of Oran cope with a worsening situation that abates only in the last months.

Describing the townspeople, the narrator remarks they "disbelieved in pestilences. A pestilence isn't a thing made to man's measure...."[36] Thus, he foresees our own struggles with denialism as it pertains to COVID-19, the false assurances that it is not as serious as we have been told, the numbing salves about its eradication, and the heated arguments over preventive measures. Despite this disbelief among his fellow citizens, Rieux labors on as he cares for the sick and dying. He is almost stoic and even dissociated from the emotional pain of what he sees while knowing his wife is away in a sanitarium being treated for another illness. Despite people's hopes that the plague outbreak will subside, it does not, and the authorities are powerless in face of it.

The quarantine of Oran comes as "deprivation" for everyone in the town.[37] This loss of normality and of freedom appearing as deprivations echoes the emotional tenor of how many have responded to the COVID-19 pandemic. In particular, the loss of human contact and social connections has deprived us of what we usually take for granted, and we too were un-prepared for this. Poignantly written, Camus describes "they drifted through life rather than lived," an accurate depiction of how many have endured COVID-19.[38] Of course, many others have rebelled against this drifting tendency by instead socializing in large groups, going to mass demonstrations, attending large political rallies, with many repeatedly suspending belief about the dangers and a looming possibility of death. Later in the book, Camus explains the roots of such attitudes as "an ignorance that fancies it knows everything and therefore claims for itself the right to kill."[39]

At another point, Camus writes, "Plague had killed all colors, vetoed pleasure."[40] This loss of everyday enjoyment coupled with ongoing confinement explains the depressive and despairing aspects of the COVID-19 pandemic. One boy told me during his session, "It sucks. Every day is like another shitty Sunday." For him, Sundays were typically boring, impatient times that he had to wait out to get to the better promise of an exciting new week. But with restrictions on movement, Zoom as a constant screen for school and work, and social distancing from those outside the immediate family, colors seemed to fade through the monotony of our isolating routines during COVID-19. More optimistically at the end of *The Plague*, Camus writes of what we learn during a period of plague: "that there are more things to admire in men than to despise."[41] I believe he meant that even when times are at their bleakest, we yet manage to love and care for one another, finding things in ourselves we would otherwise never have imagined. For many in the United States, the record 2020 election turnout and its result of a new president were powerful statements about reaching for the admirable instead of settling for dejection.

Xenophobia

There might be a biological underpinning to why we avoid what looks ill, sick, and diseased. Mark Schaller and Justin Park have described the behavioral immune response that guides our detection of symptoms of infection in the environment and leads to humans then showing avoidant strategies.[42] However, this response is prone to false-positive errors when we see dangers or evidence of infection when they are not there. Unconsciously, such mistakes lead to explicit and implicit biases and, as the authors speculated, they then contribute to ethnocentrism and xenophobia.

Xenophobia has risen around the world during the pandemic, especially anti-Chinese rhetoric and xenophobic conspiracy theories that demonize refugees, immigrants, and foreigners.[43] In the United States, Trump's frequent use of "Chinese virus" and "Wuhan virus" has encouraged hate speech against Asian Americans. By late April 2020, Asian American and Pacific Islander groups created a reporting center called Stop AAPI Hate, and they had received 1,500 reports of incidents of racism, hate speech, discrimination, and physical attacks against Asian Americans.[44] In the United Kingdom, Sky News reported in early May 2020 that regional police forces listed over 250 anti-Asian hate crimes between January and March. Similarly, in Australia, in the first two weeks of April 2020 alone, there were over 175 racially motivated incidents.

Contrary to outrageous claims about a need to defend the country, the rates of contracting COVID-19 are no higher among immigrant populations. A study at the Cato Institute found that the rate of COVID-19 cases and deaths within the United States is not correlated with the share of the local population that is foreign-born.[45] The authors also noted that research on travel bans as a response to pandemics showed that they do not limit the spread of disease because they are typically enacted after the disease has already spread. During the 1918 flu pandemic, the United States continued to allow entry to more than 100,000 immigrants and did not restrict the temporary migrant worker program, primarily for agriculture, that year. The American Medical Association has called on public officials to refrain from using racially charged and xenophobic language when discussing the pandemic, especially when such language amounts to scapegoating against Asians and Pacific Islanders in the United States and against Asian-presenting people.[46]

Berkeley Franz, a sociologist, and Lindsay Dhanani, a psychologist, conducted an online survey to examine attitudes about xenophobia and racism in the United States related to COVID-19 and they found that xenophobia seemed to increase with a concurrent perception of threats emanating from specific groups or countries.[47] They reported that pre-existing biases and discriminatory beliefs about different ethnic groups fuel xenophobia and that fears of further threat reinforce the stigma of danger from them. On a hopeful note, they also found that education about COVID-19 reduces xenophobic attitudes. Those obtaining their information primarily on social media, however, have less accurate knowledge about COVID-19.

The xenophobia seen recently in the United States is linked to paranoid fears about bigger social and demographic changes, which some groups mistakenly perceive to be apocalyptic for their traditional ways of life. Many Americans feel persecuted by outsiders, immigrants, refugees, and minorities. The nature of the threats behind these persecutory emotions is often based on beliefs about competition for various resources, which can include jobs, economic status, educational opportunities, public benefits, and media recognition. Those entering are felt to be invading and penetrating what are imagined to be safe zones. An ensuing fear of contamination makes the alleged association between COVID-19 and outsiders more insidious and difficult to speak to in a rational way because, for those who feel threatened, their responses are coming from emotionally visceral and primitive levels of experience.

Those imagined safe zones exist chiefly in fantasies, although this does nothing to hinder the talk of building walls to isolate ourselves. With COVID-19, many in the United States see outsiders as crossing perimeters related to community health and threatening to overwhelm access to medical care. Think of the various layers that make up a hospital as continuously shrinking perimeters that lead eventually to intensive care units. Those are seemingly perilous perimeters that we are terrified of, because the news media has streamed pictures of people dying in ICUs, after which they go on a reverse journey across other final perimeters of morgues, funerals, memorials, and burials. Our terror over COVID-19 is understandable. But becoming paranoid to cope with it, by projecting our fears of it onto outsiders, is a poorly adapted social response.

COVID-19 as a disease invades our bodies, crossing through respiratory airways and our lungs and affecting many other organ systems, especially densely vascular ones like the liver, intestines, brain, and kidneys.[48] These are real physiological perimeters inside us. Our lungs are where air comes and goes, a veritable metaphor for a border or a perimeter. *Pneuma* is a Greek word for breath, although in Greek tragedy it is used to mean breath of life and in the New Testament to mean spirit.[49] It is strange to think then that COVID-19 robs us of a natural and necessary flow (*pneuma*). That flow is life-giving. Further strange to think that what it means—entering and exiting to nourish and replenish—can be divisive when it comes to how we view other flows like those of immigrants and refugees.

Another religious and highly symbolic aspect of plague occurs in the Book of Revelation, in which John of Patmos has a vision of the end times and sees the four horsemen of the apocalypse.[50] The first rider wears a crown, rides a white horse, and carries a bow and arrow. Although there are varying interpretations of what he stands for, one consistent view has been that he represents a conquest of pestilence and plague. His bow is a mechanism for spreading what his arrow carries, namely deadly infections shooting outward. The conquest that he spreads over humanity is one that decimates populations through fatal illness. The fourth rider in this vision of Revelation, who rides a pale horse, is believed to represent death as well. Of course, these are gloomy and shadowy aspects for why plagues are felt as terrorizing and catastrophic. They too are important parts of the human experience during a pandemic, and they help to explain why so many of us might have felt persecuted by what has happened all around us.

Notes

1 Daniel Defoe, *A Journal of the Plague Year* (The Project Gutenberg E-Book #376, 1995, updated 2020), 72.
2 Dermont Kavanagh, "Daniel Defoe: 'A Journal of the Plague Year,'" *London Fictions*, 2012, https://www.londonfictions.com/daniel-defoe-a-journal-of-the-plague-year.html. See also Wikipedia, s.v. "Great Plague of London," https://en.wikipedia.org/wiki/Great_Plague_of_London
3 Defoe, *Great Plague*, 372.
4 "Tearing Up the Welcome Mat," *The Economist*, August 1, 2020.

5 John Barry, "Historian John Barry Compares COVID-19 to the 1918 flu Pandemic," University of Rochester Newscenter, October 6, 2020, https://www.rochester.edu/newscenter/historian-john-barry-compares-covid-19-to-1918-flu-pandemic-454732/. His book *The Great Influenza: The Epic Story of the Deadliest Plague in History* was published in 2004 by Viking.

6 John Merrick, "The Angel of History," *Boston Review*, September 4, 2020, www.bostonreview.net/philosophy-religion/john-merrick-angel-history

7 Ibid.

8 Emanuel Le Roy Ladurie, "A Concept: The Unification of the Globe by Disease," in *The Mind and Method of the Historian* (Chicago: University of Chicago Press, 1981), 28–83.

9 Ibid., 52.

10 Merrick, "The Angel of History."

11 April Thompson, "The Immigration HIV Exclusion: An Ineffective Means for Promoting Public Health in a Global Age," *Houston Journal of Health Law and Policy* 5 (2005): 145–171.

12 Sonya B. Cole, "COVID-19: Though It Exacerbated Anti-Immigrant Sentiments, It Could Accelerate Immigration's Digital Transformation," Worldwide ERC, October 19, 2020.

13 "Deportations Continue, Threaten Other Countries' Health Security Amid Crisis," Feminist Newswire, May 12, 2020.

14 Claire Williams, "4 Ways that the Trump Administration Has Targeted Immigrant Children during COVID-19," First Focus Campaign for Children, September 15, 2020.

15 Alex Nowrasteh, "21 People Died in Immigration Detention in 2020," *Newstex Blogs Cato@Liberty*, October 22, 2020.

16 Karlyn Kurichety, "Deliberate Endangerment: Detention of Noncitizens during the COVID-19 Pandemic," *UCLA Law Review: Discourse* 68 (2020): 118.

17 "ICE Guidance on COVID-19," US Immigration and Customs Enforcement, https://www.ice.gov/coronavirus

18 "DHS Announces Ten-Fold Increase in Vaccinated Workers through Operation VOW," Department of Homeland Security, April 5, 2021, www.dhs.gov/news/2021/04/05/dhs-announces-ten-fold-increase-vaccinated-workers-through-operation-vow

19 "DACA," National Immigration Law Center, https://www.nilc.org/issues/daca/

20 "Canada Sets Record Immigration Target of 400,000+/year till 2023," *Times of India*, November 1, 2020.

21 Medicaid in the United States is a federal and state program that helps with healthcare costs for some people with limited income.

22 Medha D. Makhlouf and Jasmine Sandhu, "Immigrants and Interdependence: How the COVID-19 Pandemic Exposes the Folly of the New Public Charge Rule," *Northwestern University Law Review Online* 115 (2020): 146.

23 Ibid.

24 Ruqaiijah Yearby and Seema Mohapatra, "Law, Structural Racism, and the COVID-19 Pandemic," *Journal of Law and the Biosciences* 7, no. 1 (2020): 4.

25 Samantha K. Brook et al., "The Psychological Impact of Quarantine and How to Reduce It: Rapid Review of the Evidence," *The Lancet* 395, no. 10227 (2020): 912–920.

26 Ibid., 917.

27 Tarik Endale, Nicole St. Jean, and Dina Birman, "COVID-19 and Refugee and Immigrant Youth: A Community-Based Mental Health Perspective," *Psychological Trauma: Theory, Research, Practice, and Policy* 12, no. S1: S225–S227, http://dx.doi.org/10.1037/tra0000875

28 Meiqi Xin et al., "Negative Cognitive and Psychological Correlates of Mandatory Quarantine during the Initial COVID-19 Outbreak in China," *American Psychologist* 75, no. 5 (2020): 607–617.

29 Ibid., 613.

30 Chris G. Sibley et al., "Effects of the COVID-19 Pandemic and Nationwide Lockdown on Trust Attitudes toward Government, and Well-Being," *American Psychologist* 75, no. 5 (2020): 618–630.
31 Ibid., 627.
32 Jaiqi Xiong et al., "Impact of COVID-19 Pandemic on Mental Health in the General Population: A Systematic Review," *Journal of Affective Disorders* 277 (December 2020): 55–64.
33 Kim Usher et al., "Family Violence and COVID-19: Increased Vulnerability and Reduced Options for Support," *International Journal of Mental Health Nursing* 29, no. 4 (2020): 549–552. https://doi.org/10.1111/inm.12735
34 Steven Taylor et al., "COVID Stress Syndrome: Concept, Structure, and Correlates," *Depression and Anxiety* 37, no. 8 (2020): 706–714, DOI: 10.1002/da.23071.
35 Ibid., 712.
36 Albert Camus, *The Plague*, Trans. Stuart Gilbert (New York: Vintage Books, 1991), 37. A 1948 version available at Internet Archive, https://archive.org/details/plague00camu_khb
37 Ibid., 67.
38 Ibid., 73.
39 Ibid., 131.
40 Ibid., 113.
41 Ibid., 308.
42 Mark Schaller and Justin H. Park, "The Behavioral Immune System (and Why It Matters)," *Current Directions in Psychological Science* 20, no. 2 (2011): 99–103.
43 "COVID-19 Fueling Anti-Asian Racism and Xenophobia Worldwide: National Action Plans Needed to Counter Intolerance," Human Rights Watch, May 12, 2020, https://www.hrw.org/news/2020/05/12/covid-19-fueling-anti-asian-racism-and-xenophobia-worldwide#
44 Ibid.
45 Alex Nowrasteh and Andrew C. Forrester, "No, Mr. President, Immigration Is Not Correlated with COVID-19 in the United States," Cato Institute, April 1, 2020.
46 "AMA Warns against Racism, Xenophobia amid COVID-19,"*Impact News Service,* May 6, 2020.
47 Berkeley Franz and Lindsay Dhanani, "What Covid-19 Should Teach Us about Xenophobia," National Center for Institutional Diversity, *Medium,* June 15, 2020, https://medium.com/national-center-for-institutional-diversity/what-covid-190should-teach-us-about-xenophobia-ccbff02c61a1
48 Tamar Lapin, "Coronavirus May Damage Kidneys, Heart and Liver," *New York Post,* April 15, 2020, https://www.columbianeurology.org/coronavirus-may-damage-your-kidneys-heart-and-liver
49 J. T. Valance, s.v. "pneuma," *Oxford Classical Dictionary,* March 7, 2016, https://doi.org/10.1093/acrefore/9780199381135.013.5145
50 Robert Tyminski, *Male Alienation at the Crossroads of Identity, Culture and Cyberspace* (London and New York: Routledge, 2018).

Chapter 8

Finding Safe Harbor

A mighty woman with a torch, whose flame
Is the imprisoned lightning, and her name
Mother of Exiles.

Emma Lazarus[1]

Millions of immigrants coming to the United States have passed by the Statue of Liberty on which Emma Lazarus's words are engraved as a welcome to a safe harbor. Safe harbors can be planned destinations, but not always. In Book Five of The Aeneid, the Trojan Fleet has departed from Carthage and encounters a huge storm.[2] Their ships are forced to land at the port of Eryx on the island of Sicily. Juno, who the reader may recall was strongly opposed to Aeneas and his voyage, sends a messenger to urge the Trojan woman to burn their ships because they have endured long enough and should just remain in Sicily. Four ships are set afire before Jupiter intervenes with rain to prevent the fire from spreading to the rest of the fleet. Having avoided this near disaster, Aeneas decides that women, the elderly, and any others too tired to continue can put roots down in Sicily, where a local king claims Trojan heritage and offers them protection—safe harbor.

Juno's disguised messenger riles the Trojan women by appealing to the raw emotions coming from the collective misery of their seven-year journey:

> O wretched we, whom not the Grecian pow'r,
> Nor flames, destroy'd, in Troy's unhappy hour!
> O wretched we, reserv'd by cruel fate,
> Beyond the ruins of the sinking state!
> Now sev'n revolving years are wholly run,
> Since this improsp'rous voyage we begun....[3]

She invokes their story from its tragic beginning when the Greek armies sacked Troy. Noting the passage of time—the seven years—she emphasizes

DOI: 10.4324/9781003119593-8

the enormous strain, anguish, and suffering they have faced. "O wretched we" is an emotional proclamation: they have reached their limits and do not want to go any farther. Refugees across time often report that they do not know how they found the strength to finish their journeys. In The Aeneid, the exhortation of Juno's messenger nearly works when the women set fire to the ships. This part of the epic dramatizes the extreme difficulties that the Trojan refugees have gone through. At this point, the main group separates from some of its original members who no longer want to struggle onward. The story thus shows that the heroism of Aeneas is not for everyone; a good enough environment can provide the refuge and safe harbor that they seek. The Trojans who stay in Sicily decide seven years is a dear enough price to pay. They are ready to settle where they have landed.

Although I'm referring to these Trojans as refugees, the formal term *refugee* stems only from international treaties and agreements reached in the 1950s.[4] Nonetheless, the term applies to people at any point in history who have been exiled, displaced, and sought refuge elsewhere. Many immigrants are not officially designated as having refugee status, which is regulated by the aforementioned treaties, but they still qualify as refugees based on a commonsense understanding of the word. Like the Trojans, they might have fled their homelands in search of a new beginning in another part of the world where they and their families can feel safe, have better educational and economic opportunities, and enjoy freedom from persecution, discrimination, and prejudice. And, like the Trojans who decide to remain in Sicily, not all of them will reach their chosen destination because of intervening factors, including how much hardship they can ultimately bear. *Refuge*, therefore, is a relative term for these choices when compared to a homeland that does not offer "good enough" options. *Good enough* is a concept developed by Donald Winnicott, who used it to talk about the mothering of children: that a good enough mother does a very demanding job; she will encounter a number of setbacks that lead to various disappointments for her children; and yet she enables them to grow, to learn tolerance for life's frustrations, and to develop their potentials.[5] In the context of immigration, the question might be: where is a "good enough" place to settle that will allow for safety, opportunity, and growth, while not necessarily being an imagined utopia?

Many immigrants might elect to follow the path of Aeneas, absolutely resolute in finding their chosen destination because it completes a long-held dream—like crossing a rainbow to a magical place. That choice does not make them better than those who choose to settle earlier in their journeys when they might have found another place that offers them relief from ongoing wretchedness. This chapter looks at some of the many variables that influence such choices, which can become bewildering, because of the serious risks and unknowns that are involved. One thing about rainbows is that they appear suddenly and unpredictably, but when they do, they are stunning to behold. However, they are ephemeral; they are easily obscured by clouds, and, in reality, they are optical illusions. Quite a challenge for assessing whatever risks await those hoping to cross them.

Mental health and refugees

Barbara Eisold, in her book discussing psychoanalytic views on seeking asylum, concurs with my description of the broader status of who is a refugee: "The vast majority of people who are displaced are not refugees/asylum seekers at all. These are people who have been forced to leave home because of events" that do not meet the legal criteria for refugee status.[6] Consider, for example, the migrations brought about because of climate change—the droughts, floods, and other environmental disasters that have made their homes uninhabitable; when people move for these reasons, they are not officially refugees. In addition to discussing the asylum-seeking process in the United States, Eisold reviews the effects of trauma, especially its intergenerational transmission when children grow up and unconsciously live out traumatic pieces of what their parents had experienced before, during, and after their migration.[7] The clinical examples later in this chapter illustrate some of the remarkable elements of this unconscious familial transmission.

Beltsiou, in the edited volume that I reference in Chapter 1, discusses how immigrants often encounter the "uncanny" when they arrive in a foreign land where they seek to make their new home.[8] This experience reflects an immigrant's resettlement into so many things that are new, unknown, and foreign to them and their feeling deeply unsettled as they do so. The resettlement process can be frightening and disorienting, much like an uncanny encounter, which includes, for instance, experiences of déjà vu or synchronicity. Concurrently, for a native or local population in a receiving country, immigrants can likewise represent something of the uncanny. Residents may feel frightened and disoriented by the foreignness of new immigrants. Thus, aspects of the uncanny resonate for both, and discomfort can lead to othering and avoidance. Othering results when we exaggerate differences, look down on those who remind us of those differences, and project feelings of inferiority onto them.

Encounters with the uncanny can also arise around differences in language and communication. When an immigrant uses a foreign word unexpectedly in a conversation—perhaps as a placeholder for a forgotten word in the new language—or when an immigrant has a strong accent, a native speaker listening to them might feel confused or even irritated because something is not immediately understandable or conversational flow is interrupted. Of course, how someone reacts in this situation is varied and unpredictable, but often enough, non-English-speaking immigrants can recollect instances where they have been dismissed, brushed off, condescended to, and so on, when evidence of the foreignness of their language surfaces. When I lived in Germany, native Germans often guessed I was from a Scandinavian country. Sometimes they would be curious about my accent, but I also received frowns, skeptical looks, and questions about why I was studying in Germany, as though that would have made no sense. Many of my immigrant patients have often lamented their accents being mis-understood and feeling devalued when a native English speaker apparently distances themselves after hearing them speak. Language can become a troubling shorthand for whether a person fits in or not because it literally makes the difference audible. Tolerance of difference is not a given. Developmentally as well as culturally, many individuals struggle to accept and tolerate differences. I will say more about the uncanny in relation to immigration in the last chapter.

Irene Cairo, an analyst in New York who is from Argentina, gives ex-amples from psychotherapies when a patient's language of origin is con-nected to emotional responses that have not yet found means of expression within the new language of the receiving country.[9] She notes that she had to make space for "the old language, because nothing would better serve as a vehicle for the reintegration of affect."[10] I have at times worked in German with patients whose primary language was German, and I have found that quite different emotional experiences emerge as a result. Sometimes, these have allowed for earlier developmental memories and attachments to con-solidate in a newer form. For example, a man from Germany once said to me, speaking in German, that he remembered looking out a window at a bird in the rain when he was in school. I asked what he saw, and he replied, "*Ein Rotkelchen*"—a robin—and I asked him how he felt seeing it. He began to cry and said he worried it was alone in the cold rain. This memory led to exploration of his loneliness as a child; he was able to access a part of himself that he had not allowed himself to know more fully before then. His saying the word in German (*Rotkelchen*) was crucial to linking his memory with feelings that in turn brought up further memories. I doubt it would have happened this way in English.

Others have written about how another language can do exactly that, namely hold other parts of ourselves that we keep secret or unconscious while living with a second language in our day-to-day lives. Sarah Hill, another New York analyst, writes, "Much of our primary body-based, af-fective selves and relational configurations are deeply and sonorously en-coded in our mother tongues ...."[11] Language can be a key to other parts of the psyche that immigrants might have repressed or dissociated because they are too painful to recall. Verbalization of those fragmented parts can assist immigrants in psychotherapy and analysis to reclaim them and enrich their experiences of themselves. When I do not know my patient's primary language, I sometimes ask, when it feels particularly important, "What would that word (or phrase) be in your first language?" This exploration, more often than not, taps into memories and feelings tucked away long ago.

Seeking asylum is difficult. In a review study spanning twenty years of research into the mental health of asylum seekers, authors from Ireland concluded that "the asylum procedure is inherently damaging to mental health" because of the multiple stressors—financial, emotional, educational, family—that arise during the asylum-seeking process.[12] This kind of administrative abuse negatively affects children who are born while their immigrant parents are waiting for permanent status.[13] A particular problem for families in this situation is the asymmetry created between parents and children when the latter must live with the threat of losing their parents to possible deportation.[14] Interpersonal dynamics in these situations can be characterized by fear, vigilance, and avoidance. In regard to the draconian policies of the Trump administration, one study cites "dire mental health consequences" that can impair integration into US society and threaten to leave children traumatically abandoned.[15] A phenomenological study of undocumented immigrants to the United States found that many reported mental health symptoms as well as feelings of low self-worth and devaluation.[16] These studies demonstrate the monumental resettlement problems now facing immigrants coming to the United States, especially those seeking asylum.

Some researchers explore which type of psychosocial interventions, aside from advocacy for political change and submitting legal challenges to existing rules, can help immigrants and refugees nowadays. One study examined sixty research articles to see which trends and correlations exist for supporting refugees from developing countries.[17] Surprisingly, it found that psychosocial support interventions that build communities and networks appear to outperform programs that address mainly trauma symptoms. The authors hypothesize that this is because stressors of daily life can be more urgent for refugees than an immediate focus on trauma, which is better addressed individually.

Another question that arises for immigrants and refugees is to what extent do those exposed to trauma then discuss it within their families. Thorup Dalgaard and Edith Montgomery advocate an approach based on "modulated disclosure" that attends to children's developmental levels and allows for appropriate timing for parents to talk about their trauma with their children.[18] Here, *modulated* implies not saying either too much or too little and finding a "just right" amount to tell. These authors reviewed twenty-five articles, covering a wide range of cultural backgrounds, on the topic of disclosure and silence around trauma. The majority of these studies point to modulated disclosure as optimal, indicating that either silence or full disclosure confuses children more. However, there is an additional caution that a Western assumption of openness and talking things through does not fit many other cultures, and this assumption bears reevaluation depending on the family's cultural context.

A newer area of research is the concept of posttraumatic growth. Some refugees report that after resettlement and the processing of traumatic events they experience positive psychological shifts as well as interpersonal gains.[19] These changes are not the same as resilience because they appear to result in internal rearrangements of self-concept and relating to others. As this field is developing, more research about it will likely be published. Many preliminary findings are either mixed or inconsistent.

Case example—Unsettled

When I met Galit she had recently turned nine. I worked with her for two-and-a-half years. She was in a fourth-grade special education program at a public school because she had an autism spectrum disorder, one referred to as Asperger's syndrome.[20] Notably, children with Asperger's are unusually verbal, although their nonverbal capacities are significantly lower, and Galit had this profile. Her father worked in finance, and her mother was a teacher. She had a brother who was three years younger. Galit's parents had left a part of the former Soviet Union and immigrated to Israel, where she was born. They then left Israel when she was four and moved to the United States, settling near Chicago. The family spoke a Slavic language at home, and Galit had learned some Hebrew. When they moved to the United States, she initially refused to learn English, perhaps as a form of protest that it was simply too much for her young mind to take in. Around age seven, her family moved yet again to the San Francisco Bay Area.

Prior to seeing me, Galit had undergone much speech and language therapy as well as occupational therapy; these therapies continued during her psychotherapy with me. She was fairly uncoordinated, often stumbling and flapping her hands to discharge anxiety and tension. In her first drawings with me, all the people had extremely long arms, disproportionate to the rest of their bodies. This emphasis on arms seemed indicative of several trouble spots in her young life: fine motor and coordination difficulties, a lack of impulse control, and an avoidance of contact with other people—long arms to keep them at a distance. Galit also had a specific phobia of birds. When asked to draw a picture of herself, she drew a pterodactyl and said, "It's a predator," most likely as a defensive expression, turning passive into active, to control her own fears of being preyed upon. During her first sessions with me, she was aloof and avoidant, making limited contact and using a dismissive tone to reply to my questions or comments: "That's silly. Why would you ask that?"

She had no history of any traumatic encounters or accidents with birds. Her parents thought this specific fear arose after they had come to Chicago when Galit ran terrified from a flock of pigeons while at a park. Her parents were understandably anxious about Galit's mental health and other special needs. I asked how the relocations had been for them. Galit's father sighed. He said he moved to find better work opportunities as if he had no other choice. Her mother, who appeared somewhat depressed, mentioned that it was hard learning "new ways and new languages," although she too seemed to feel she had little agency about any of these moves. I wondered how Galit had reacted upon moving to Chicago. Her mother replied that Galit had not liked it and kept telling them that she missed her grandparents who were in Israel. They thought that although she had shown signs of having developmental issues in Israel, in their minds these clearly worsened after coming to the United States. They had left their home country to flee anti-Semitism and for better economic opportunities. When I inquired about the language they used at home, they spoke of it as the one constant in their lives, a kind of fond living memory of where they were from. Yet, this Slavic language was one that Galit heard primarily at home.

I asked how they had explained the moves to Galit. They simply told her, "We're moving," and that it would be exciting. They did not appear to feel much self-determination about these moves; they were more like passengers in the back seat of a car that someone else drove. Their narrative appeared to contain a split: on the one hand, the change was going to make life better, yet on the other hand, both parents seemed attached to what they had left behind. Galit dramatically split her play and stories in sessions with me. Beyond the typical "good" versus "bad" in children's play, she was fascinated by right and wrong, wicked and pure, and love and hate. These states of play often felt unbridgeable as if they were too far apart; they made me wonder how Galit made sense of changes that might have felt too disruptive and unexplainable. Early on, her parents alerted me that her father's work might take them to Asia, and I wondered how yet another relocation would affect Galit.

She worked consistently on her phobia of birds, playing in my office with bird toys, such as a stuffed bird and a plastic pterodactyl. She reported about her run-ins with various birds, and together we tried to figure out which kind of bird had frightened her. What color was it? How big was it? Was it alone or with other birds? After a few months, Galit came in one day and told me there had been a bird near the steps of my office building. She said, "I wasn't afraid because I knew I could walk by it and come talk to you." Although birds, of course, build nests, they do not typically reside in one spot for very long. They represent migratory behavior, and I sometimes speculated whether Galit's bird phobia, arising after her family came to the United States, might have been a communication about her terror of moving around, once again having to learn "new ways" while feeling foreign and outside.

I encouraged her parents to talk more with her about the family's history, to look at old pictures together, and to remember the different places where they had lived. Her parents liked this idea and perhaps found it therapeutic to settle into a common narrative about their travels. Soon Galit's phobia diminished, and she no longer ran away when a bird landed on the sidewalk. Her mother said that sometimes Galit would look right at the bird and say aloud, "I'm not afraid" and then tell her mother, "I'm going to tell

Dr. Tyminski I wasn't afraid." When her class went to a petting zoo, Galit took a risk and petted an owl. Later, she insisted on calling her grandparents to tell them she had done this. She was getting a handle on a fear with multiple meanings. For example, she understood that although birds usually had sharp claws and beaks, they were unlikely to attack her. As we shifted away from birds as sources of fear, I thought about migration, and in her sessions, I found ways to comment on how many places Galit had lived. I invited her to tell me what she remembered about each place. She told me she liked the weather in Israel, she liked her school in Chicago, and she liked her house in San Francisco. I encouraged her to draw something about each place, as I thought about how a child builds internal bridges between different locations. One day, Galit came in with photos of where she had lived in Israel and in Chicago. We talked the entire session about memories she had of these places.

Soon thereafter, Galit announced, "Let's play house!" She imagined a scenario in which she and I were married, thus connected and not easily separated, and we had two nineteen-year-old daughters, Sarah and Debra. Debra was devoted and dutiful, whereas Sarah was a troublemaker. This split in our imaginary family was a useful way for Galit to process how emotional bridges are built between people, especially when they seem far apart. She became openly curious about me, asking if I were married. When I declined to answer and instead asked what her guess would be, she replied, "Oh, it's secret" and laughed sweetly.

Another bridge for Galit at this time was puberty. Over a year into her therapy, she experienced her first period. Shortly thereafter, she became fixated on my Adam's apple, asking me repeatedly about it: What's it called? Did it hurt? Why was it shaped like that? How long had I had it? She was both fascinated by it and repulsed, once saying, "It looks like a pencil's stuck in there." I thought her questions about my Adam's apple were a way for her to process another bridge she had to cross now as her body changed. I remarked that her interest in my Adam's apple showed her curiosity about bodies when they change as we get older. Galit denied this, but suddenly, our house play evolved when Galit announced our daughter Sarah was having a baby. This development within dramatic play showed, I believed, a symbolic bridging of Galit's relationship with her body, in her transference to me, and to a growing capacity for building links within her own experience. Sarah's "baby" also represented a specific way of making a story about a family with a beginning, a past, and a present, all of which showed promising growth in Galit's psyche. Her family's moving around had left Galit feeling deprived of important details for such a story about herself and she wanted to create one.

About two years into Galit's treatment, her parents informed me that her father had a job opportunity in Taiwan. This news disappointed me because I thought relocation would be disruptive for all of them. At first, her parents were not telling Galit, now eleven, much about this. My concern grew when one day Galit said that Sarah was getting a divorce from her husband, and Galit was even considering divorcing me. I intuited that she had picked up something about a possible relocation. She began to regress, using a childish voice, acting silly, and becoming argumentative over simple things. This change occurred at school, in her home, and with me. She began identifying with a baby doll among the toys, and I remarked that the baby felt helpless and didn't know what was going on. Galit would nod yes when I made comments like this.

Consulting with Galit's parents, I emphasized that they too had grown and could handle talking openly in the family about the possibility of moving to Taiwan. Her father was unsure, but surprisingly, her mother insisted and seemed to grasp its importance. They began carefully sharing a story with Galit and her brother about their father's work—that he might find a new job. They looked at maps together and spoke about what it would be like in Taiwan. Galit's mother told me this was unlike anything they had ever done before their prior moves. I continued to encourage them to prepare themselves and her for what such a change would mean for them. Galit asked if she would have to learn Chinese and seemed upset about this idea. I indicated to her parents that she had had a difficult time with English, and perhaps they could begin planning ahead to find a school where English was used. Her father went to Taiwan to finalize his job offer, and Galit told me, "My father's gone. He's coming back in August, and we're all going to Taiwan." She did not appear distraught and instead acknowledged she felt both sad and excited. This statement of two different feelings at once also felt like another indication of her ability to build bridges in her inner world.

During the last period of Galit's treatment, she expressed anxiety about the upcoming changes. For example, she spoke about Asian American people she saw in the city as being "mean"; she said she did not like Chinese food and even wondered if some of it was "poisoned"; she used a ninja character from the toy collection to attack the baby; and she told me pandas "could bite you and hurt you." I related each of these fantasies to her mostly unconscious feelings, such as being scared about meeting new people (who might at first seem "mean") because she did not understand how different and alike they each were. I offered that once she got to know someone who at first looked different to her, she might be surprised to find herself liking them and discovering they were not so different. I spoke about her persecutory fear of having something unknown ("poison") get inside and terrorize her—because she was angry and worried this new place could be awful for her because of all she'd have to take in again, like a taste of bad food. And I mentioned how vulnerable she might feel (the baby) because she would have a lot to learn while worrying about making mistakes and feeling misunderstood (the ninja's attacks and the biting pandas). In these interactions, I attempted to speak to Galit's complicated feelings while also showing that she had grown and learned how to deal with emotional challenges such as her fear of birds.

Within the house game that we played, the topic of divorce, which she brought up more, led to me commenting that she and I would soon be saying goodbye. I told her about her many good qualities that I would remember. I added that a goodbye could seem like a divorce when a person chose not to remember, but our memories helped us to hold on to what was important and meaningful. Galit said in one of these sessions, "I know that new things can also mean there's hope." I empathized with her missing me and said I would miss her too; she cried when I said so. "I'll be okay."

In our final session, as we talked about funny moments that we had shared, Galit turned to me and said, "I feel mixed up inside." I said that meant we cared about each other and it was hard to say goodbye. Before she left, she asked her mother to take a picture of the two of us. Her mother again remarked that this move was different from their previous ones because they included Galit in their planning for it and talked through her worries. I felt it was a new experience for all of them in creating a story together about their family.

Luckily, I was able to locate a referral for Galit in Taiwan. The psychologist, who had trained at the day school where I had worked earlier in my career, was Taiwanese and had returned home after finishing his training. I found another bridge for Galit to connect old and new.

Discussion

In an early session, I asked Galit's parents to tell me something about their home country. They both described oppression and discrimination that they wanted to escape. The mother's grandparents had died in a death camp during the Holocaust, and her parents were displaced near the end of the war and forced to live in a resettlement camp in another country. The father's parents hid in a cave for months after the war. Thus they both reported significant intergenerational trauma. I had the impression that they had not spoken about this much. Their own history of repeated moves seemed less driven by seeking professional opportunities than by something they carried within themselves about the dangers of staying in one spot too long. Coupled with this pattern was their reluctance to talk about their prior moves with their children, who were left to helplessly experience them as sudden changes.

This tendency to avoid communication within the family led them to enact a story rather than tell one. Their surprise at my suggestion of constructing a family narrative together was significant because it revealed how unconscious they had been about the traumatic suffering within their own families. There was a notable lack in valuing a story as purposeful, creative, and helpful. One additional consequence of this attitude was a passivity about fate because both parents tended to view their moves as inflicted on them—by the father's job opportunities—rather than chosen. The missing links in their lives and their stories complicated Galit's development as well because she struggled initially to form cognitive and emotional links within herself.

Although I would not assert that a bird phobia necessarily means just this, for Galit birds represented unpredictable creatures that could fly at you and then fly away, a fantasy that terrified her. They were not at all stable. A similar unpredictability characterized Galit's early life, moving at four and then at seven, by putting her into new situations where almost everything a child considers important would change (school, language, friends, family members, environment, culture, foods). These basic elements of a childhood environment instead were torn apart, scattering like a flock of birds, with no connecting pieces to form a meaning out of what was happening. Her subsequent terror of a world without meaning partly reflected the inter-generational trauma that her parents had unintentionally passed on to Galit. Fortunately, they were open to working on not repeating this pattern and instead communicated with each other about having a future in another place. For their previous moves, this future was murky at best, and its absence was another missing link, a temporal one. Trauma often deprives those who suffer from it, a perspective on the future.

Case example—In the middle of the night

Mariam was in her mid-forties when we met. We ended up working together for more than four years. She had contacted me because she wanted to work on personal issues she felt she had in relationships and with intimacy. Mariam told me, "I struggle with being close to women." She was lesbian, worked in the tech industry, and had been single for quite a while. Mariam had spent her childhood in Lebanon, where she was the younger of two children; she had a brother four years older. Her father was a government official. They were a Christian family and had to flee during the Lebanese Civil War when Mariam was eleven. Her family resettled in the United States in a suburb of Detroit where there was a large Lebanese community. Mariam realized she was gay after her family moved to the United States.

Over the course of Mariam's analysis, I learned that the Lebanese Civil War began in 1975 and lasted until 1990. The coastal areas of Lebanon were a mix of mostly Sunni Muslims and Christians. Fighting erupted between the Maronite Christians and Palestinians, who had fled Israel, and their allies. Lebanon had once been part of the Ottoman Empire; it then came under French control after World War I. It became independent in the 1940s with control split between the Maronites and Muslims. In the late 1940s, there was an influx of Palestinian refugees because of the Arab-Israeli War. Powerful families dominated the political scene and patronized their supporters. Many more Palestinian refugees arrived from Jordan by 1970. In 1975, battles broke out between the Palestinian Liberation Organization and the Christian militia in Beirut. The fighting eventually resulted in more than 100,000 fatalities and over 1 million displaced residents who fled Lebanon.

Mariam attended college in the Midwest. She had her first relationship during that time, with a woman who was bisexual and who eventually rejected Mariam to marry a man. Their relationship had lasted more than two years. Mariam had not had another intimate relationship since then. She dated women but lamented that she felt "no passion" for them. Mariam's parents separated around the time she left for college.

In her first dream, Mariam reported, "*I am talking with a woman friend about another woman who I had been dating. I am describing her flaws, and my friend argues with me. You came into the scene, and you listened to us. I think you agreed with me, and I then felt better about my decision to break up with her.*" I asked Mariam how she understood this dream. She said she tended to be critical of others, that she looked for flaws in people, and that she did not have much patience for imperfections once she spotted them. I wondered whether she was talking about her first impressions of me and possibly whether she might also be afraid I would make these kinds of judgments about her. In either situation, aggressively appraising someone and cutting them down when they didn't measure up appeared to be a concern as she began psychotherapy. I asked her what she thought about being critical of others, and she replied that she viewed herself as "blunt" and "direct." I wondered how she understood using this approach. She said she was "competitive" and added, "I like to win." Because of these interactions, I believed Mariam would be very cautious in therapy until she felt safer with me.

I inquired about her earlier life. She told me that she grew up in an exclusive part of Beirut where she lived in a villa. She said, "It was paradise." I asked what she meant by that. She told me, "I could've had anything but then the war came." This sounded like she lived in an idealized situation before being driven out by violence. To myself, I wondered about Mariam's sense of entitlement because she described her privileged status without even a second thought to what it might have meant for others. Perhaps too, she was warning me about how she might react to limits in our relationship when she would not be able to have something she wanted from me. Instead of speaking directly to that, I asked if she could say something about how she felt coming to see me.

Mariam: Well, I had to wait to get an appointment with you. I guess you're busy. [Mariam had called me three months prior when I didn't have any openings. When she checked back with me more recently, I did.]

RT: Could you say how you feel about that?

Mariam: I'm glad to be here. It's sort of glamorous.
RT: How so?
Mariam: Well, your office is in this neighborhood with mansions, and I imagine your schedule is hard to get into. So I feel like I scored a lucky ticket.
RT: I hear you reacting to waiting for an appointment with me and then seeing where my office is located. I wonder if maybe you're putting a lot of weight on appearances and not letting yourself have whatever other feelings are there?
Mariam: (Grins slightly) I don't think so. I'm feeling impressed, and there really isn't anything more to it. (Mariam looks down as though she is finished with this conversation.)

In her slight impatience with me, I seemed to be regarded as a servant, someone who does their job and just accepts whatever she believed without questioning her. I chose to be quiet after she said this, although I wondered when our disagreements might become more apparent. At this point, it was important for Mariam to voice her idealizations unchallenged. Her initial dream alluded to her wish that I validate her, not stir the pot. Importantly, whenever I asked Mariam to describe more about her early life in Beirut, she repeatedly told me, "I don't want to go into that now."

A couple of months later, another dream brought her idealizing tendency into sharper focus. Mariam had been complaining about unsatisfying dates she had gone on, about coworkers she believed were lazy, and about her father who she thought was narcissistic. She started her session by mentioning this dream. "*I am staying in a huge, fantastic house on Lake Michigan. I notice that water has come into the surrounding area and flooded it. I went onto the deck, and I jumped off into the water and started swimming. There were naked people swimming but I avoided them. Then I noticed the water was too warm, and that bothered me.*"

I asked if she could tell me what came to mind now as she spoke about the dream. Mariam said, "Oh, that house was like a lodge. It was glamorous, visually stunning." She was excited about how grand the house was but then mentioned that the water temperature made her anxious because she knew it was wrong for the lake. As I listened, I began to have some ideas about the state of Mariam's psyche at that time. She described a separation—she was alone at the lake house—as wonderful and idyllic, which could be a defensive way to cope with loss and feeling alone. She also noted that she avoided contact with the naked swimmers; perhaps this was also a way to distance herself, a protection against attaching and forming a relationship. I wondered whether Mariam might have regarded me as someone to avoid because implicit in the dream was a heat that made her uncomfortable when she jumped in. Perhaps the "bath" of analysis would become too much for her. The lake's flooding made me consider the affective overwhelm that might have been associated with whatever trauma Mariam had experienced in leaving war-torn Lebanon and coming to the United States.

RT: You used that word *glamorous,* and I recall you also said it when I asked about coming to see me. Any further thoughts now about it?

Mariam: It's your office, the way it's furnished, the wall hangings, the decor. It all does seem glamorous to me. I saw this therapist ten years ago, and in her office, there were these faded posters, and the fabric on the chairs was so worn.

RT: What else do you notice about me?

Mariam: Well, how you dress. You're not a shlumpy therapist in baggy clothes. You're stylish. And your cologne. I don't know what brand it is, but it just smells expensive.

RT: You notice a lot here that makes you feel impressed.

Mariam: Yes, and your role at the university too. That's impressive. I mean, most people don't realize how significant a place [the university] is.

RT: I sound like a catch, although possibly imposing too.

Mariam: A little. But I'm not afraid in here. I am embarrassed to tell you these things.

As I listened to Mariam, I found myself thinking that the large house on the lake might be symbolic of my office and me. If so, then Mariam jumping out would have been both moving away from what felt imposing and an expression of feeling left to swim for herself with naked strangers. I also wondered whether the dream portrayed something of her trauma from the Lebanese Civil War because there seemed to be a representation of her being alone coupled with an abrupt departure into heated surroundings. I did not comment on these thoughts. Instead, I asked what Mariam made of feeling embarrassed. She replied, "I'm worried I'll become pathologically dependent on you. I don't want that. It's such a cliché of therapy, isn't it?" Mariam's remarks here seemed to affirm an aspect of the aloneness that her dream portrayed, as well as a transference of fearing yet wishing for someone like me to depend on. I also thought that her attraction to me was based mostly on appearances, and this made me think of how she might struggle when a relationship became more substantive. She appeared to be saying that her desire only went so far because she was anxious about where else it might take her.

I continued to think about the unnaturally warm lake water and what it might imply about Mariam's memories of her country. A few weeks after this session, I thought there might be an opening to ask Mariam about her life in Lebanon.

RT: You haven't told me how you left Lebanon.
Mariam: I've already said that I don't like talking about it.
RT: I imagine it could've been awful leaving a war zone. [I wanted to explore if she could overcome her resistance to the topic.]
Mariam: Yeah, it was. But I think people make it out to be more than it was.
RT: What do you mean?
Mariam: It just happened a long time ago. Other people have gone through worse. I don't see a point in dredging it up.
RT: It's part of your story.
Mariam: I wish it weren't.
RT: My interest in it feels out of place to you.
Mariam: Yes. I like to think about proportions. And I lived in Lebanon about a quarter of my life, so that 25 percent shouldn't be over-emphasized.
RT: It was your childhood.
Mariam: (Sharply) Okay. But, I don't believe that a person's childhood is determinative. It's just a part of a life. And how we live later is based on our choices.
RT: It feels like we're arguing now.
Mariam: (Smiles and relaxes) I agree! How's that for irony? I agree we disagree.

This adversarial tone characterized many of Mariam's sessions during the first year that we worked together. After this exchange, she came into a session and told me she was anxious about flirting with a younger woman at work. She imagined she might have overstepped, and this woman would then report her for sexual harassment, although Mariam described them as mainly exchanging a few flirtatious innuendos. I asked her if she had any idea why this situation would worry her so much, and she replied that she was afraid of turning into someone like her father. I had no idea what Mariam was referring to, so I gestured with open hands for her to explain.

Mariam: He had a mistress.
RT: (Silent)
Mariam: For a long time. A long time, since I was maybe six or seven.
RT: I think there is a longer story about this. (Pause)
Mariam: Yes. (Pause) He started cheating on my mother when I was young. He met this woman. I think she was a singer. He was always flirting with other women, right in front of my mother. It makes me ashamed to think I'd flirt like him. I so do not want to be like him. He was a cheat. My mother knew, and it made her feel like she was the problem. She was constantly dissatisfied with herself because she felt she didn't have enough of whatever to

satisfy my father. She became more reclusive as I got older, and then, somehow, I ended up being like her best friend. She confided in me about their marriage, and I knew things I wish I hadn't—like about his mistress and where he went weekends when he wasn't home. I became codependent with her. When I came out, I told her, and she said, "Oh, I knew that a long time ago." It was such a buzzkill, and it made me think, how did she know when I just figured this out? I haven't come out to him. I don't know why. I'm just ashamed he'll think we're somehow equivalent sexual outlaws, him with his mistress and me being gay. It's my last closet to come out of.

It was astonishing to hear Mariam speak at such length, nearly a year into her analysis, about her parents, because she had previously curtailed any longer discussions of them. She carefully edited that part of her life into an abridged version. Now, it seemed she had found a way to test the waters with me. Perhaps, she felt I would be there for her if she felt flooded or overheated.

Mariam talked more about her prior life interspersed with regularly in-sisting that she also report on events at work and dates she had gone on. When she came out as lesbian during college, she did not feel she could immediately tell anyone in her family and she was quite anxious about it. Middle Eastern values and social attitudes about family and gender roles felt constricting to her, and she was not confident that she would not be re-jected. She believed that a basic flaw in women she had dated was that they were "not inspiring." I asked what that meant, and Mariam told me that the woman she had been in love with during her college years believed that a primary relationship had to be inspirational. Mariam said, "If they're not inspiring, that's a deal breaker." *Inspiring* meant they were passionate about some aspect of their lives, adventurous and, of course, good-looking, and even better, charismatic. I thought about Mariam's privileged background in Lebanon as a potential source for this idealistic fantasy of love, although it seemingly contradicted the affairs she described her father and others having. Mariam said that she had met inspiring women and tried to date them, but this glow would inevitably fade and she would become discouraged. As I heard her say this, I recalled her description of my practice as glamorous, and I wondered when that too would fade. Were we in analysis on borrowed time? I mentioned to Marian that perhaps her critical voice would interfere with her tolerating someone's flaws and the loss of an initial glow. She agreed. "The problem is in me." That seemed like a promising insight, and I encouraged her to elaborate. "I have a fear of closeness. I'm stuck on that one relationship I had in college. Being critical keeps me fixated on it."

In Jung's volume on alchemy, *Psychology and Alchemy*, he writes meta-phorically about what happens when we experience this loss of a glowing object, meaning one we have idealized. He posits that we are then confronted with rust, which, as imperfection, strains our beliefs and emotional responses when we prefer to have something idealized. "In the alchemical view rust … is the metal's sickness."[21] Jung's linking of alchemy to fundamental psychic states can be challenging to comprehend, but if a reader sticks with him, his insights are truly compelling. For example, in this instance, he is describing a human tendency to desire ideal things rather than grapple with what feels imperfect, diseased, tarnished, or worn down. Mariam's rust included being gay as a woman from a conservative culture and her experiences of being a war refugee coupled with all that she lost as a result. She felt ambivalent about integrating these experiences in her analytic process. Jung adds, "To round itself out, life calls not for perfection but for completeness; and for this, the 'thorn in the flesh' is needed, the suffering of defects without which there is no progress."[22] Although it may sound simple, acceptance of the scope of our individual shortcomings is a never-ending process that many of us rebel against with refusal. The cost of an ongoing rebellion, as Jung states, is our own psychic wholeness. He emphasizes the pain that this process of accepting the rust involves as being necessary for psychological growth.

As we talked more about her being gay, Mariam revealed she had a lesbian aunt who lived in Boston. This aunt had a chronic form of cancer in which her health often varied from better to worse. Mariam felt close to her and had visited her several times during her analysis. Yet I had not heard about this aunt until well into Mariam's second year of analysis.

RT: Hmm. I wonder how come you've not mentioned her before now.
Mariam: I guess I forgot.
RT: (Silent)
Mariam: I know how that sounds. I'm not a forgetful person, so there is probably a reason I didn't tell you.
RT: What comes to mind about that?
Mariam: It's not the gay thing. I love that my aunt is lesbian. It feels like an anchor in my family and makes me less an outsider.
RT: (Silent)
Mariam: (She seems more uncomfortable, wiggling in the chair, and then stretching out her arms in a jittery way.) I don't know. Maybe we can talk about it some other time.
RT: You're aware of avoiding something.
Mariam: I am. (She seems annoyed with me.) All right. It's about how we left Beirut. (Long pause) We left at night. It was probably after midnight. I remember my mother telling me earlier that evening to pack one bag. She was very clear. She said, "One bag only. Take what feels precious to you." She actually said "precious," and I was what, eleven, and I thought, how do I know what's

precious to me? (Pause) A government car picked us up at our home. My mother and aunt—she's her sister—were both crying. My brother was a teenager, and he understood it better than I did. He looked like he'd seen a ghost. We could hear explosions in the distance in the city. I asked where we were going because no one had told me. Can you believe it? No one even thought to tell me where we were going. I mean, maybe they thought that was better to not upset me. (Pause) We went to the airport. I recognized it from our trips when we'd gone to [different places in Europe and the Middle East]. But we went through the passenger terminal and into another hangar. I remember thinking, this isn't right, this isn't how we get on planes. There was a plane waiting in the hangar. I can't remember if it had any markings on it. We got on, and we took our seats. There were others too—I don't remember how many—but it was almost full. (Mariam looks out the window for a bit. We sit in silence during a longer pause. I felt attentive to hearing what she had not spoken about for a long time.)

RT: Where was your father?

Mariam: (Sighs) Yeah, he didn't come with us. He stayed in Beirut for another two months or so. Maybe a little longer. The plane landed at Dulles [Washington, DC, airport]. All I remember is that we got into a car and were taken to an empty apartment. I think it was in Virginia. Funny thing is I remember more about that night in Beirut than I do about what happened after we landed in the US. It's like those days after we arrived are wiped away.

"Wiped away" aptly describes what refugees often report about aspects of their journey to a new country where they resettle. It is as if parts of their experiences have been erased, although not completely, such that only traces remain. Mariam was sad during this recounting of her leaving Beirut, and we spoke more about her grief at losing her home and her shock at how abruptly it happened. She became more openly depressed after that session. She felt stuck, irritable, and "in a bog" that made her also feel trapped. She noted how little community she had now, and she missed that because she realized she was more isolated than she wanted. She reported dissatisfaction in almost all areas of her life, including her relationship with me. When I commented on this, she responded, "Life is depressing. What do you expect?" I found openings when I could say that her feelings were not only about her current life but also about her earlier memories of traumatic relocation. She replied, "Oh," and seemed forlorn. Her awareness of these complicated feelings sometimes led to her rebuffing my interest in knowing more. She told me, "I just want to be left alone."

Mariam:	Therapy is such a chore.
RT:	It is difficult work to be conscious of things we'd prefer not to see or talk about.
Mariam:	You're way too detached.
RT:	Hmm. You feel I don't really care and that I only listen without any feelings myself.
Mariam:	Sometimes. I know you have feelings. But I guess I'm expecting something more.
RT:	Yes, I recognize that sometimes being with me is disappointing for you.
Mariam:	It's just pointless!
RT:	You're angry, and even when I try to connect, there is something you feel wanting to break us apart.
Mariam:	(Laughs) That's kind of funny.
RT:	How so?
Mariam:	You take me seriously, more seriously than I take myself. I like to think I'm just being ironic and no one gets me.
RT:	That's lonely. I don't think I want to see your important experiences as funny or ironic.
Mariam:	Most people just don't understand me. I mean, isn't it obvious I'm being sarcastic?
RT:	Not always.
Mariam:	(Looks surprised) Oh. I should probably think about that then.

Mariam often felt misunderstood by me, and this scared her because she realized we were relating more deeply. In this exchange, the glamor had faded, and she found me disappointing. In her remarks about being taken seriously, however, I thought she was revealing her longing for just this kind of experience and expressing her conflict about that longing. In other words, could someone see her traumatized eleven-year-old self and not turn away from her? She had explained feeling left too much alone around the particulars of that event, and at this time, her memories evoked how painfully lonely and isolated she had felt then. Perhaps, her surprise over the impact of her sarcasm revealed her wish that someone see around it so as to glimpse the profound hurt inside her.

Well into her third year of analysis, Mariam began speaking about a desire for closure with her past and with her family. She was more open about her grief at the multiple losses resulting from their abrupt departure from Lebanon. She reflected on how unhappy her mother was with her life in Michigan. "It's like she's stranded, and now because of that, she's become very bitter." She contrasted this with the circle of a close family that her mother had in Beirut. She said that her father had practically abandoned her mother when they separated. He claimed to be preoccupied with business deals that he was secretive about and that supposedly involved other Lebanese immigrants in the United States.

Although Mariam continued to date women, she found herself "obsessed" with younger women. She asked, "Why am I looking for a twenty-five-year-old to date?" She connected this question to her college relationship as well as to her crushes at boarding school. When she spoke about these things, it was as if she were frozen in time. Her "obsession" with younger women seemed also to remind Mariam that she had unfinished psychic work from that earlier period of life. Around this time in analysis, Mariam reported a dream about us.

Mariam: In this dream, *you were my psychiatrist but actually you were faking it. You were really an electrician. And you weren't even here to work on something. You were another therapist's patient.*

RT: I was pretending and misleading you in the dream.

Mariam: Yes. I felt duped that I hadn't figured it out.

RT: So you'd not be able to trust me because in the dream, I played a trick on you. I wasn't who I claimed to be. Your sense of what was real was undermined.

Mariam: Yes.

RT: Does that remind you of anything else, trusting in someone only to have the rug pulled out from under you?

Mariam: Funny you put it like that because it does remind me of when I was sent to boarding school at twelve. We had this throw rug just inside the entrance to our house, and I was standing there waiting for the mailman when my mother came into the hall and told me they had enrolled me in a boarding school on the East Coast. I remember the rug slid a little and I almost fell.

RT: (I was surprised by her memory of the rug and wondered about this synchronicity as potentially meaning how very unstable her life had felt to her back then.) Everything seemed so uncertain, I imagine, and after leaving Beirut and coming to Michigan, you learned that you'd be going to another strange place.

Mariam: It was difficult. I had no preparation, and I didn't understand about boarding schools in the US—that the kids going to them are essentially groomed for that and it's supposed to be a prestigious thing. I had no idea.

RT: What comes to mind about going there?

Mariam: I idolized all the popular girls. They seemed glamorous and naturally on top of their adolescent drama. Not like me. The first couple years, I associated with the Goth girls who were more the losers there. We got made fun of, and you really couldn't cross into other groups much.

RT: Isolating.

Mariam:	Very much. And I had the darkest skin of anyone. There were no minorities at this school. I kept thinking, Why did they pick this place to send me to? I felt I stood out because my skin was darker, and it's not even that dark! But I looked foreign to them, and I could tell. In my third year, I made friends with a girl, Julia—she was athletic, popular, and preppy. I mean, she even looked fashionable in uniform. I loved her.
RT:	You look sad right there.
Mariam:	Maybe. She went to college on the West Coast and died in a boating accident.
RT:	(Silent)
Mariam:	(Fighting tears) I guess when I heard that, it was kind of devastating. I have such vivid memories of staying up until dawn talking with her.
RT:	You lost someone very important to you.
Mariam:	I did. I lost her and I felt cheated.
RT:	Tricked again.
Mariam:	(A single tear on her cheek) Yes, horribly tricked.
RT:	No wonder it's hard to trust now. You had all these experiences of life being turned upside down.
Mariam:	I guess that explains, at least partly, why I can't let myself be more attached.

Following this exchange, Mariam shared other memories of leaving Beirut. For example, she recalled how confusing it had been that her father stayed behind. She worried about his safety and whether he would make it to the United States. Mariam, her mother, and her brother sheltered temporarily in an apartment in Virginia. Since she was not in school, she watched television almost all day. She heard the news about Lebanon—explosions, executions, and militia attacks—and she felt helpless and numb. She told me that not all of her family made it out. She added, "I never talk with people about Lebanon." I asked what stopped her from doing so. "It seems like a hopeless conversation." But she had been talking about it with me, and I thought this showed progress at integrating some complicated aspects of her trauma around leaving and resettlement in the United States, experiences when she had, indeed, felt hopeless. Slowly but steadily, Mariam was telling me her story about fleeing a place she had once called home.

After this, more negative transference emerged, perhaps in an effort to push me away after feeling closer to me. It may also have been a test to see whether I would get turned off and lose interest in her. Mariam became argumentative with me, and she often showed flashes of unexplained anger. I thought this made sense because her story was now more out in the open between us as a shared experience. I not only represented a listener but also someone who knew about the unwanted feelings from her trauma.

RT:	Lately, I notice we've been disagreeing more.
Mariam:	Yes, I know! (Dismissive)
RT:	It seems the more I try to understand your pain about Lebanon, the more you become upset with me.
Mariam:	I don't know if I'd put it that way.
RT:	How might you put it?
Mariam:	(Angry) I don't like talking about the war!
RT:	Yes, I hear your anger about it. You feel I focus on it too much.
Mariam:	Right.
RT:	(After a long silence) I wonder too if you are anxious that I won't get what you went through, that I don't understand just how awful it was for you.
Mariam:	(Pause) Possibly. I mean, I know you're trying to draw me out and offering me a chance to talk about it. It's kind of amusing because this week, I've been fantasizing about what it would be like to date a therapist.
RT:	Hmm. Can you say more?
Mariam:	Well, I was thinking about you. (Pause) You're analytical. I like that. I can tell you have a good mind; you're not flakey or New-Agey like my previous therapist. I mean she had crystals on a table in her office, and the first time I saw them, I thought, oh boy, I guess I'm really in California now. (Pause) You're also reasonably in shape. And you know about [a musician who was not that well known].
RT:	You're describing various ways we connect, and that sounds positive, helpful. What would you say gets in our way?
Mariam:	(Pause) I have a fear of being trapped. That you'll know me too well, and I know it makes no sense, but somehow, that feels like a trap.
RT:	I hear our getting closer could feel like a trap—that you might feel stuck or frozen by it. Maybe that worry is also about the war, that you could've been trapped in Beirut. You had such a close call escaping from there, and then you came to the US, where there were all kinds of other traps awaiting you. [I was thinking here about how her mother had told her about boarding school and then sprung it on her, and about her realizing she was gay, which put her in conflict with many of her cultural traditions.]

Mariam reported feeling closer to me after this session. She had a pleasant dream *about visiting her grandparents and trying to help them resolve their estrangement.* She said they had an arranged marriage that appeared loveless. Her grandmother had doted on Mariam, and Mariam loved going to their home. She cried some as she spoke about these memories, which she said were "fragrant" because she could smell the spices, pet birds, and flowers in their house. Mariam's dream seemed to express a hope of reconciling a divided couple, which made me think about the recent negative transference that we had weathered. She spoke about her feelings of anger and disappointment at me, and I believe this helped her to shift her perspective around relating by not necessarily feeling trapped by closeness. On the contrary, estrangement in her dream now seemed a problem to her.

Mariam also shared poems she had written. A common theme expressed in her writing was about losing one's way, nightmares, and trying to find the light. Poetry was a creative outlet for her to further process and metabolize her traumatic losses. Sharing the poems also showed her willingness to take a risk with me and become more vulnerable. She spoke in detail about how it had felt to lose her culture, which she cherished. She often noted that Lebanese people in the United States did not feel the same to her as those she had known in her homeland. She became more conscious during this period, now in her fourth year of analysis, of the ways she isolated herself and pushed others away.

Thinking about finding a partner, Mariam recognized that her ideal one was a combination of the women she had loved in high school and college. She commented on this as a wish that could not be re-created no matter how hard she tried. She expressed sadness at losing those loves, but she remarked they remained sweet even though unfulfilled. Sometimes, she wished for a do-over, a way to rewind the clock or time-travel so she could choose another path. This wish is probably not at all uncommon among refugees and immigrants who have suffered great losses during their resettlement to a new country. Mariam's wish for a do-over was a step in mourning what her life had once been in Beirut, an ache for that life, nostalgia.

Mariam ended therapy with me a bit like how she left Beirut, except now I was the one receiving the surprise ending. She moved somewhat suddenly for a new job in another part of the United States. However, we had some time to terminate our relationship, although I felt not enough. She joked with me, "I guess it must be hard for you. [That she was leaving like this.] But at least you'll know I'm able to take more than just one suitcase." With that remark, she seemed to allude to what had changed in our relationship. It seemed promising—both that Mariam empathized with my position as someone being left and that she used a relevant personal metaphor to let me know she was taking away from it more than she had ever expected. Afterward, I often wondered if she could have ended it in any other way; perhaps she had to leave feeling in control of her exit. She was no longer an eleven-year-old girl rushing onto a plane at night.

Discussion

Idealization can be a defense against unwanted feeling or anxiety, especially related to separations and differences, and relying on it has certain ramifications for the psyche. We think of idealization as putting someone on a pedestal where they are superior to us. This serves to set them apart and possibly to cast us in their glow. In other words, we too are special because we can relate to an idealized person. Children naturally do this at a young age, when, for example, they imagine their parents to be secretly royal, superheroes, or possess magical powers. Soon enough, they discover this is not the case, and they learn to cope with their disillusionment about it. A tendency to idealization persists; we all have aspects of it in us.

When idealization fails, the psychic energy attached to it usually turns to the opposite: an attack on the previously elevated person who now is viewed as worthless, fraudulent, or despicable—anything to distance ourselves. Idealization might hold our feelings of anger, competition, and envy in check for a while. Awareness of conflict, disappointment, or even a simple mistake can break this emotional compromise. When it does, a person can feel overcome by their own anger. Rage at not having an infantile or child-like need met can flip into devaluing what once was idealized. In the wake of idealization comes persecution, much like a zealot scorns a prophet to urge them to be cast out or worse.

Idealization can be a reaction to loss too. The lost situation can, for instance, become idealized as irreplaceable, and all potential substitutes have to be devalued to ensure the magnificence of the lost thing. We all are capable of this; it is a utopian fantasy. Mariam idealized her life in Beirut as paradise. She was quite open about it. She felt as though nothing could measure up to what she had lost at age eleven. Her idealization of that life protected her somewhat from awareness of her trauma at losing it, although it kept her isolated by degrading potential current opportunities as insufficient. Her early dream of the huge lake house represented aspects of this dilemma in which she was alone in a kind of castle as the overheated water engulfed her. Those hot waters symbolized difficult aspects of her trauma at leaving Lebanon, such as emotions of anger and panic. In that dream, she acted oblivious to those, using both denial and avoidance to cope with her situation. Perhaps that was the best her eleven-year-old self could do under those circumstances. In idealizing her life in Lebanon, Mariam protected herself from becoming flooded by rawer emotions that were quite near and felt overwhelming.

Earlier, I introduced Jung's idea of psychic rust as one way to understand the loosening of idealization. Rusting does not usually happen quickly; it emerges over time. Mariam gradually let me know about her rusty areas, which included the trauma of leaving Lebanon the way she had as well as her being gay. Her revealing them to me showed a willingness to come out of a self-imposed hiding. Through this process, she discovered more about what had felt "wiped away" in her psyche. She did not want to be like her father, who she felt kept too much hidden and secret, and that desire was healthy in her. She was similarly afraid of becoming bitter like her mother, and her desire to differentiate from her was also positive.

Idealization can become something of a trap for a refugee or immigrant when their homeland is exalted as a paradise that is forever lost and never can be reclaimed. Nostalgia. Nothing will compare and stand a reasonable test of being "good enough." Recall that previously I mentioned Winnicott's notion of "good enough" in relation to migration and place. Here, in terms of idealization, it refers to not being ruled by impossible standards for perfection. This kind of psychic trap freezes a person in time, reinforces isolation, swells the tide of nostalgia, and can foreclose a future elsewhere. Mariam came to see many such traps in her work with me. For example, she understood that her mother felt "stranded" in Michigan because she could not reconnect with others there while she was caught in melancholic longing for Beirut; her nostalgia trapped her. Mariam described a pattern of relational traps she repeated because her desire remained entwined with experiences from boarding school and college. One of those women had died, and the other had rejected Mariam to live a straight lifestyle. Mariam recognized her preference for things past and she felt frustrated by it. That frustration showed a possibility to heal if she could mourn her traumatic losses and become conscious of how these had shaped her life. It helped therapeutically when she made the connection that she worried about her feelings for me as possibly trapping her. In the transference, I noticed a gradual evolution from her seeing me as glamorous to be instead a pretender who faked it and eventually, someone she could feel close to, which then made her worry she would not have a way out if needed. Articulating these ideas and the feelings that went with them helped Mariam experience new things in her relationship with me: differences, conflicts, and disappointments that were not traumatizing. In a way, I slowly went in her mind from being idealized to being good enough, with a lot of doubts and negativity in between.

How Miriam left was interesting, to say the least. It might have seemed like an unconscious recapitulation of her leaving Lebanon. However, she and I were able to speak some about it, and I came to believe that she understood there was an element of reversal in what she was doing. She decided to move on, rather than have an ending—out of her control—hijack her life. Perhaps the way she ended with me expressed a bit of her hopelessness about Lebanon—that she still feared an unpredictable outcome and wanted to instead take charge. Her remark about the suitcases made me think that this time she was going better prepared than she once had been.

Fertummelt

Fertummelt is a Yiddish word meaning confused or befuddled. Henry Roth's novel *Call It Sleep* is about a young boy, David, whose family moves to New York City in the early twentieth century from the area of Galicia in Austro-Hungary.[23] It begins in 1907, which ranks as the peak year for immigration to the United States, when David, seventeen months old, arrives at Ellis Island with his mother, Genya. His father, Albert, a bitter and angry man, awaits them at the pier in Manhattan. They speak Yiddish at home, but of course, David must learn English, a task that Roth captures with great imagination: "Land where our fodders died." A reader knows David and his mother will have many hard times when just after their arrival, Albert snatches the hat David is wearing and throws it into the water. Most of the novel covers a three-year span in David's young life, from ages five to eight. He and his parents come to live in the gritty Lower East Side, where his father works as a milk delivery man, the horse and wagon kind, not the truck kind. David is afraid of him: "Nothing about him ever changed ... always the thin inscrutable mouth, always the harsh pride of taut nostrils, heavy lidded eyes."[24]

David becomes aware that there are many family secrets, including an affair his mother had in Galicia with a gentile, speculation about David's own parentage and who his father might truly be, and Albert's role in his father's death when he was gored by a bull. This secrecy about what happened in the old country is almost archetypal for immigrant families. These stories usually are vague like passing clouds and can leave children wondering exactly what happened. Roth depicts these dynamics poignantly. David's imagination turns to God. After starting Hebrew school, he becomes fascinated by the story in the Bible (Isaiah 6) when an angel holds a hot coal to Isaiah's lips to purify him of his sins. David even comes to think that sparks from the electric rail tracks are signs of God's power, like the hot coal. The rabbi tells him otherwise.

David meets an older Catholic boy named Leo who he starts to idolize: "My name's Leo Dugovka. I'm a Polish-American. You're a Jew, ain't-scha?"[25] Leo tells David that crosses are holy, and Christ is the Savior. David is captivated by this information, and Leo shows him a medal of Mary, also called a Miraculous Medal, which convinces David that this is what makes Leo unafraid. Beset by fears, David wishes he had something like that to help him. Roth's portrayal of David aptly describes his many anxieties and ever-present sense of lostness. David concludes such talismans must mean that God can be with a person instead of far away. Promising him the medal, Leo thus manipulates David to introduce him to his female cousins, a meeting that disturbingly ends with Leo raping the older cousin.

After David tells the rabbi (Reb Yidel Pankower) that he suspects his mother is really his aunt and his true mother is dead, the rabbi decides to go to David's home to confront his parents with this information. Along the way, as the rabbi sees boys and girls lolling around the stoops of tenements, he thinks, "What was going to become of Yiddish youth? What would become of this new breed? These Americans? This sidewalk-and-gutter generation? He knew them all and they were all alike—brazen, selfish, unbridled."[26] Here, the rabbi gives a nostalgic voice to the home country while noticing the obvious differences among the young and disapproving because he thinks they have lost intangibles of great value. They have seemingly forfeited their traditions. Again, Roth hits upon a common immigrant dynamic of heightened tensions between generations over values and lifestyles.

The denouement of *Call It Sleep* takes David, by then extremely distraught at his parents' mutual accusations about fidelity, infidelity, and rumors that reinforce his own lack of understanding about what is true and what is not, to the electrified trolley tracks, where he again searches for what he thinks is the spark of God. David desperately wants to know some truth about his life and believes only God will share it. Instead, he is severely shocked by the voltage in the tracks. People rush to aide him, and an ambulance takes him home. Albert, seeing his injured son, finally shows remorse, and while his mother looks after him, David drifts into a slumber—to rest, to have release: "One might as well call it sleep. He shut his eyes."[27] In this fairytale landscape of coming to America, Roth sketches for us as readers the incessant struggles that greet an immigrant child. And after a near brush with death, David can be reborn after letting go of his troubles by calling all of it sleep.

The Picador edition of *Call It Sleep* includes an essay by Hana Wirth-Nesher as an afterword.[28] She remarks that this novel shows cultural interactions that occur "linguistically, thematically, and symbolically" and that Yiddish literature is often characterized by bilingualism because within every Yiddish text there is the presence of another language.[29] Roth uses not only English, but also Yiddish, Hebrew, and Aramaic; he grew up with Yiddish before going on to study at City College in New York. Roth was three years old when his family came to New York from Galicia. Wirth-Nesher notes, "It [the book] is about an immigrant child's quest for a personal and cultural identity apart from his parents; it traces the arduous and bewildering path of assimilation."[30] The work is written in English, the language of the other, and a reader is likewise confronted with this otherness when they encounter within the text, transliterations of Yiddish, Hebrew, and Aramaic. In a way, this intermingling of languages creates an opportunity for a reader to empathize very closely with David's confusion and the various ways he feels distanced from the dominant culture and language of America.

Further, this interplay of languages is what makes *Call It Sleep* unique. The novel directly transports a reader into the topsy-turviness of being an immigrant child in the United States who has to learn English. When David starts attending Hebrew school, we see another level of his initiation into sacred texts, whereby he learns yet another language. This multilingualism is characteristic of many immigrant households, for example, when parents might speak different languages themselves and immigrate to a country where another language is used predominantly. The stimulation that David finds in learning Hebrew and reading Biblical texts arouses in him a numinous interest in Christian symbols, such as the cross, medal of Mary, and rosary. His young mind is curious about these religious differences and what they might mean about God because he believes God can reveal truth to him.

In the final section of Roth's book, David appears to transcend all these differences by his act of touching the electric "light" or coal of Isaiah; he undergoes a symbolic death, after which he awakens in a symbolic rebirth. David imagines and, to some extent, dreams while unconscious, that this electric jolt provides a unifying version of the God he knows from Isaiah and the God that Leo introduced him to. This example of transcendence represents a positive outcome for an immigrant's attempt to bridge two cultures, two traditions, two languages, and so on. Wirth-Nesher, however, believes that in this final scene, David becomes American and "is destined to live a life in translation, alienated from the culture of *his* language."[31] That interpretation indicates David has to choose and cannot comfortably have both, a position that I think would be unfortunate and impoverishing. On the contrary, I do not think that just because he has access to all the incongruent parts of himself David has to choose any one over the others. Rather, from our modern perspective, such a choice itself potentially becomes alienating when it means the disfavored parts have to stay in the unconscious. Sadly, Wirth-Nesher's idea about David's assimilation into American culture may be historically accurate for the era in which the novel takes place.

O wretched we

In this chapter, I discuss cases in which children come to the United States. They did not decide this, of course; they are following their parents. Over 18 million children in the United States, or about one in four, have at least one parent who is an immigrant.[32] In The Aeneid, many of the women, children, and elderly do not follow heroic Aeneas to Italy and instead settle in Sicily. They had grown weary and wanted to get on with living their lives without the labor of heroic endeavors. They represent a contrast to Aeneas and the others following him, who pursue a heroic ideal. Both aspects, however, moving toward an ideal and simply becoming exhausted, apply to many immigrant and refugee stories. Children do not typically have deciding votes in such matters.

Galit's family appeared to enact their intergenerational trauma through repeated moves. Her bird phobia not only brought her into treatment but also provided an opportunity for her parents to break a cycle of moving places without communicating with their children. An absence of verbal communication characterizes intergenerational trauma. Much of what transpires in this process is communicated nonverbally and thus leaves family members feeling bewildered and passive about their roles. In some sense, the women who set fire to the fleet in The Aeneid were trying to interrupt a heroic cycle in protest so a choice could become conscious.

Haydee Faimberg, a French analyst, asks about intergenerational trauma. "How can the transmission of a history which at least partially does not belong to the patient's life ... be explained?"[33] She hypothesizes that a part of the parent's psyche intrudes unconsciously into a child's mind, and there, it becomes a burden for the child to carry without their knowing why. Along with this intrusion, a parent unconsciously comes to regard their child as identified with their own unwanted history. Such parents then keep their distance emotionally to protect themselves from contact with what they have warded off, while their child is left feeling baffled and confused by their remove. Like David's father, this parent views their child negatively and fears that the child will somehow bring to light a history that the parent has rejected. The child is pressured in this projective process to be what the parent does not accept in themselves, a shadow entity that the parent avoids. A child is a suspect but has no idea what the crime was. The generations stand at odds, alienated, and misunderstood.

Mariam's family left Beirut under traumatizing conditions. Again, there occurred a barrier within her family to communicate what was happening such that she did not even know exactly where they were going. Imagine the disorientation this causes in children. Knowing a destination provides perspective and hope. Without that, a child is left to fantasize about bad things and feel uncontained with their anxieties about a place they know nothing of. Family stories contain us psychologically at least as much as common history, language, religion, and culture. By the end of her analysis, Mariam was able to tell a more conscious and coherent story about herself and she was more accepting of the rusty parts of her life. Her recollections brought the events of her earlier life into some daylight.

Language is such an important human experience because it enables a shared mode of being for the finer peculiarities of sayings, idioms, jokes, folklore, songs, and familiar turns of phrase all to find expression. Of course, there are the larger elements of language including vocabulary, sentence structure, punctuation, grammar, and syntax. But those finer elements usually include how a language voices things that can feel beyond translation. Children typically struggle in expressing what once felt known in a previous language that is no longer captured by the oddities of a new language where words don't come easily. David from *Call It Sleep* shows us fantastic dimensions of an imaginal world that immigrant children inhabit as they jostle between languages. Being bilingual is a psychological experience as much as it is a skill or talent. Ways of describing the world are reordered, words take on cryptic meanings, alphabets can seem a bit strange, and sentences can become like physical exercise. In his search for "light" and truth, David shows us a child's insistent request for answers to life's mysteries. Like Galit and Mariam, he too wants to simply know, Why am I here? Often enough, children have not been told and are only left to wonder about it.

Notes

1 Emma Lazarus's 1883 poem "The New Colossus" appears on the Statue of Liberty, Liberty Island, New York City, New York.
2 Virgil, *The Aeneid*, trans. John Dryden (Project Gutenberg E-Book #228, 2008), 291–372. Hereafter, references to Dryden's translation of The Aeneid will appear as Dryden and page number.
3 Dryden, 349.
4 UNHCR, "What Is a Refugee?" https://www.unrefugees.org/refugee-facts/what-is-a-refugee/
5 Donald W. Winnicott, *Playing and Reality* (London: Tavistock Publications, 1971).
6 Barbara K. Eisold, *Psychoanalytic Perspectives on Asylum Seekers and the Asylum-Seeking Process* (London and New York: Routledge, 2019), xiii.
7 Ibid., 54.
8 Julia Beltsiou, "Seeking Home in the Foreign: Otherness and Immigration," in *Immigration in Psychoanalysis: Locating Ourselves,* ed. Julie Beltsiou, 89–108 (London and New York: Routledge, 2016), 96.
9 Irene Cairo, "The Place across the Street: Some Thoughts on Language, Separateness, and Difference in the Psychoanalytic Setting," in *Immigration in Psychoanalysis: Locating Ourselves,* ed. Julie Beltsiou (London and New York: Routledge, 2016), 135–148.
10 Ibid., 146.
11 Sarah Hill, "Language and Intersubjectivity: Multiplicity in a Bilingual Treatment," *Psychoanalytic Dialogues* 18, no. 4 (2008): 453.
12 Dermot A. Ryan, Fiona E. Kelly, and Brendan B. Kelly, "Mental Health among Persons Awaiting an Asylum Outcome in Western Countries," *International Journal of Mental Health* 38, no. 3 (2009): 106.
13 Luis H. Zayas and Molly H. Bradlee, "Exiling Children, Creating Orphans: When Immigration Policies Hurt Citizens," *Social Work* 59, no. 2 (2014): 167–175.
14 Susan Mapp and Emily Hornung, "Irregular Immigration Status Impacts for Children in the USA." *Journal of Human Rights and Social Work* 1 (2016): 61–70. DOI: 10.1007/s41134-016-0012-1
15 Alexander Miller, Julia Meredith Hess, Deborah Bybee, and Jessica R. Goodkind, "Understanding the Mental Health Consequences of Family Separation for Refugees: Implications for Policy and Practice," *American Journal of Orthopsychiatry* 88, no. 1 (2018): 27.
16 Widian Nicola, "Living 'Illegally': On the Phenomenology of an Undocumented Immigrant," *Clinical Social Work Journal* 45 (2017): 293–300. DOI: 10.1007/s10615-017-0618-5
17 Khalifah Alfadhli and Joan Drury, "Psychosocial Support among Refugees of Conflict in Developing Countries: A Critical Literature Review," *Intervention* 14, no. 2 (2016): 128–141.
18 Nina Thorup Dalgaard and Edith Montgomery, "Disclosure and Silencing: A Systematic Review of the Literature on Patterns of Trauma Communication in Refugee Families," *Transcultural Psychiatry* 52, no. 5 (2015): 579–593.
19 K. Jacky Chan, Marta Y. Young, and Noor Sharif, "Well-Being after Trauma: A Review of Posttraumatic Growth among Refugees," *Canadian Psychology* 57, no. 4 (2016): 291–299.
20 Sue Fletcher Watson and Francesca Happé, *Autism: An Introduction to Psychological Theory* (Cambridge, MA: Harvard University Press, 1998).
21 C. G. Jung, "Individual Dream Symbolism in Relation to Alchemy," *Psychology and Alchemy*, vol. 12, *The Collected Works of C. G. Jung* (Princeton: Princeton University Press, 1968), para. 207.
22 Ibid., para. 208.

23 Henry Roth, *Call It Sleep* (New York: Farrar, Straus and Giroux, 1934).
24 Ibid., 274.
25 Ibid., 303.
26 Ibid., 374.
27 Ibid., 441.
28 Ibid., 443–462.
29 Ibid., 443.
30 Ibid., 447–448.
31 Ibid., 460, italics in original.
32 "Part of Us: A Data-Driven Look at Children of Immigrants," Urban Institute, March 14, 2019, https://www.urban.org/features/part-us-data-driven-look-children-immigrants
33 Haydee Faimberg, "The Telescoping of Generations," *Contemporary Psychoanalysis* 24, no. 1 (1988): 104.

Chapter 9

Images of Immigrant Experiences

We are such stuff
As dreams are made on; and our little life
Is rounded with a sleep.[1]

Prospero in The Tempest

Shakespeare's *The Tempest*, published in 1623, deals with the travails of Prospero, a magician from Milan stranded on an island in the Mediterranean. Virgil's The Aeneid echoes many times within this play, for example, with themes of sea journeys and shipwreck, mention of the North African queen Dido, as well as gods and goddesses manipulating various characters. There is also a motif of colonization and subjugation in the figure of Caliban, a native of the island before Prospero arrived; he is something of an earthy wild man (and, far removed from Shakespeare's time, also a modern comic book character).

Prospero enslaves Caliban, treats him cruelly, and regularly insults him, such as when saying, "thou poisonous slave, got by the devil himself," meaning a devil raped his mother and Caliban is their child.[2] Thus, Caliban, the subjugated native, represents someone who is perceived through a radical othering. In that way, he characterizes what can happen during many rude awakenings that not only the colonized but also immigrants sometimes endure. In an afterword to the Folger's edition of *The Tempest*, Barbara Mowat writes that, at a time of militarized empire-building and migration, *The Tempest* offers a perspective on the fates of "the colonizing and the colonized."[3] Images of immigrants' dreams unfortunately have the potential for being corrupted and destroyed when foreignness is colonized by a dominant culture.

The magician-slave relationship between Prospero and Caliban illustrates the tragic dynamics of immigrant experience when there is an encounter with the foreign that goes badly and turns into othering. What happens when a foreigner or newcomer is subjugated by a process of forcible assimilation without acknowledgment of who they might have been within a

DOI: 10.4324/9781003119593-9

different culture? Caliban is a complex character who knows and sees things that are quite beyond Prospero. If Prospero portrays the domineering biases of the so-called enlightened Western culture, then Caliban offers a useful dramatic foil because he has access to nature, its beauties, and the supernatural. The crude interactions between them make palpable the emotional pain of othering when the recognition of differences collapses and there is a refusal to accept what is seen as other and a devaluing of what is foreign. Caught in this loop, acting as equals becomes impossible, and questions that prompt discovery—What is their unique view of the world? How might they bridge their differences?—go unanswered.

Coming to a receiving country as foreigners, immigrants usually face similar questions around acculturative stresses and resettlement problems. No one would wish to go through what Prospero does to Caliban—subjugation, othering, and cruelty. Up to now, I have provided chiefly data and examples about immigration from academic sources and literature and vignettes from clinical cases. Here, I review the results from a questionnaire that I distributed to self-identified immigrants.[4] Part of my focus was to capture aspects of the imaginal and symbolic. For example, which images retain valence for immigrants when they resettle and make a new life elsewhere? And what are some of the challenges they have in adjusting to a new country?

Figure 9.1 A crowd of European immigrants and their luggage on The Imperator, then the world's largest ocean liner, arriving in New York Harbor on June 19, 1913, with over 4,000 passengers, June 1913 (Shutterstock.com, Everett Collection).

Questionnaire

This questionnaire is designed to gather descriptive information about images and impressions that are associated with immigrating to a new country. Other questionnaires I have helped to design have been used for evaluating social growth in children with autism spectrum disorders (ASDs).[5] The purpose of this survey is to obtain information about the lasting images associated with immigration as well as feeling responses to that experience. A survey like this provides a snapshot of a topic and is not intended to establish correlations between variables.[6] This survey uses open-ended questions to elicit subjective written impressions from the respondents.

The survey does not allow for statistical analyses other than calculated means, modal trends, and frequency percentages. The method of gathering respondents was primarily through social media and different affinity organizations like colleges and career-based groups. Thus, this study has neither a random sample nor an experimental comparison group. The survey was not constructed for use with an experimental design, which is a limitation. Participants signed a consent form, explaining the purpose of the study, to permit the inclusion of their responses in both this study and this book.

Sample

The sample included thirty-seven respondents with a ratio of fourteen males to twenty-three females. The mean age at immigration was 22.2 years; the mean age currently was 52.4 years, meaning that most of their lives have been lived in the receiving country and outside their home countries. Nine immigrated to the United States from North, Central, and South America; fifteen came from Europe; three from the Middle East; ten came from Asia, Australia, and New Zealand. Thirty-four immigrated to the United States; one to Canada; two to Denmark. These immigrants often went back to visit their home countries. Sixteen went at least yearly; eleven went every two to four years. Five planned on moving back to their home countries. Thirteen immigrated for work; twelve immigrated for family; three for education; six for political reasons; three for adventure.

Images

Among these respondents, there were three main areas of imagery regarding what came to mind about their new country. These are summarized in Table 9.1. Frequency percentages do not add to 100 because many respondents listed more than one image as enduring and meaningful.

"Features of the landscape" included buildings like skyscrapers and houses, street scenes, bridges, local geography, paths, space, emptiness, and dimensions of size such as bigness. Emptiness occurred as a representation of

Table 9.1 Imagery associated with new or receiving country

Type of Image	Number	Percent
Features of landscape	26	70
Transport	11	30
Economic life	10	27
Cultural symbols	6	16
People	4	11
Safety threats	3	8
Miscellaneous	5	14

disconnect and isolation. "Transport" referred to highways, roads, buses, cars, and other vehicles. "Economic life" included observations about poverty, wealth, and inequality. "Cultural symbols" referred to flags, money, statues, and other signifiers of "Americanness." The category of "People" included social characteristics such as being friendly, unfriendly, accepting, and avoidant. "Safety threats" were primarily images of guns. The "Miscellaneous" category included images about food, protest, and color tones of the environment. There were sixty-five images in total reported for the new country.

Table 9.2 shows the main visual categories for the responses about images of the home or original country. As expected, there were some differences as to how these clustered when compared with images about the new or receiving country. Interestingly, there were fewer images reported overall (38) about the home or original country. These are grouped mostly into the categories of "Features of the landscape" and pictures of "People." Again, the percentages do not sum to 100 because of multiple responses.

"Features of the landscape" included towns, cities, specific buildings, nature, and geography. There was less emphasis on dimensions of size in these than with the images of the landscape for the new or receiving country. The category of "People," however, referred more specifically to respondents' families and ancestors, and this distinguished these images from the people

Table 9.2 Imagery associated with home or original country

Type of Image	Number	Percent
Features of landscape	17	46
People	11	30
Religious symbols	2	5
Transport	2	5
Economic life	2	5
Miscellaneous	4	11

images about the new or receiving country, which were more generic. "Religious symbols" were churches in this sample. "Transport" meant public transport and not highways, individual cars, or trucks. "Economic life" referred to poverty and hardship, not wealth. The "Miscellaneous" category included food, sports, chaos, and color tones of the environment.

Acculturative impressions and challenges

Question nine of the survey queried respondents about challenges that they would describe as aspects of acculturation that were not smooth or easy. Responses to this were often vivid, clear, and specific. Table 9.3 describes the main groupings. Interestingly, many responses mentioned opportunity as a challenge, perhaps because it seemed like a test about succeeding in an entirely new setting. However, opportunity was further described affirmatively by many respondents. Responses do not sum to 100 percent.

"Opportunity" appeared as a theme in various responses, such as "It was up to me to take advantage of the choices I had" and "The education I got made me prove myself and work hard" and "It was an opportunity to explore and re-invent myself." Respondents seemed aware of having opportunity and feeling responsibility for using it to achieve. Occasionally, freedom was mentioned as an opportunity and a responsibility. "Alienation" and "polarization" were described by statements about racism, feeling alone, or like an outsider, not truly fitting in. One respondent remarked, "The image is a person on an island." "Othering" included observations about being excluded and treated differently for no obvious reason but being an immigrant. "Confusion" was mentioned as associated with experiences of othering. "Language" here meant statements about difficulties in learning and using English. "Shallowness of Americans" included comments about apparent friendliness that did not develop into anything deeper. "Lack of a social safety net" referred to the sparse social supports available within most of the United States. The challenges described in this sample also differ from other significant hurdles that many immigrants face if their legal status is uncertain and revocable. This sample appears more highly educated and

Table 9.3 Acculturative challenges

Type of Challenge	Number	Percent
Opportunity	15	41
Alienation and polarization	14	38
Othering and confusion	7	19
Language	6	16
Shallowness of Americans	5	14
Lack of social safety net	4	11

thus not representative of immigrants as a whole coming to the United States. A revision to the survey should include an item about number of years of education to clarify this possible slant among the respondents. Further, the survey reported on here does not ask about race, religion, or ethnicity, and it thus omits to gather important demographic data that would potentially help to understand when respondents encounter biases and have experiences of racism.

Discussion

I do not intend to suggest that there is a single kind of archetype for migration or immigration. Rather, immigration is such a momentous experience that the psyche will naturally react to it by activating different archetypal tendencies, which can express themselves in countless ways. Some of those can be quite polarized too. Looking at The Aeneid has illustrated, I believe, many archetypal characteristics that emerge from relocating after a great journey. Elsewhere, I describe some of the theoretical variations that Jung attributed to how he viewed archetypes, shifting over time from seeing them as primordial images to their being instinctual impulses that shape observable patterns of behavior, including what we find in myths, dreams, and art.[7] Importantly, for Jung, an archetype is something like a piece of nature.

> It is a great mistake in practice to treat an archetype as if it were a mere name, word, or concept. It is far more than that: it is a piece of life, an image connected with the living individual by the bridge of emotion… the archetype is living matter.[8]

This lived experience of an archetype is what informs how I examined the imagery that the immigrants in this study reported. Note that emotion has a central and natural role in giving an archetype meaning and valence within the psyche. For Jung, archetypes are part of the structure of the psyche, and they reach deeply not only into the unconscious but also into our emotional lives.[9]

The images of the new and receiving country appear centered on perceptions about the landscape for its excitement and size—towering skyscrapers, big bridges, and vast distances between places. To some, it seemed too large, perhaps intimidating, reminding the immigrant of the huge task of starting anew and coming to terms with the risks of relocation. For example, one respondent remarked, "I had never seen such a big bridge before"; another commented, "Everything is so much bigger in the US"; yet another added, "Everything is supersized here"; and someone noted, "This country is vast." There were images about the large size of portions in restaurants, the hugeness of "big box stores" like Walmart and Costco, the enormous geographic distances between places, the towering redwoods, and the overwhelm of too many choices. Symbolically, gigantic sizes often bring to mind the great effort required to master a task or endeavor. In addition, they can remind us of being a child—smaller in stature and with much less power—who has much to learn before growing up. It is as if the emphasis on these large physical dimensions communicates just how much immigrants have to absorb—a great task—to orient themselves to a new life in the United States.

The idea of not belonging occurred many times in reference to emptiness. Will an immigrant find connection, or will they get lost in a desolate space? For example, "There is a strong sensation of emptiness," and another respondent added, "The constant consumerism [encourages] constant work to earn more for an empty goal... a feeling of emptiness." Such feelings express disappointment with American society. Comments respondents made about images of city streets suggest ambiguity because there is life flowing somewhere, but there is also a potential for dead ends and being caught nowhere.[10] This duality about moving in a direction and then possibly getting lost represents one of the great tasks of immigrating. It is also a recurring motif in The Aeneid, as Aeneas and his followers endure years of detours before reaching their chosen destination. An immigrant might just wonder over an extended period of time if the journey has been worth it.

Landscape images also might portray an immigrant's desire to blend with a new environment in seeking continuity rather than rupture. The spaciousness some remark on could be inviting in this regard by offering "a sense of openness." Mistakes would not be so terrible because there is plenty of room to try again. Space can positively imply experimentation without rigid boundaries and confinement of the past. It can mean freedom. One respondent described the positive feelings of being "in an environment free of political turmoil and unrest." Fleeing from danger in another country or part of the world has long been a factor in why immigrants chose to move to the United States.

Similarly, roads and highways appeared in many images as passageways between here and there, past and future. They represent movement, change, and transition. These roads symbolize a bit of searching for a path, perhaps like a hero's path, to be able to actualize an immigrant's dream or desire.[11] They indicate a persistent meaning about the effects of moving, relocating, and coping with new directions, sometimes with no map at all. One person explained, "Every time I move, I must redefine who I see myself to be." Someone else neatly portrayed a fairytale aspect of relocating when describing an actual memory: "[I am] walking down a path in the snow. Birds are chirping. A stranger, a girl, introduces herself and walks with me to school." The unfamiliar is blended with friendliness that eases the tension surrounding newness and possibly makes a path less cold, less foreboding. Many fairytales and myths include such friendly guardians and helpers who shepherd a person along uncertain routes.

Of course, there are important images that illustrate the potential for danger in the new environment. The survey responses that mentioned guns, homelessness, and poverty made visible a kind of jarring reality that an immigrant might not have anticipated. "There are too many guns everywhere and too much racial violence." These images express uncertainty about whether an immigrant will eventually feel safe in the new place. They also emphasize a sobering reality of losing an idealized situation that would be free from such dangers. "I don't understand how a country of open and friendly people feel comfortable with shooting each other." These impressions and perceptions can be difficult experiences to process because they often create doubts and worry about survival. One respondent noted, "There is abundance of everything, yet there is such poverty and homelessness." These are unavoidable pictures of contemporary life in the United States, where too many tragedies stem from gaping inequality, widespread gun violence, and terrible poverty.

Respondents' images of their home or original country coalesced in two main ways. First, the familiarity of those landscapes often portrayed a place where an immigrant feels, or felt, at home. The natural geography and images of towns, cities, and their buildings can evoke the feeling of a cultural wrapping that holds a person in place, language, customs, and history—like a treasured blanket. Often, vibrant colors were part of these depictions, more so than was reported for images of the receiving country. I will discuss this idea of a cultural wrapping, derived from French psychoanalyst Didier Anzieu's work, in more detail in the last chapter.[12] These pictures of places and locations may be cherished parts of the home country that motivate an immigrant to visit often and even to consider a return. Such feelings can be powerful because they are often associated with belonging to a group, in a uniquely physical way, and with knowing a place in fine detail, which are things that an immigrant gives up, minimally for a time and quite possibly for longer, when they migrate elsewhere.

Second, the images of familiar people signify the basic details about a person's development within their families and communities. One respondent wrote, "I see my parents' crying faces at the airport when I flew back [to the US] for the first time." Another also mentioned an image of saying goodbye to their father at the airport. Ancestors are a part of this psychological experience of historical continuity reaching into a past that an immigrant knows from stories passed on usually at young ages. If landscapes represent a dimension of cultural wrapping, then these images of closely known people form a familial wrapping. Taken together, they constitute outlines belonging to a personal narrative that is usually quite different from the one an immigrant has in their new country. Within the context of a home country, these images typically would not require any translation, by which I mean multiple kinds of translation: culturally, socially, historically as well as linguistically. Whereas respondents' images associated with the new country show elements of journey, facing a gigantic task, and managing unforeseen dangers, those of the country of origin seem to indicate deeply felt continuity and self-knowledge. In considering these images of old and new, there is a definite contrast that emerges between known and unknown, certainty and risk.

The acculturative challenges that respondents described were notable for showing a range of experiences between taking advantage of possible choices and having awareness of various obstacles that could thwart this. A feeling response that was frequently noted was confusion, which could indicate disjuncture between expectations and reality. Understandably, such gaps in experience, when multiplied, would create a degree of alienation. For example, it could appear that having a choice implies a person can move toward a thing they want—unless other social factors, such as othering, racism, and biases, intervene to prevent that. Observing recent racially motivated attacks in the United States, one person remarked, "My 'belonging' is threatened and I have become conscious of the ugly side of what I thought I was gaining." Several noted that they have had experiences of being looked down on because of their accents. One explained, "I feel like I am seen differently because of my appearance and accent." Another concurred, "I have felt invisible or misrecognized in terms of a social identity. The expectation that immigrants need to assimilate feels like being asked to have a 'false' self." This process is not just one about ideals that are dashed; it also describes what happens when subtle and implicit biases are at work in discriminating against immigrants. Then opportunities can instead seem like false promises that dupe the unsuspecting. Confusion makes sense as an emotional response when an apparent opportunity turns out to be a trick.

A particular level of acculturative challenge also shows up in the social realm with respondents' observations about the social norms of Americans. Friendliness typically can be quite misleading in the United States. It is not always, and perhaps rarely, an invitation for follow-up or deeper connection, even when people appear to have struck a chord with one another. Although it is beyond my scope to address this outward social falseness within American culture, many immigrants are rightfully confused by it until they learn that a hopeful indication of friendship will often not pan out, despite what might have been said. Immigrants to the United States frequently must learn as much about the alienating ways of American society as about the appealing ones. One person noted, "I was surprised that many Americans asked me whether my family would like to come to live here, and they were surprised when I told them no." Many lament the racism in the United States as well as the antagonistic political environment. "The hardest aspect of living in this country is the political climate." On the other hand, many respondents commented on the support and kindness they found in people when they came to the United States. And several remarked about the diversity that they found: "The USA is definitely a multicultural country," and "I've met people from all over the world which has allowed me cultural richness and has taught me tolerance." Part of an American social archetype is the contradictory mix of welcome and hesitancy.

There were many reflections among the survey responses about the difficulties of immigration. "Immigration is not easy to cope with. You leave behind all your life history… and open a new page. It's like going to kindergarten and learning from scratch." Another respondent said the image they have of migration is limbo: "You don't feel like you fully adapted in either place [country of origin or receiving country]. You feel you do not belong either there or here." These images—kindergarten and limbo— represent an emotionally trying experience of immigration that is fraught and hard to bridge. Kindergarten truly turns back the clock on life experience by becoming a young child again, whereas limbo suspends a person from feeling at home, settled, on solid ground. Both depict a state of powerlessness and perhaps an accompanying longing for acceptance that many immigrants feel upon resettling. I wish that citizens of the United States could be more openly grateful that so many are willing to undertake immigration as they attempt to build new lives here.

In the spring of 2021, the Cato Institute published the results of their immigration survey that included 2,600 adults in the United States.[13] Many of their findings show that the United States is a cautiously welcoming country for immigrants, although accurate knowledge among Americans about immigration appears woefully lacking. The percentage of Americans wanting to increase immigration has risen from 7 percent in 1975 to 29 percent now, with roughly the same percentage wanting to keep it at the current level (37 percent in 1975 and 38 percent now). However, 46 percent of Americans prefer a low level of immigration of less than 100,000/year, whereas the current level is actually about one million/year. Americans overestimate the share of the population who are immigrants, believing 40 percent are, when only 14 percent are. Further, xenophobia is not negligible as 13 percent of Americans view immigrants as either intruders or invaders. This picture is complex, just like the US immigration system. It shows cognitive biases and misinformed opinions that dictate how Americans feel about immigration and how they express their views politically. Another finding of the Cato Institute survey is that equal proportions of Americans (42 percent) believe that immigration is good or that it is equally good and bad.

This survey is rich in details about the social divide surrounding this topic. Many fears that Americans have about immigration center on prospective losses, such as loss of government services that could become overburdened, loss of status and privilege for whites, and loss of social cohesion, although the latter may be due to something of a retrograde belief shaped by reactionary fantasies about the supposed past. Fifty-nine percent of Americans want the United States to be a country with essential American values that immigrants are expected to adopt. These include loyalty, self-reliance, and English fluency, none of which is completely unreasonable—many other countries demand similar or more from immigrants. However, beneath these numbers lurks a requirement that immigrants assimilate, and the meaning of assimilation often is tantamount to giving up aspects of an immigrant's heritage culture. This assimilationist viewpoint is usually at odds with a tolerant and openly multicultural society, especially when aspirations for loyalty, self-reliance, and fluency become rigid demands in order to be accepted by the native populace. The Cato Institute survey makes note of the shadow side of a social and legal emphasis on assimilation, namely, othering. Among first-generation immigrants, 67 percent endorse a statement that "people like me are not seen as being American enough." Apparently, Americans' willingness to welcome immigrants is tentative and rather conditional.

Closing notes

The immigration survey I conducted has sketched some of the archetypal trends that appear within the imagery of a sample of immigrants. I have noted many of the study's limitations, including those of the survey's design itself. Another methodological drawback is that I alone coded the survey responses into categories and did not use independent coders for this, so I am asking a reader to trust in my ability to be somewhat objective. I hope that I have been reasonably faithful to this task.

To close, I suggest that archetypal elements related to immigration experiences are discernible within this sample. These include

- Relocating as a task that seems psychologically out of proportion or gigantic
- Looking for a foothold in a foreign environment that is both appealing and intimidating
- Entertaining great uncertainty about how a journey will eventually unfold
- Wishing to avail oneself of choices not previously available or imaginable
- Resolving feelings of belonging and not belonging
- Mourning the loss of various things from one's home country that provided familiarity and continuity

These lived experiences and memories find emotional expression in the many vibrant images that respondents reported on the survey. I am grateful for their participation and acknowledge their generous contributions to my research.

Appendix: Immigration study questionnaire

1 In what country were you born?_____

2 In what country do you live now?_____

3 How old are you now?_____ What is your gender?_____

4 How old were you when you immigrated?_____

5 Briefly, in one or two sentences, why did you immigrate?

   _____

6 What is an early and notable memory *with images* you have of your new
   country? *An image* refers to a visible picture, art, visual memory, part of
   a dream, something seen, or a vision.

   _____

7 What is *a lasting image* you have about your new country, something
   that really has stayed with you?

   _____

8 Do you plan on moving back to your home country?_____Briefly,
   why or why not?

   _____

9 What would you say has been the most challenging thing to adjust to in
   your new country and in a few words, what would be *an image* you have of
   that?

   _____

10 What is *a lasting image* that you have about your home country,
   something that has really stayed with you?

   _____

11 As you think about your experience as an immigrant, in a couple of
   sentences, what has been the biggest meaning for you to relocate and
   settle into a new country?

   _____

12 How often do you visit your country of origin? Please check which best
   applies for you.

Never	Less than every four years	Between every two to four years	About every two years	About every year	More than once a year

Thank you for your responses. Would you like to add anything?

Notes

1 William Shakespeare, *The Tempest/The Works of William Shakespeare [Cambridge Edition]* (Project Gutenberg E-Book #23042, 2007), Act IV, scene 1, p. 111. These lines are spoken by Prospero.
2 Ibid., Act I, scene 2, p. 37.
3 Barbara A. Mowat, "The Tempest: A Modern Perspective," in *The Tempest* by William Shakespeare, eds. Barbara A. Mowat and Paul Werstine (New York: Simon & Shuster, 1994), 185–199, 195.
4 Questionnaire included in the Appendix.
5 Robert Tyminski, Tyminski Social Skills Checklist, Washington, DC, Library of Congress, 2007; Robert F. Tyminski and Philip J. Moore, "The Impact of Group Psychotherapy on Social Development in Children with Pervasive Developmental Disorders," *International Journal of Group Psychotherapy* 58, no. 3 (2008): 363–379.
6 Charles Stangor and Jennifer Walinga, Chapter 3, in *Introduction to Psychology* (University of British Columbia, 2014). Accessed via open publishing online, www.opentextbc.ca
7 Robert Tyminski, *The Psychology of Theft and Loss: Stolen and Fleeced* (London and New York: Routledge, 2014), 37.
8 C. G. Jung, "Symbols and the Interpretation of Dreams" (1961), *The Collected Works of C. G. Jung*, vol. 18, *The Symbolic Life* (Princeton, NJ: Princeton University Press, 1976), para. 589. Hereafter, references to Jung's *Collected Works* will appear as Jung, title, date, and volume number in the *Collected Works* (CW).
9 C. G. Jung, "The Psychology of the Child Archetype" (1963), CW 9i, 160.
10 Ami Ronnberg and Kathlen Martin, eds., *The Book of Symbols: Reflections on Archetypal Images* (Köln, Germany: Taschen, 2010), 630.
11 Ibid., 454.
12 Didier Anzieu, *The Skin-Ego,* trans. Naomi Segal (London: Karnac, 2016).
13 Emily Ekins and David Kemp, "E Pluribus Unum: Findings from the Cato Institute 2021 Immigration and National Identity Survey," accessed April 28, 2021, https://www.cato.org/survey-reports/e-pluribus-unum-findings-cato-institute-2021-immigration-identity-national-survey. References are to the online version of this report. Readers are encouraged to view this survey, which contains a wealth of valuable data about contemporary American attitudes toward immigrants.

Chapter 10

Two Roads

Do the gods inspire this urge, or make we gods of our desire?

Nisus, Book IX, The Aeneid

Often, immigration is an attempt to relocate, but sometimes a permanent resettlement process is interrupted by events that preclude staying in the receiving country. Financial strains, legal barriers, family ties, and cultural divides that become too large to bridge, among many other causes, lead to emigration. This chapter explores what happens when an immigrant comes to the United States and subsequently emigrates elsewhere. *Emigration* is the reverse of *immigration*; it is thought that there are between 3 to 9 million US citizens who live abroad, although this number does not include non-citizens who leave the United States.[1] Many of them have various motives for wanting to live elsewhere. Some retire abroad looking for a lower cost of living; some move because of their political convictions; some seek thrills and adventure. They aren't compelled to leave; they choose to do so. A problem with this number range (3–9 million) is that it does not capture the flow of foreign-born residents who leave the United States. Gathering data on this is difficult because there are no international agencies dedicated to tracking it. One report from the Congressional Budget Office (CBO), using data on reported earnings, estimates that there is an annual emigration rate of about 1.3 percent of foreign-born workers from the United States.[2] Importantly, this approximation does not include undocumented immigrants who emigrate because frequently they are not steadily employed and thus wouldn't show up in the data. Further, these immigrants' wages are underreported, or not reported at all. Additionally, various actions taken during the Trump administration resulted in more voluntary departures for foreign-born residents who were awaiting legal proceedings to determine their status. In 2018, voluntary departures reached a seven-year high of almost 30,000.[3] Voluntary departure offers emigrants a chance to obtain another visa to re-enter the United States, whereas deportation means a mandatory wait of many years before being able to re-apply.

DOI: 10.4324/9781003119593-10

For immigrants, relocating back to their home country is undoubtedly very stressful, emotionally and financially draining, and even traumatic when they must return to a place of significant social unrest and violence. It is as if they become twice displaced, at least. Monica Luci, a Jungian analyst in Rome, writes about displacement among refugees, accentuating the loss of home along with a change of place. As a consequence, refugees experience a separation from those internal parts of the psyche represented by home and place.[4] Emigration implies going through this disruptive psychological task yet again, by uprooting and journeying to another place altogether. In many cases, this might mean returning to a home country. But when that is not possible, it might necessitate relocating to a second and different receiving country. This cycle of displacement makes "home" difficult to embrace, and it usually disrupts the psychic equilibrium. Amanda Dowd, a Jungian analyst in Australia, describes displacement trauma as a kind of psychological alienation that can create ruptures at two levels, the individual and the cultural.[5] Displacement has the potential to interrupt a sense of continuity within the psyche and threatens a sense of inner containment, which we hopefully have within ourselves when we feel stable in our environment. Depending on how long a refugee or immigrant has resided in their initial receiving country, subsequent relocation can bring powerful emotions of anxiety, despair, and confusion. It is like having to scrap an entire project that someone has worked on for years, with no certain outcome for a new attempt, and with high stakes for a person mental health.

The resilience of immigrants is a recurring theme that I believe is very important to bear in mind. Even when immigrants or refugees must emigrate from the country where they first resettled, they do not leave as blank slates. They have grown and developed during their time in the country where they have resided in the interim, and these changes can empower them moving forward. Posttraumatic growth implies significant internal changes that positively transform who a person is; it is not just a reflection of hardiness or optimism.[6] Such transformation enables individuals to construct ongoing narratives about who they are and to apply what they have learned to ever-evolving life circumstances. The cases in this chapter will, I hope, demonstrate that psychological growth can occur in face of a relocation, which often enough involves exchanging one dream, home, and place for another.

Case example—On top of the mountain

Adam was a British man in his late thirties who worked in the tech industry. He had been born in Scotland, but his family had lived all over the world while he was growing up because his father had worked for a large multinational corporation, and his numerous foreign postings meant they moved a lot. Adam was the youngest of four children, and during adolescence, he attended boarding school in England. He was married to a British woman. Adam phoned me because he was worried he was having "a nervous breakdown." He indicated that he and his wife were thinking about their future because they wanted children and were considering moving back to London where they had met ten years ago.

In our initial meeting, Adam told me he was worried about impressing me. He said at the next session that he was sure he had not. He described himself as "stiff, like most English men." I noticed that he engaged in a lot of self-criticisms that were deflating his ego. His fear of breaking down stemmed from memories of an earlier breakdown in adolescence when he had been hospitalized for depression. After telling me he worried he was "needy", he spoke about performance issues he had with sex:

Adam: I get anxious and then the gig's up, with sex I mean. My wife puts up with it because she has her own hang-ups. I suspect she's relieved when we actually don't have sex.

RT: Can you tell me more about feeling anxious?

Adam: I think it's my go-to feeling. I've always been anxious, even as a child. I was shy. I was socially awkward and not very comfortable meeting new people. I wish I weren't such a dip. I mean, I'm not a loser, I know that, but I need to be more confident.

RT: You have some strong judgments about yourself.

Adam: You might say that. I don't think I'm harsh.

RT: Hmm… "Shy, awkward, stiff, a dip."

Adam: Oh, I see. Well, better beat myself to it before anyone else! [Laughs]

RT: You think your self-criticism can be funny?

Adam: Not exactly. I use humor to deflect. Jokes are my way to cope. You didn't laugh though. I find jokes and satire help to get something out.

RT: I wonder if you're sometimes angry when you joke.

Adam: My wife sure thinks so.

In this session, I noticed Adam wanted to impress me by being witty and charming. I thought he was frustrated by my relative lack of emotional response to what he was saying. I even felt he was angry with me, although I didn't know why, but it seemed early to broach that because we were just getting started. It was clear he was angry about many things. His rush to express various negative judgments struck me as somewhat counterphobic and he did not settle into thinking much about his anxiety with me. I wondered if he might have felt I was somehow like his wife, along the lines of imagining I might be relieved we were not connecting more deeply. He described a series of interactions at work that were similarly themed; he wanted more from a person, did not get it, felt anxious, and then tried to laugh about the situation. I felt Adam's humor was edgy and that to others it might come across as aggressive and punchy.

A few sessions later, a source for his recent fear of breakdown became apparent. He had been up for a promotion and was afraid of both not getting it and getting it. He was not sure he could handle the extra responsibilities, but he dreaded losing out to someone else as a sign of weakness. He was promoted and soon afterward became sad and irritable. I noted that perhaps he was feeling depressed because the promotion was not a solution to a psychological issue, one that he was not sure he wanted to deal with. He liked this idea because he felt I was "seeing behind my mask."

RT: You want something hidden to be noticed and seen.

Adam: My parents were terrible that way. They did not like it whenever they saw I was sad. I think that's one reason they sent me to boarding school, so they wouldn't have me around them. Both of them said I was a burden when I looked sad. How British is that?

RT: That memory comes to mind now for some reason. Any ideas?

Adam: I'm not sure. It strikes me as unbelievably tragic that the content of your character is all behind you. Isn't that what most psychotherapists believe? [He sounds a bit angry.]

RT: You sound upset about that.

Adam: [More aggressive] Just answer me!

RT: Now you are angry with me.

Adam: Well, it didn't take much to figure that out, did it!

RT: It seems you're angry because I was curious about your sadness. You recalled your parents not wanting to see that in you. I'm wondering whether you might almost sound like them now because I'm being something of a burden for wanting to hear more about why you were sad.

Adam: [Calmer] I see. The intensity of my judgments, which you're describing, does resonate with how I feel them.

RT: There was something else too, that you felt I was avoiding you and you showed your anger with sarcasm.

Adam: [Uncomfortable, seems to be sweating] Oh. [Silence] My father was quite distant. He was always preoccupied with his work, never available for us children, and sometimes it looked like he was frantically passing through life chasing a departing train.

RT: And you're concerned now I'd be like him.

Adam: Yes. I was angry with you because I wanted a direct answer from you [about what psychotherapists believe]. My father didn't even bother to pretend to answer my questions. He'd look at me, roll his eyes, and walk away.

RT: I'm sitting right here with you.

Adam: I get that. I guess I want an outline from you. What's the program? How will I know if I'm making progress? Do you give grades?

RT: You're worried I'll hold back too much on you.

Adam: Right! [Quiet] I was thinking that you think I'm fragile.
RT: [Here, I decided not to say anything and see what happened.]
Adam: I saw you work with children. I bet a lot of them throw tantrums and are impossible with their parents. It's admirable you do that kind of work. It can't be easy.
RT: Maybe you're wondering how much of you I could handle.
Adam: [He notices the time is almost up.] Yes, and I'm waiting for that moment when you tell me I'm gay.

There wasn't any time left in the session to go into Adam's comment about his idea of my telling him he was gay. Thinking about the meanings of what he had said, I wondered how intensely Adam might have longed for a father who saw him, who did not walk away from him, and who could deal with feelings; a father who did not avoid possibilities for loving male-to-male contact. This kind of father would have been different from the one who scolded him for not measuring up to certain standards. Adam told me he had a very difficult father. His father now lived in England, and I became curious about which part of Adam's immigration story had to do with separation from his father. In the following session, I found a way to mention that Adam had ended the prior session with an interesting comment about my view of his sexuality.

Adam: I wanted to work with a bloke in therapy, and I was glad when S [friend who was a therapist] suggested you.
RT: What else comes to mind now?
Adam: I like that you're a man who's comfortable with feelings. It's so unusual in my experience. Plus, you seem to have really gotten how tied up in knots I get around performance issues.

Adam went on a brief trip to England around this time, about six months into his work with me, and he briefly saw his parents. He was disappointed when his father left the dinner table to go to bed early. He was upset at another dinner when his British friends called him "posh." As he recounted these events, he spoke in a sharp tone and scowled.

RT: I think you're angry right now.
Adam: I just wish you'd do something besides ask me questions. It just seems so… [Trails off]
RT: What's the word that comes next?
Adam: Smug.
RT: [Silent]
Adam: I don't know. That's just what I thought at that moment. You don't really seem all that smug when I think about it.

RT: We've been talking about our relationship, and you had recently joked about my telling you at some point you're gay. I wonder if after having just seen your father and experiencing his remoteness, whether being here now is making you anxious about how we interact. Maybe you wonder whether I'm gay or not.

Adam: You could be either in my mind. You don't seem like a typical gay person for San Francisco, if you know what I'm saying. I mean, you're not flamboyant or dramatic. I don't think it would exactly matter to me, but when I think of you as straight, I feel a bit more nervous how you view me.

RT: Meaning?

Adam: It's almost cultural. Men in Britain—I'm talking about straight blokes—don't talk about sex except to make dirty innuendoes and boast about their conquests. They're mostly reluctant conversationalists unless it's some totally heady topic, maybe history facts, football, or hobbies like gardening and bird watching.

RT: You're aware of our having different cultural backgrounds.

Adam: Yes. I imagine I'd like more encouragement from you because there are so many subjects I'd prefer to avoid.

RT: That's one way to tell you're in therapy.

Adam: [Laughs] That's quite funny.

Adam was increasingly conscious of cultural differences at his workplace and in sessions with me. I thought that his calling me smug was a projection of a restrained and cerebral father who was less involved with his children, less fun. This projection seemed a mix of his experience of his father's emotional distance and his own feeling of discomfort at how his friends recently saw him (posh). Although not yet clear, our cultural differences accentuated his complicated feelings about his father and about his self-image as a new-comer/immigrant to the Bay Area. Implicit in much of what Adam had to say to me was a curiosity, almost an ache, coupled with a persistent fear about what kind of man I was and what kind of father I would have been.

RT: I wonder what sort of ideas you have about me as a man, especially compared to the men you knew in England?

Adam: You're quite different from them. I think you may be from the East Coast, maybe the area around New York but not from the City. Your accent is hard to place. At first, I thought you were Midwestern, and that turned me right off because the Midwest of the US is like the uninteresting bits of a suit. I also think of New Yorkers as being rather direct, and even though I sometimes whinge about it, you are pretty direct with me. British men are usually direct only when being critical, arguing, and commenting on football. [He sees me looking puzzled.] Do you know that word *whinge*?

RT: No.

Adam: Brits say it for complaining and whining. I've never heard it here.

RT: You found another difference between us—how we use language even though it's mostly the same.

Adam: I can tell you're educated; I think well educated. You don't speak with the sloppy sentences most Americans have when they're talking, like their thoughts are struggling to break free of the brambles.

After about eight months of psychotherapy, Adam began acting more assertively at work and in his marriage. For example, in a discussion with his wife about their finances, he stood up for the cost of his psychotherapy when she suggested he cut it back. And at work, he showed greater skill at handling conflicts between employees. As I thought about his recent sharing of his impressions of me, I noted that he was speaking up more directly and finding it helpful. He agreed but worried that he could not sustain this change, that he was "doomed to fail." I asked him why he thought so, and Adam recalled that his mother frequently berated his father. She also put down his interests as boring, and she bought all his clothes because she believed he had no taste. As he talked about this, Adam recognized that his harshly critical voice was identified with hers, and this unsettled him.

RT: What would you say now about your father?

Adam: He was a materialist but in the philosophical way. He was a scientist who thought only facts mattered to how someone saw the world and spoke about it. My wife constantly worries that I'll turn into him. She doesn't care for his dryness and says he is like a desert nomad who doesn't know how to interact with normal people. [Pause]

RT: What else would you say about him?

Adam: [A little shaken] He was lonely, is lonely. He has no friends. He had one, but that fellow died a few years ago. One friend who's gone. How sad is that?

I thought Adam was weaving between his parents and how he held them internally in a new way, seeing his critical voice as similar to his mother's and fearing how much like his father he might be. Coming on the heels of our discussion about his perceptions of me, it seemed that Adam was actively contrasting me and his father and that the differences he saw in me spoke to a dawning awareness of his hunger for more of a father. For example, his recent assertiveness seemed to show he was taking in our work and starting to change as a result. This felt promising.

Around a year into his therapy, Adam said that his wife was often bringing up her desire to go back to the United Kingdom. Speaking of her isolation, she told Adam she felt Americans were difficult to form friendships with and she missed her family in England. He was continuing to do well at his job, and he resisted her pleas that he consider going back. He attempted to rationalize their situation by offering her practical suggestions and explanations for how Americans interacted. As he told me about these conversations, I wondered how much he sounded like his facts-oriented father, and I mentioned this to him. He agreed and noted that he was also proud of his career successes, which he thought surpassed those of his father's. As we talked, he had a sudden memory of himself and his father.

Adam: I was a clumsy kid, not very confident. When I was around ten, I was carrying a bowl of creamed potatoes from the kitchen to the dining room table. I dropped it, and the potatoes and sauce went everywhere. My father scolded me for being spasmatic.

RT: Did you know what he meant by that?

Adam: Not really. I knew it was bad. [Pause] I cleaned it up. I think my mother helped me. Then I went into the kitchen to get another bowl to bring to the table. The same thing happened again! I dropped it. He just started shouting. I cried, and he yelled, "Stop crying because it upsets your mother!" I didn't know what to do. I put a towel over my head and cried.

RT: You wanted a very different response from him than you got.

Adam: [Crying] Yes. I just wanted some... attention, just some blasted attention, not being scolded and humiliated.

RT: I think you mean loving attention. You wanted that.

Adam: Yeah, I did.

Following this session, Adam spoke more about getting what he wanted from others. He related this theme of pursuing a desire to his marriage, his work, his successes, and to where he wanted to live. Our sessions too began to reflect his desire for having more because they started running over. I tried to end them on time and realized we were enacting something about fatherly love and attention. Adam was clever at distracting me right near the end, and we would often run over by several minutes as he tried to finish his train of thought. I eventually mentioned that I could tell he wanted more from me, and I offered him additional sessions, which he took. The enactment of our running overtime subsided, and Adam started to discuss his alienation from his father. He repeated one statement frequently: "He was not ever there even when he was."

Around this time, as Adam recalled episodes related to his estrangement from his father, my father had a stroke and died suddenly. I was devastated. My father and I had our ups and downs through the years, but during the last seven years of his life, we became closer during my mother's illness and her subsequent death. I had to leave my practice for periods of weeks to travel to the East Coast, first for his hospitalization and planning care for him, and then, soon thereafter, for his funeral. I am sure I was not fully there for Adam during this time of my bereavement. I did not know how to speak with him about my upset and distraction. I seemingly waited for him to notice, but he politely avoided bringing this up. After my return from the funeral, Adam said he wanted to ask me something.

Adam: Are you all right? You haven't been yourself, and I understand you're the doctor and things about you are private, and I shouldn't even be asking you. But could you just let me know if you're all right?

RT: Adam, I don't know how to answer you. I want to say yes so you don't worry, but I am not myself. You are correct. I am doing the best I can, and I realize you have noticed that I am different with you. I appreciate you asking me now. I am mostly all right [and I thought to myself, except when I'm not—but did not say this part].

Adam: OK. Did someone die?

RT: Yes, someone I loved dearly died. [I teared up, and Adam did too.]

Looking back, I understand that I did not completely address Adam's observation and take up an important link with his father that then appeared true about me—that I must have felt to him that I was not there even when I was. At the time I saw Adam, I was still very involved in a school for emotionally disturbed children where I had worked as the director. I was overwhelmed by my loss and the demands of my work, although I will note that I felt at my best whenever I was seeing patients in my practice. John Beebe, a Jungian analyst who was my consultant then, told me that this was an indication of the Self in action.[7] In other words, something from deep inside can guide us through the worst of times when we let it. I have also learned since then that patients typically react with grace and kindness when entrusted with just enough knowledge about us and that such an exchange rarely disrupts their process. It often leads to an important deepening. I wish I had known that better when I worked with Adam.

Perhaps because of this unresolved issue in the transference of a checked-out father, Adam kept to the subject of his father, speculating how many of his successes were not only about besting his father but also about living out what his father would have wanted. He spoke about not wanting to be trapped in a demanding job that "sucked the life out" like he thought it had for his father. I had been using the word *manic* in our discussions when things he described at work sounded so, such as coworkers not sleeping for days, wild imaginings about the magnificence of the Internet, great wealth when an IPO happened, the intellectual superiority of people working in tech, and so on. Now, Adam too began to comment on the manic pace of his work. He laughed once when I noted something was manic and replied, "They [his company's owners] would feed you crack cocaine if it made you more productive." He mentioned that all their work retreats occurred at mountain resorts, up high, where he felt "oxygen-deprived." Although he was joking, I noted that thinking is difficult when our brains do not get enough oxygen.

For Adam, there were several aspects of his troubled relationship with his father that also appeared closely linked to his immigration to the United States, almost as if England represented his father, one that Adam preferred to keep at far more than arm's length. He recalled that when he was a child, there had been talk in the family about his father wanting to move them to the United States, but it never worked out. Our talking about this relationship began to shift Adam's understanding of why he immigrated. He began to question why he had done so and whether he truly wanted to stay in the United States. Being up on the mountain with his career successes now seemed less gratifying. He fantasized about returning to London, although he lamented that in five years' time, he would have the same problems there as he had in San Francisco. He also wondered about moving to other countries but gradually came to recognize that doing so would mean living as his father had—that he would be continuing to chase achievements and pressuring himself into higher performance without regard for the rest of himself and his marriage. He thought himself different in many ways from his father because he was more emotionally attuned, he had several good friends, and he got on well with his coworkers. During these discussions, Adam remembered that when he was a teenager, he had been bullied as a sissy and bookworm, but then he decided to take up swimming, joined the school team, and did well at it. The bullying subsided. His swim coach took a liking to him, and Adam came to see him as a mentor and father figure. This reevaluation of his personal father and other father figures, which seemed to have begun with me, opened a new perspective for Adam on his attitudes about England and his coming to the United States.

He began to deepen his understanding of who his father was. For example, Adam wondered why he felt so hurt by his father's flaws and deficiencies—his social awkwardness, withdrawal, lack of emotion, and unrelatedness within the family.

Adam: I know we all have those sorts of things because we're human and ridiculously imperfect. I don't know why I let his problems affect me so much. He was not a good father but he tried. I believe he tried.

RT: You've described your father as a man with emotional wounds that he didn't know how to address himself or get help for.

Adam: Yes, he was wounded.

RT: And he is the father you know, the father you love, the father you wish you could protect and take care of. It is hard to reconcile those feelings with someone being so flawed.

Adam: [Cries] I did want to take care of him. I remember thinking if only I found the right way, he'd be proud of me.

About fourteen months into our work, Adam got another promotion. This led to a phase of grandiosity in which he claimed he felt "powerful" and "vindicated" for triumphing over rivals. Soon, however, he began to feel overworked and exhausted. He became subject to much gossip, jealousy, and accusations he had benefitted from favoritism. Being in the limelight in this way was not what he had dreamed it would be. He had a panic attack on a street corner and phoned me barely able to speak. The shadow of his ambition appeared to reach out and choke him with a message that he was making risky choices. He decided to take a week off for a holiday and go with his wife to see their relatives in London.

   Upon their return to San Francisco, they were both nearly deported because Adam had not filed documents to extend their visas. At the airport, he somehow slipped past a border patrol officer who was paying more attention to his wife's lapsed visa. She was detained and almost sent back to England. Adam rushed to contact an attorney who assisted her in being able to re-enter the United States. As I mentioned in earlier chapters, the array of forms and documents that the US Immigration and Naturalization Service (since renamed to US Citizenship and Immigration Services) requires is mind-boggling, and many immigrants struggle to stay apace with deadlines and other documentation requirements. Still, Adam knew better because he had an attorney who had told him weeks before that these forms needed updating so he and his wife could extend their visas.

   Initially, Adam tried to make a joke about what had happened. I listened and empathized with his panic that his wife could have been deported during those hours while he and his attorney hurried to sort the visa issue. I mentioned that it could have ended differently because of the seriousness of the problem, and he looked deflated after hearing me say this.

RT: You had been feeling almost manic before you went to England.
Adam: Yes. I was revved up and full of myself.
RT: Do you think forgetting to update the forms could be linked to that?
Adam: Oh, maybe. I was telling myself, "This is great, you are fantastic, everyone's so impressed." [Pause] I'm not at all sure that's how I really felt about things.
RT: [Silent]
Adam: [Sighs] Truth is I'm actually quite ambivalent about my job and that promotion. The pressure is God awful, and I don't like how tired I am every fucking day. [Pause] I don't like this. I'm in a crucible.
RT: That's an image in which things melt and lose their form.
Adam: [Nods] I don't want that.

After this exchange, Adam told me that he enjoyed writing short stories. He had not let many others read them, and he even kept them from his wife because he was not sure "how good" they were. We talked about how his sadness about his work seemed familiar and that it echoed an earlier bout of depression in his psychotherapy with me. He felt oppressed by his role managing others, irritated by their conflicts, and angry at his boss for expecting so much from him.

About eighteen months into his psychotherapy with me, Adam found an opportunity with a company in London. He applied and was offered the job.

Adam: I'd love to go home now.
RT: You've decided.
Adam: Yes, and that bit we did talking through about my father—that helped me because I think I was unconsciously trying to prove something to him. But it was the him of twenty-five years ago, not even the him of today!
RT: That was an important and lively recognition for you.
Adam: Of course, England can make you crazy, so I'm preparing for that too,
RT: Crazy, eh?
Adam: All the class nonsense and the attention to hierarchy. I'll miss the Americans' casual disdain for hierarchy in how they organize themselves.
RT: What else comes to mind about going back?
Adam: I should have time to write. I'd love that.
RT: Can you say more?
Adam: The freedom I feel when I write. It's like I lose myself. Actually, I lose my self-consciousness. Does that make any sense? [Pause] I become less focused on how I seem to others. I just get into where the writing takes me.
RT: Sounds good.
Adam: Yeah, I think it's the right choice for me to go back.
RT: Where did you see yourself headed if you stayed?
Adam: An awful, awful place. I'd become overweight because most managers sooner or later give up their healthy lifestyles to work more and they start eating crappy food. Plus, there'd be no break from endless drama. Americans have this can-do thing; they're entrepreneurial, optimistic, but man, can they be bloody competitive, cutthroat. [Sighs] It's a tradeoff because the English can be backward looking.

Adam's appraisal of his decision sounded balanced as he considered what he would miss, what he would get instead, and what some of the differences would mean for him. His wife was relieved and very pleased at the idea of their moving back to London. For both of them, there appeared to be a mix of feelings, such as sorrow, ambivalence, and desire when they spoke about being nearer to their families. In the last two weeks of our meeting, Adam showed up for his appointments twice on the wrong days.

Adam: [The second time this happened.] I can't believe it happened again!
RT: I wonder if you're anxious about our saying goodbye.
Adam: [Looking down, he blushes.] Yes, I guess so. You've helped me, and I want to say thank you but it sounds lame.
RT: Not to me.
Adam: I'll miss you. You weren't like my father. I guess sometimes, I thought you might have been, but it turned out you weren't. It would be nice if we had more time.
RT: That is part of goodbye when it's been meaningful.

We spoke some about the visa incident months before. Adam now understood it as a wake-up call about the psychologically perilous path he had been on. He now thought he had been unconsciously following his father in chasing ambition and career, and he decided he did not want that. In one of his last sessions, Adam told me that weeks before, he had seen a suit at a well-known San Francisco department store and that he had wanted to buy it. He realized, however, that he no longer had enough time to shop for it because of packing at home and finishing up loose ends at work. I asked him what he thought the suit represented, and he replied, "I have absolutely no idea." For a moment, I wondered if it could have meant something about psychotherapies and analyses that end before they are finished. Before the goods are really delivered. Adam asked me to find him a referral in London, and that seemed a promising intention on his part.

Discussion

In previous chapters, I described others (Hans, Ursula) who returned to Europe after living for a long while in the United States. It is no wonder that many people do not stay in the United States given all the complications of immigration laws, cultural adjustments, career obstacles, financial hurdles, and the meaningful attachments to their families who remain abroad. Unlike Hans and Ursula, Adam was an immigrant in a different category because he had a very good job with a large tech company that provided a generous income and that had an in-house legal department to help him and his wife with visas. His decision to be in the United States was bolstered by external supports that gave him freedom of choice and options that many immigrants here do not have. Adam was drawn to San Francisco because of ambition and career pursuits, and he enjoyed privileges that most immigrants outside this category do not have. He was often not conscious of these privileges and how they distinguished his experience from that of most other immigrants. I occasionally brought up this subject with Adam, and he would agree he had important advantages whenever I mentioned it, but I felt his manic attitude precluded deeper conversations about it. For example, he sympathized with the immigrant women who cleaned their apartment because he suspected they might have been in the United States illegally. He said thinking about them made him feel "crummy" because his circumstances were so much better than he imagined theirs were. He often gave them large tips after they had cleaned the apartment. Now, when I sit with someone whose situation is similarly privileged like Adam's was, I look for opportunities to explore how privilege enters into their immigrant narrative and what meanings they either do or do not make of it. This has not always been easy during an era when a large part of American political and social discourse has endorsed xenophobia and immigration restrictions.

Adam's manic attitude seemed partly predicated on unconsciously repudiating his father. He would be more successful than his father had been, and thus, Adam could bask in an imagined oedipal triumph over him by becoming what he thought his father was not. Adam was in the grip of both a repudiation of and an identification with his father. His initial period of treatment with me involved repeatedly challenging and testing me to see, among other things, (a) how distant I would remain; (b) how unemotional I would be; (c) how I would respond to Adam's boyish demands for attention; and (d) how I would react to Adam's rages. I believe that our relationship was able to pass most of these transference tests. My own father's death was apprehended by Adam in his question, "Did someone die?" I now see that he may well have believed it had been my father who died. It would have potentially been a rich exploration if I had taken this up in more detail with Adam because he might have been able to see me dealing with the loss of a loved father and related it to his own experiences of his father. These pivotal points in therapy usually assume more clarity in retrospect. However, I think Adam got to where he needed to go, especially when he brought up his own hurt about his father's deficiencies. Adam's question then—"Why [do] I let his problems affect me so much?"—showed the beginnings of a shift in how he held his father internally. No longer just a parent to be vanquished, his father was a human figure who was wounded and who nonetheless "tried." This reappraised father, not good in many ways, but wounded and yet trying, allowed Adam to reconsider his situation in the United States as representing both avoidance of his father and replicating his father's destiny, not his own.

Following another promotion, this hard-won awareness succumbed temporarily to yet more manic flurry that resurrected Adam's ambition and resentment of his father. The near deportation experience after the visit to England offered him a chance to reorient himself through an exploration of why he had overlooked filing the overdue visa forms. The crucible was an arresting image of Adam losing himself, perhaps melting into identification with his father, and it became a conscious symbol of what Adam did not want: a pressure cooker that burned him out. His creative secret of writing stories emerged here as a desire, one that also helped to shape his decision to return to England. Adam's psyche presented another intriguing image as we concluded our work together, namely the unbought suit. Looking back at it, I wonder now if it expressed a step toward relinquishing a persona he had felt confined by as well as recognition for his being different from his father and not needing to assert this artificially. He had worked through what we might think of as a negative father complex, and his thanking me explicitly referred to this (that is, "you weren't like my father" could have signified "you weren't cut from the same cloth").

Adam's situation demonstrates how our internal parents remain with us in complicated ways that affect decisions about where we live and why. Adam actively disavowed being like his father so intensely when we first met that he could not see how he was actually living like him. His relocation was both a proclamation of dissimilarity and an unconscious identification with the man he did not want to resemble. Adam's story is evocative of that image from The Aeneid when Aeneas carries his father Anchises as they flee; the son shoulders the father knowingly and unknowingly.

Case example—Looking for the light at the end of the tunnel

Marco was a seven-year-old boy whose parents contacted me because he was anxious and avoiding school. Marco's mother was from Quebec and his father was from Spain, and he had a three-year-old brother. Marco's parents described him as sensitive and shy. He startled at unexpected noises and strong odors. He had tantrums at home in which he thrashed around the house until he broke down crying.

Two years before we met, Marco's parents had moved to San Francisco from Washington DC. Both parents were on work-related immigrant visas. His mother was a nurse and his father an engineer. They both expressed worry that Marco, who was finishing second grade, felt like an outsider at school because he had few friends and tended to stand off on his own rather than engage in reciprocal play.

I met Marco's parents first and asked them about their life here. They each hesitated, and I inquired why. They replied that they were always "dreaming" of where to move next. They did not feel settled in San Francisco and indicated they were unsure of a future here. Marco's father said, "We feel out of place. It's not really been a smooth adjustment." I asked them to tell me more about that, and Marco's mother responded that they had not even unpacked completely. I look puzzled, and she added that there were still full cardboard boxes in the hall and some of the rooms.

When I asked what kept them from unpacking, the father said, "It just seemed we weren't going to be here long." Marco's mother noted that they had not even hung many pictures on the walls of their home. I asked if they talked with Marco about why the boxes were unpacked and few pictures hung, and Marco's father said, "No, not really. Do you think we should say something to him?"

I had not even met Marco yet, and I was already wondering how this environment would feel to him—perhaps uncertain and possibly unstable. Children like to have structure around them, not just in terms of their relationships and their school, but also in the components of their physical environment, which gives them a sense of a visible and perceptible container. When I met him, Marco was soft-spoken and very introverted. I soon began to wonder though about the difference between introversion as a personality trait versus inhibition as a psychological mode for cautiously navigating one's surroundings. He seemed to have some of both in him. He gradually took interest in my office and the toys there, but I had to encourage him to explore. In the initial sessions, Marco slowly warmed up to me and the office. He looked at the pictures on my wall and asked about many of them. For example, he wondered about the location of a park in one image and the museum in another. He commonly formulated many of his first questions with "Where?" These interactions made me think about living in a house with unpacked boxes and little on the walls. Might Marco have been thinking about *where* his family was headed if they weren't staying here?

Marco also liked a map that hung in my office. He pointed out where Spain was and Quebec, and he told me he had visited both places because his grandparents lived there. He spoke French and Spanish and brought in various comics he had in these languages to show me. I had the impression that Marco knew about places and locations, but he did not feel settled where he now lived. He more readily spoke about playgrounds in Madrid than, for instance, he did about the one closest to his house in San Francisco. I speculated how frustrating it might feel for a child to know more about a place on a map than the place where he actually lives. Perhaps, I wondered, Marco's anger and thrashing around had to do with venting this frustration. His problems with changes and transitions made sense in this context, because he would likely worry about where he was going next and feel unprepared for it.

I met regularly with Marco's parents, and in one of these meetings, I recommended that they either unpack the boxes or put them away. At first, they were surprised when I said this because they were not sure the unpacked things held any significance for Marco. I mentioned it would be like living out of a suitcase even though you planned to stay for a longer period of time, and this analogy helped them understand that the boxes could represent transition and an impending move. I encouraged them to hang up some pictures too, and they agreed that had been on their agenda for some time but they had never gotten to it. We discussed too how unsettled they felt, and they each endorsed that this was true. There were things about San Francisco that they did not like, and they felt it would be difficult to raise children here. I suggested they form a narrative about their family that could express that, a story they could share with their children as a containing narrative about the four of them. I cautioned them against discussing too much about possible moves to places they might have dreamed about because Marco's mind could not yet process what that meant. He might get that a move meant packing and going somewhere, but for a seven-year-old to imagine a real environment would require a lot of extra imagination. In such situations, imagination and fantasy can sometimes trick children into believing quite scary things about the world.

Later, Marco became more willing to talk with me about his angry feelings and his frustrations. During these interactions, I noticed he often asked me if he could lean against a hard surface—he said his back hurt otherwise—like a wall in my office, the base of the couch, or the side of my desk. He seemed reassured by having this hardness at his back, that it comforted him. I mentioned to his parents that Marco might have been showing me that he felt a need for firmer support to help him feel less worried by what seemed unconscious, that is, behind him. Marco's parents began expressing clearer expectations with him and simultaneously enrolled him in various afterschool activities like a sports club to build his confidence. These tasks might sound basic enough, but for families not living attuned to the present, they can easily slip aside. We all let such things slip into unconsciousness. Marco needed support for his developing ego so it could master the environment he lived in, not one he might imagine moving to at some uncertain date. As I talked with his parents, I also encouraged them to seek support here. I reflected on their feeling unsettled, and I noted that building ties within their community could help them feel more settled, while not foreclosing their dreaming about other places to live. They both felt such intense work pressures that they were unsure how much they could do this.

After about a year of psychotherapy, Marco was doing better and his parents decided to stop his treatment. They had seen many improvements but still wished he was not as angry as he was at home. I mentioned that he had told me that he "liked the dark side" in the Star Wars saga because those characters showed their anger physically. I mentioned to Marco and later to his parents that most of those characters have complicated stories about where they came from. Marco's interest in them suggested an ongoing need to talk about the family narrative, where they were from, where they had lived, and where they were now living. I suspected that Marco might have remained angry as long as his origin story felt murky and dark. In one of our last meetings, Marco's father agreed they had moved around perhaps without taking stock of the effects on all of them. He said, "We have been living a long, long time with the light at the end of the tunnel." I commented that the image was notable for both the darkness and the sense of not being out yet, not having arrived at a good destination. He agreed. A year later, Marco's family relocated to Canada to be closer to his mother's family and closer to traveling to Europe for the father's.

Discussion

Since approximately 2008, several of my patients who were immigrants to the United States left this country and moved to Canada. I believe this is not an accident of geography. Rather, I think that the Canadian approach to immigration has been, during this time period, more welcoming, tolerant, and less xenophobic than in the United States. Also, important social supports for healthcare, school, preschool, and early childcare are more uniformly built out as parts of Canadian society than in the United States. As mentioned previously, as a percentage of their population, Canada now accepts more immigrants than the United States.

Marco's parents came to me because of his behaviors, yet they too were in distress over their situation in San Francisco. None of them felt settled here, and they each felt unsupported. This is a lonely circumstance for a family to be in. Marco's interest in my map and my pictures almost literally communicated his desire for orientation and clarity about his environment. He felt that this was missing at home, and his angry outbursts were partly to protest this uncertainty. His parents readily worked with me to change their home and to support him in actively reaching for the community life of a child. Donald Winnicott writes about children who act out:

> [It is] as if seeking an ever-widening frame, a circle which had as its first example the mother's arms or the mother's body. One can discern a series—the mother's body, the mother's arms, the parental relationship, the home, the family including cousins and near-cousins, the school, the locality with its police-stations, the country with its laws.[8]

This image of concentric circles is one of my favorites because it depicts the multiple layers necessary to embed each of us within families and communities in order to ground social and emotional development for what is our shared humanity.

I believe that Marco was protesting because he wanted to experience this kind of containment beginning at home. What is a home with unpacked boxes and bare walls? Less a home and more a temporary residence. Helping Marco to develop more connections within their community was a smart move by his parents in establishing another layer to this image. I believe that a missing piece for Marco's parents was associated with the final layer Winnicott mentions, "the country with its laws." This circle—including a country's social values and institutions—is salient for immigrants, because how can anyone feel settled without it, settled enough to begin unpacking to make a new place more like home? A country that does not welcome and support immigrants and refugees will not fully provide this circle of containment, and its absence will affect them. When this is not available, they might feel they are spending too long in a dark tunnel waiting for the light.

Leaving from America

Chimamanda Ngozi Adichie's award-winning novel *Americanah* tells a fascinating and complex story of immigration and subsequent return to the main character's home country, Nigeria.[9] The protagonist, a young woman named Ifemelu, leaves Nigeria at a time when it is ruled by a military dictatorship. She comes to the United States to study in Philadelphia, where she works various jobs, especially doing childcare, and begins to write a blog that chronicles her observations about class, race, and differences in the United States. Like many and probably most immigrants, she often experiences significant worries about money and her finances. Ifemelu's high-school boyfriend, Obinze, is denied a visa to the United States after 9/11. Instead, he goes to London where he lives as an undocumented immigrant. Obinze is eventually caught and deported from the United Kingdom, and as this happens, he reflects on the word *removed*, which is the formal term for his deportation, and that this feels like he is "a thing."[10] In sections such as these, the author transports a reader into a world where humanity is seemingly absent and people are regarded and treated as things.

This novel is impactful because such details are subtly slipped in to explain the various pressures operating on immigrants. For example, Ifemelu's friend Jane who is from Grenada tells her, "If you are not careful in this country, your children become what you don't know."[11] Jane unassumingly remarks on the acculturative stresses that families face in orienting to their receiving country, particularly around what happens to their children. Like the rabbi in *To Call It Sleep*, Jane notices changes in the children that force discomfort and unfamiliarity upon her. Children become "others" within a family that is already experiencing othering because of their imported differences and cultural ways, which their new neighbors, coworkers, employers, and friends might struggle to understand. Jane voices how this lands internally within a psyche as an unknown, which can feel eerie and unsettling. Such references to the uncanny often typify what many immigrants go through psychologically as they resettle into new locations; this uncanniness can also reflect some of what citizens and established residents of the receiving country feel when they interact with immigrants. I will explore this idea of uncanniness more in the last chapter and discuss its relevance to immigration.

What happens to children is of great concern for immigrants because they are central to a family's emotional life and, as I discuss in Chapter 5, they represent the future. In *Americanah*, some of this symbolism is carried by Ifemelu's younger cousin, Dike, who lives in the United States with his mother, Aunty Uju (actually Ifemelu's cousin). Thinking about his future, Ifemelu wonders if Dike will be thought of as American African or African American. "He would have to choose what he what was, or rather, what he was would be chosen for him."[12] She introduces an idea about racializing, and somewhat like Appiah, she considers the social forces around labeling when an identity is externally given rather than chosen. In other words, what might happen to Dike if he is *identified* before he himself decides who he is? This process, which I discuss in Chapter 6, can create all kinds of confusing binds that make a person less an individual and more of a type or category in ways that hurt and impinge on a psyche's capacity for development and well-being. Later in the novel, Dike attempts suicide, shining a spotlight on the struggles immigrant youth frequently face during acculturation and afterward—because this process continues for a long time—when they feel torn apart by the social demands of the receiving country. Their mental health is often at high risk during such struggles.

Another aspect of acculturation is the acquisition of specialized knowledge about the new surroundings. What makes this fresh location tick? Are there key pieces of information that once obtained will ease painful contrasts around not knowing/knowing and not belonging/belonging? Adichie writes about Ifemelu, "She hungered to understand everything, to wear a new, knowing *skin* right away..."[13] This reference to skin caught my attention because it invokes another layer of psychic change, namely a kind of group skin, which a new member longs for, because it signifies fitting in—being similar and accepted. Didier Anzieu writes about how the individual psyche comes to be organized at a level of what he calls "the skin-ego"; in the final chapter, I will discuss how an analogous "group skin-ego" incorporates social aspects of membership, recognition, and belonging.[14] Lacking this skin, a person will often feel excluded and even scapegoated for not wearing what is acceptable—in other words, a recognizable skin that conveys specialized knowledge and affiliation.

Adichie gets that this level of group skin-ego is powerful and formative. Ifemelu writes in her blog, "Dear Non-American Black, when you make the choice to come to America, you become black. Stop arguing. Stop saying I'm Jamaican or I'm Ghanaian. America doesn't care."[15] Although Appiah might refer to this naming as labeling, I think it also addresses what a group skin-ego might obscure by blurring one's individuality. Being put under an umbrella that includes "Black," a person who is Black and an immigrant might feel something is askew, when, for instance, something essential about their background is unrecognized. Adichie describes these social perceptions as part of acculturation; however, these important differences, which belong to who we are, are then covered up. Such deeply personal dilemmas speak to the value of Crenshaw's ideas about intersectionality (see Chapter 6).

Less a reader concludes this is unique to the United States, Adichie wryly positions Obinze in the United Kingdom, where he observes,

> They [British] would not understand why people like him, who were raised well fed and watered but mired in dissatisfaction, conditioned from birth to look towards somewhere else, eternally convinced that real lives happened in that somewhere else, were now resolved to do dangerous things, illegal things, so as to leave....[16]

She captures in this poetic section an immigrant's hope, their dreaming about a better place to relocate to because their aspirations cannot find adequate expression within the circumstances of their home country. Like Aeneas and the Trojans traveling for over seven years, they look for somewhere else where real lives can happen. Mythic potential characterizes some of the best intentions of immigrants because it inspires them to search by stepping outside what the vast majority are comfortable with, namely keeping to what is entirely too familiar even when real life appears not to happen there.

Sections of *Americanah* occur in a hair salon where Ifemelu is getting braids put into her hair. Symbolically rich, this braiding evokes the entwining of two things to create an image of another thing that is whole, beautiful, and desirable. An immigrant might wish to weave different strands of their experiences into something like this. During a visit, a stylist asks, "How did you get your papers?" Ifemelu thinks to herself, "A sacrilege, that question; immigrants did not ask other immigrants how they got their papers."[17] Here, too, Adichie homes in on the secrecy that many immigrants feel a need to maintain regarding their legal status and their papers. In the final chapter, I will give a personal example of the delicacy surrounding these papers, which can create hiding dynamics within immigrant families. "Papers" are associated with many complicated reactions for immigrants, including but not limited to luck, fear, trickery, guilt, and anxiety about discovery, even when they have not done anything wrong.

Americanah is also about emigration—leaving places. Having returned to Lagos, Ifemelu notices the many changes that have occurred since the time she left. A friend tells her, "You are looking at things with American eyes. But the problem is that you are not even a real Americanah. At least if you had an American accent we would tolerate your complaining!"[18] Real Americanahs might wear a group skin-ego that more obviously showed they had been living in the United States. They would have a different accent and might have picked up other cultural signifiers that they knowingly wore and that revealed their differences to native Nigerians. At a level of the group skin-ego, of being able to tell something about who a person is by the signs of where they have lived, Ifemelu does not show many evident traces of having lived in the United States because she has retained essential qualities of her home country even after living away from Nigeria for a long while. Still, her return brings with it unusual sensations and revised feelings along with a different perspective. She is aware of feeling estranged and disoriented around how Nigeria has changed. These impressions of unfamiliarity strike her as uncanny.

There is so much to recommend about *Americanah*, and I have quoted from it in some detail because its themes of leaving and returning, immigrating and emigrating, having a place and being displaced, are tightly embedded within the psychic experiences of the main characters. Back in Lagos, Ifemelu explains to Obinze about how she now views the United States. "The best thing about America is that it gives you space. I like that. I like that you buy into the dream, it's a lie but you buy into it and that's all that matters."[19] "Space" implies freedom, room, movement, and options; it is an image of many tempting possibilities, a factor in some of the images discussed in Chapter 9. Certainly, that is a large part of what brought Adam and Marco and his parents to the United States. Ifemelu's conclusion that America's offer of space is both a dream and a lie is an interesting combination because a dream, in the conscious sense of this word, usually means potentialities for what could be, whereas a lie is quite different. A lie typically covers an untruth, a thing known or suspected to be false. We often lie to fool ourselves because truth can be painful. Combining an understanding of America as both a dream and a lie, Adichie describes an ambivalence about what the United States can mean, one that seems fairly common among immigrants. At times, it looks like a dream about possibilities, and at others, it seems a big lie when dreams prove to be beyond reach.

Concluding thoughts

Why might someone come to a new country and later decide to leave it? When evaluating this, a significant factor to keep in mind is whether traumatic experiences have motivated their choice to immigrate. In the examples in this chapter, trauma was not a prominent background factor. When someone must leave because of persecution, as in the case of a refugee, or when someone must leave because they have felt fundamentally unsafe at home because of violence, religious biases, climate disasters, intolerance of their sexual orientation, or massive economic collapse, then a desire for a better life operates at a level of basic needs; it is driven by causes that determine survival. That is not the case for an immigrant who is looking chiefly for improved economic and educational opportunities. Although there appears to be little data about emigrants from the United States, it would be useful to find out how many who leave have had traumatic experiences and concerns for personal safety. I would imagine this is rarer. It makes sense that refugees would desire to never go back to a place where they felt persecuted and targeted violently. Likewise, immigrants from places with various kinds of environmental devastation might never want to return. We would scarcely imagine that Aeneas or his descendants would decide to go back to Troy.

When motives to immigrate center on education, career, and improved opportunities, immigrants probably have more freedom to choose where they want to live. In these circumstances, relocation after a trial of living somewhere could be appealing. Notably, being able to do this comes from a position of privilege that most immigrants do not have because they lack what it assumes: resources, money, transferable and highly desired skills, and connections with other privileged groups.

In Adam's case, it seemed that his home country was intimately and unconsciously associated with his negative feelings and memories about his father. As he became more conscious of these linkages, Adam felt freer to decide to return because he came to feel differently about his father—not exactly positive, but more ambivalent and more compassionate for his father's limitations. He recognized that he was also perpetuating a way of life based on his internal father, one that chased career and ambition in moving around to find the best opportunities. As he succeeded, Adam felt he had surpassed and beaten his father. These psychological complexities, once they were more consciously appreciated, permitted a reevaluation of what life path Adam found himself traversing. His decision to return to England therefore seemed to assert his desires in ways that were more connected with what he actually hoped for himself once he was not stuck in an avoiding-competing cycle with his father.

Marco's parents appeared themselves, though only semiconsciously, to openly express ambivalence about living in the United States. Their "dreaming" (as conscious fantasizing) about other places to live was similar to what Adichie's character Obinze voices about thinking "real life" happens somewhere else. This impulse to find "real life" gave their current situation a tentativeness that made Marco feel anxious, even a little unsafe, when he hesitated about going to school or out in the neighborhood. He might have experienced separation anxiety around a fantasy of their leaving without him (boxes packed and ready to go). Marco's visible interest in places he saw in pictures and maps in my office further underscored his sense of dislocation and a need to orient himself. He could not relax enough to feel settled here because what he saw in his home environment indicated an imminent move.

As his parents made changes to become more settled, Marco became less anxious, although his temper remained something of a challenge. His attraction to "the dark side" of Star Wars characters appeared uncannily linked to his father's metaphor about living for a long time in a dark tunnel. To Marco, darkness as a personal characteristic became attractive and functioned as a psychic compensation for not knowing when they would make it into the light. It was as if the family system was kept in suspension awaiting a time when they would find a location to settle in and call home. Canada frequently came up in his parent's dreams about places to live (his maternal grandparents also lived there). Hopefully, the family's eventual relocation there addressed their lack of connection in the United States, replacing it with a more secure life in Canada. As I mentioned earlier, several patients in my practice who were immigrants have left the United States for Canada because of its welcoming attitude toward immigration, its tolerance of different lifestyle choices, and its European-like social-welfare systems. Certainly, in the past six to ten years, Canada has become a more telling contrast with the United States around these issues.

During our digital and Internet era, variations of defining immigration have shown up to describe the movement—*emigration*—of attention and time to online platforms and screens. Digital immigrants are often characterized as those who grew up before the Internet became widespread. As a result, they have had to learn and "move," that is, migrate, their interests online by learning new ways of doing things. In contrast, digital natives are those who have grown up with the Internet since they were children, which includes many millennials (born between 1980 and 1995) and Generation Z (born between 1996 and 2012).[20] *Native*, in this terminology, means that those children had access to digital technology from when they were children since the Internet launched publicly in the early 1990s. Natives are supposedly almost naturally attuned to the Internet, social media, working online, and videogaming.

A problem, I suggest, to this way of defining "natives" as opposed to "immigrants" is that the definition of native presupposes anyone born after a certain date can more easily relocate parts of themselves into a virtual world away from the real world. The term *native* becomes based solely on a historical date. To my way of thinking, there is a psychological relocation that is involved for any of us using digital technologies because we have to project aspects of our experience online. This process happens even for so-called digital natives. Everyone immigrates in this fashion when spending time online. Therefore, it seems more accurate to speak of first-generation immigrants (those who are older) followed by second, third, and subsequent "generations" of digital immigrants (each one younger than the preceding). Otherwise, we overlook that the Internet and its various platforms require all of us to move something—attention, time, involvement, interest—out of the real world. We are all immigrating "digitally" when we use it, regardless of our age, or when we first learned about it. The COVID-19 pandemic has shown both the uses and the limitations of this migration into the digital world. We have had to rely on online resources and platforms to communicate with one another during a time of sheltering and social distancing. Using my conceptualization about "digital generations," it is understandable that younger generations of digital immigrants might have an easier adjustment to this technology because they have grown up with it. After all, a similar ease with acculturation usually occurs for younger immigrants who actually move and relocate in the real world.

Nowadays, a form of legal digital immigration has emerged as an option for people who want to operate their businesses online. Countries such as Estonia and Georgia now offer what is called *e-residency* for the purpose of starting a digital company, having a bank account in the country, and by-passing a person's home country's regulations including certain taxes.[21] This has become something of a trend among entrepreneurs, freelancers, and independent contractors providing various professional services. Estonia has had such a program since 2014, with the benefit that it is a member of the European Union and thus enables its e-residents the prospect of conducting business on equal footing with other EU firms and companies. Perhaps, in the wake of the COVID-19 pandemic and the proliferation of online work, such digital immigration might become more prevalent. Assuredly, this is a long way to have come from the journeys described in The Aeneid.

Notes

1 Wikipedia, s.v. "Emigration from the United States," accessed April 2, 2021, https://en.wikipedia.org/wiki/Emigration_from_the_United_States
2 Jonathan A. Schwabish, "Identifying Rates of Emigration in the United States Using Administrative Earnings Records," Congressional Budget Office, March 18, 2009, 31.
3 Christie Thompson and Andrew R. Calderón, "More immigrants Are Giving Up Court Fights and Leaving the U.S.," *The Marshall Project and Politico,* May 8, 2019, https://www.themarshallproject.org/2019/05/08/more-detained-immigrants-are-giving-up-court-fights-and-leaving-the-u-s
4 Monica Luci, "Displacement as Trauma and Trauma as Displacement in the Experience of Refugees," *Journal of Analytical Psychology* 65, no. 2 (2020): 260–280.
5 Amanda Dowd, "Displacement Trauma: Complex States of Personal, Collective and Intergenerational Fragmentation and Their Intergenerational Transmission," *Journal of Analytical Psychology* 65, no. 2 (2020): 300–324.
6 Richard G. Tedeschi and Lawrence G. Calhoun, "Posttraumatic Growth: Conceptual Foundations and Empirical Evidence," *Psychological Inquiry* 15, no. 1 (2004): 1–18.
7 Noted with John Beebe's permission.
8 Donald W. Winnicott, "The antisocial tendency," in *Deprivation and Delinquency,* eds. Clare Winnicott, Ray Shepherd, and Madeline Davis (London and New York: Tavistock Publications, 1984), 125.
9 Chimamanda Ngozi Adichie, *Americanah* (New York: Random House, 2013).
10 Ibid., 345.
11 Ibid., 137.
12 Ibid., 173.
13 Ibid., 166; italics are mine and not in the original.
14 Didier Anzieu, *The Skin-Ego,* trans. Naomi Segal (London: Karnac, 2016).
15 Adichie, *Americanah*, 273.
16 Ibid., 341.
17 Ibid., 450.
18 Ibid., 475–476.
19 Ibid., 536.
20 Quin Wang, Michael D. Myers, and David Sundaram, "Digital Natives and Digital Immigrants: Towards a Model of Digital Fluency," *Business & Information Systems Engineering* 5 (2013): 409–414, doi: 10.1007/s12599-013-0296-y
21 Zoha Khan, "Eresidency—Top 3 Countries that Offer Eresidency." *FDN Life Magazine,* January 14, 2020, https://fdnlife.com/eresidency-top-3-countries-that-offer-eresidency/

Chapter 11

Relocation Mysteries

All shall be Latium; Troy without a name;
And her lost sons forget from whence they came.

Jupiter to Juno near the end of The Aeneid[1]

You road I enter upon and look around, I believe you are not all
that is here,
I believe that much unseen is also here.

Walt Whitman, "Song of the Open Road"[2]

At the end of The Aeneid, Juno concedes to Jupiter that the Trojans will have to give up their Trojan identity and become something else, essentially citizens of Latium, or Latins. Revoking a claim to their history, Jupiter further states that they shall soon forget it, and as a result, they will lose memories of their Trojan heritage. Thus, he seemingly advocates an assimilationist perspective on how a migration should finish with a renouncement of what came before. He goes so far as to insist that even memories of that prior time should succumb to forgetting, relegating them to the realm of the unconscious. As if offering a counterpoint to Virgil's lines about lost memories, Whitman writes that roads are not just what we see, but they also conjure up what is unseen, which can include things that are uncanny as well as unconscious. The unseen often points to the power of the unconscious to preserve mysteries, which we might sense through the struggle to bring them into awareness. Whitman reminds us that appearances can deceive.

In this closing chapter, I discuss the interplay of those aspects of migration that make a person's story about it more of a mystery—namely, through omissions and lies about events surrounding migration that continue to simmer within the unconscious, and by other experiences of the uncanny that create shifting realities not only for immigrants and refugees but also for people in a receiving country. The uncanny is a potent psychological experience that shakes our understanding of what we believe to be real; it can be disorienting when it shows other realities that we would prefer

DOI: 10.4324/9781003119593-11

to deny or keep unconscious. Before discussing these topics, I offer a brief update on where many American immigration policies now stand after Trump's defeat in the 2020 election. This, of course, is really something of a moving target because such policies are inevitably rewritten, and I hope that readers will recall both the vexatious complexity and numerous contradictions of American immigration policies and procedures as presented in previous chapters. There is no Jupiter to bring order to the fragmented US immigration system, and we might keep in mind that this is not entirely a negative thing. My book was completed prior to the 2022 Russian invasion of Ukraine and it does not address that event's effects on refugees and asylum-seekers.

Forward, Not Smoothly Upward

Following Joe Biden's election victory over Donald Trump and the subsequent flip of the US Senate to Democrat control, there has been speculation about the need for overarching immigration reform. It is impossible that will happen without some Republican support because of the narrowness of the margins in Congress. The Trump administration made over 400 changes to US immigration policies to maximally restrict immigration: They suspended DACA, decreased asylum applications (through a procedure known as *metering* or *asylum turnback*), barred immigrants from many largely Muslim-majority countries, and built a wall along the US–Mexico border, which was only partially completed. His administration also capped the number of refugees allowed at 15,000 for 2020 (by comparison, from 1980 when the Refugee Act was passed into US law through 2016 the average was about 95,000 per year); ended the protected status for 400,000 people who came to the United States after disasters; designated countries in Central America with significant domestic unrest and violence as "safe" (so their citizens would not qualify for asylum); deported immigrants testing positive for COVID-19; and separated hundreds of immigrant children from their parents at the border.[3] The family separations done at the US–Mexico border were a runaround of the 1997 *Flores Settlement* that requires minors to be released quickly to a parent, guardian, relative, or licensed care facility; this refusal to follow *Flores* is what led to children being detained in jail-like conditions.[4] Further, those seeking asylum at the US–Mexico border who were not Mexican were compelled to wait in Mexico for the duration of their immigration proceedings.[5] A *New York Times* editorial before the 2020 election posited that "the Trump administration has pursued the destruction of immigration in America"; between 2016 and 2019, immigration to the United States fell by nearly half to a level last seen in the 1980s.[6] With foreboding, the editorial predicted that the Trump administration's changes might be in effect for years to come.

Figure 11.1 The concept of illegal migration from Mexico to the United States by Fishman64 (Shutterstock.com).

The Biden administration has continued Trump's policy of expelling many asylum-seeking families from Central American countries back into Mexico and, ironically, has possibly incentivized many children to try to enter the United States on their own because the only exception to expulsion has been unaccompanied children traveling without a parent.[7] David Bier of the Cato Institute, a libertarian think tank supportive of free and open immigration, writes that the Biden administration has not increased the processing of asylum seekers at ports of entry to the United States and might be maintaining the "metering" of applicants, which restricts daily their incoming numbers at each border crossing.[8] Asylum seekers, whose numbers have risen sharply over the last decade, used to travel primarily to neighboring and bordering countries; however, they now travel farther and show greater geographic dispersion as they flee violence and oppression in their home countries. This trend holds true for the United States as well as for other high-income countries.[9]

During the first three months of the Biden administration, over ninety executive actions have been taken on immigration, fifty of which undid policies from the Trump administration.[10] Immigration enforcement within the United States has been redirected to noncitizens who are considered security risks. As a result, arrests and detentions by Immigration and Customs Enforcement (ICE) are down. There has been a move to end the long-term detention of families. Biden terminated several travel bans from predominantly Muslim and African countries; he also lifted bans on visa issuance for immigrants, granted Temporary Protected Status (TPS) to immigrants from Venezuela and Myanmar, and permitted children from Central America with a parent in the United States to receive refugee status.[11] The Biden administration reversed changes to the public-charge rule that would have scrutinized new immigrants' likely future use of public benefits. Additionally, the Remain in Mexico program for asylum seekers has been terminated so asylum seekers with active asylum cases can again enter the United States during their legal proceedings. The problem of unaccompanied minors entering the United States and overwhelming shelters has yet to be fully addressed in a uniform way. The Biden administration recently indicated it will increase the number of refugees admitted to 62,500 from 15,000. Positive actions on asylum seekers who transit via Mexico (whose applications were denied under Trump) and who are victims of gang and domestic violence (whose applications were also denied under Trump) have also been taken. Construction on the border wall has been halted, although there are still funds to continue building it. Access to citizenship for those who qualify under DACA and TPS would have to pass through Congress and thus is uncertain, although the Biden administration has taken some steps to protect those enrolled in the DACA program (undocumented immigrants who came to the United States as children). The fate of the DACA program remains tied up in various court proceedings.

Prominent Bay Area immigration attorney Marc Van Der Hout, in an interview, noted that it is "too early to tell" what the effects of the Trump years will be and that the Biden administration is "making changes all the time."[12] He indicated that Attorney General Merrick Garland has the power to change rules and procedures that the former Attorneys General (Jeff Sessions and William Barr) made to restrict immigration, and he expects that many of them will be overturned. He added that immigration legislation is unlikely to pass Congress and explained that many undocumented Latinx immigrants are effectively trapped in the United States because they cannot leave the country since they would not be permitted to return. The Biden administration is attempting to garner support for targeted actions in Congress to expand lawful residency or citizenship to select groups such as DACA recipients. Because so many US immigration policies result from executive actions, they are unpredictable, subject to administrative whims, and not solid ground for immigrants to plan upon longer term.

Those against allowing more immigration to the United States frame their case by asserting immigrants' negative effects on the society, the economy, and their version of American culture. Xenophobic tendencies are thereby dressed up in political and economic arguments about the preservation of American values and supposedly looking after the rights of lower-income workers who are US citizens. It is extremely difficult to counter these prejudices because the Internet allows for mutually exclusive echo chambers in which misinformation and lies persist.

Immigrants and refugees are exceptionally adaptive and contribute greatly to the United States, but this viewpoint is much less widespread than the evidence for it would otherwise suggest. Alex Nowrasteh and Benjamin Powell argue that there is no economic case to be reasonably made against immigration.[13] Looking at historical data across many countries, they found that greater shares of immigrants within a population in 1990 were associated with more economic freedoms and growth twenty years later.[14] They found no evidence that immigrants are unproductive nor do they bring social habits along with them that lead to corruption, terrorism, or decreased economic growth in the receiving countries. They discovered that immigrants have actually expanded the free market in the United States, have over time countered socialist trends in the United States, and have preserved important economic institutions underpinning a free market economy. Nowrasteh and Powell conclude, "The new economic case against immigration is essentially a conjecture."[15] Or perhaps convenient for xenophobic propaganda.

Omissions, lies, and mysteries

In this book, I have provided twelve main examples from my practice and from literature about quite different migration experiences (chapter is indicated in parentheses): Hans (1), Nasir (4), Arturo (5), Miguel (5), Ichiro (5), Ursula (6), Galit (8), Mariam (8), David (8), Adam (10), Marco (10), and Ifemelu (10). Within this small and distinctive group, two-thirds have experiences of trauma or traumatic events, including medical ones such as HIV seropositivity, governmental oppression, and state-sponsored violence (a category that both Nasir and Ichiro belong to), and intergenerational trauma such as with Galit's family. The presence of trauma in a migration experience almost inevitably leads to gaps in psychic processing, either through dissociation or through other defensive and protective mechanisms. Often, body-based symptoms come to express aspects of lived trauma. These can be extremely difficult to understand consciously and to represent psychologically within a personal narrative because literally the body is where a story is held. Traumatic experiences usually have an edge of unreality because of the real terror of what actually occurred—they are life-threatening, and the ensuing gaps in a person's story are understandable as ways to cope with something unbearable.

Other nontraumatic immigration stories, however, also can be overwhelmed by omissions and lies that create similar gaps within a psyche. Omissions are often choices that are probably subject to both conscious and unconscious motives about what to tell in a story. Sometimes omissions protect others, although they can also protect the teller. A family or group history thus can become distorted when important details, facts, and historical events are left out of the story. Yet these omissions retain power by existing unconsciously, even when not included within spoken history or memory. Immigration stories can feel like mysteries when something does not add up because of a perception of missing pieces. Many immigrants know well a kind of encounter within their families that ends with a re-cognition that something is simply not up for further discussion—it is off the table or, better yet, under the table.

Lies fall into a different category of story editing. Rather than leaving out something essential, a teller creates an alternate version of what has hap-pened. History is thus fabricated, and this is repeated as accurate to cover up an unpleasant truth. I am not particularly interested in the morality of lies. On the contrary, their psychic functions are much more compelling for how we deceive ourselves, trick others, and shift reality to suit our personal ends. The implication of a lie is that the actual reality is intolerable for some reason—it could be humiliation, loss, trauma, shame, injured pride, bitter disappointment, or almost any other shadowy emotional territory from which we might want relief. Lies therefore are defensive but they are also creative. Aside from protecting something about the past that we would prefer to overlook, they conjure up a different reality in which we can feel more at home, in control, at ease, and safer. In Greek mythology, Odysseus is known as a cunning liar who uses deception in many creative ways. And Oedipus lives out a tragedy of omission about his origins.[16] Virtually all the cases and examples covered in earlier chapters contain elements of either omissions or lies as part of their narrative of migration. Notably, it is Ichiro's refusal to lie, when it would have been convenient, that leads to his cruel and unjust imprisonment.

As a child, I was often confused by what I heard of my grandparents' immigration stories. My Polish grandparents, on my father's side, claimed a nationality that did not officially exist at the time they came to the United States because Poland had been partitioned between Prussia, the Austro-Hungarian Empire, and Russia. I have a copy of my grandmother's "alien registration card" since she never became a US citizen—I remember often wondering what it meant that she was an "alien" and why she had "to register" herself at a government office. Her immigration documents list her as coming in 1911 from a town in Austria called *Krzywe*, which means *crooked* or *curved* in Polish. She never learned English, and yet, I loved visiting her because she was warm, generous, and intuitive. I did not know my Polish grandfather well because he died when I was seven. His immigration documents are murky, sometimes indicating he was from Austria, and sometimes from Russia. He arrived in the United States in 1910. While researching this book, I learned that he came into the country using a neighbor's name and documents; thus he entered the United States under another person's identity. That may ac-count for the murkiness. This neighbor of his, apparently could not leave their town in what is now southeastern Poland because of a dying parent, and he gave his travel papers to my grandfather. My last surviving aunt, who died not long ago at the age of ninety-seven, confirmed that she had known of this story when she was a child, although she told me it was not ever discussed openly in the family. From today's perspective, he would have been an illegal immigrant, although that would not necessarily have been the case in 1910.

My mother's parents were German and Irish, and they lived with us. My German grandfather died when I was six. His mother was born in Saxony (Germany) and came to the United States around 1886. His father was born in the United States, although his father's parents both had immigrated from Germany to the United States earlier in the nineteenth century. Because my maternal grandmother lived with us, I heard many stories about Ireland and Irish folklore and songs. However, whenever I became more openly curious about her family, she would evade my questions, change the topic, or just go quiet. I only knew that her mother's family had immigrated from Ireland to Canada, and she rarely said anything of substance about her father. He was a blank. When I was a child, we sometimes visited her cousins in Canada who were related to her mother and did not know her father. In researching about her parents, I learned that her father had been born in Canada, had come to the United States years before 1900, and brought her mother to the United States in 1895. On later US census forms, he falsely claimed that he had been born in the United States. This lie to census takers about having been born in the United States seems relatively benign, unlikely to account for my grandmother's vigorous avoidance of discussing her parents, especially her father.

My grandmother's mother was a Catholic. Years after my grandmother died, I was surprised to discover that her mother very possibly had been born in Ireland, not in Canada. When I tried to learn more about her, I found that the 1871 Canadian census, when she was a year old, lists her birthplace as Ireland. In looking through other Canadian census documents, I stumbled upon evidence that my grandmother's father was a Protestant (a person's religious faith was indicated on these forms). His family traces to County Monaghan in Ulster province; this county is part of the Republic of Ireland, although most of Ulster is now in Northern Ireland. During the nineteenth century, all of Ireland was governed by the United Kingdom.

More importantly, interfaith marriages were highly problematic for Irish families well into the twentieth century. A wish to omit this detail about her parents' marriage does offer a likelier explanation for my grandmother's unwillingness to talk about them as people with life stories to be told and remembered. Perhaps, she was ashamed about her father's Protestant faith and so she decided to hide it from us. According to Catholic Canon Law, "mixed marriages," or interdenominational marriages, required approval from the Catholic Church as well as a promise that any children from the couple would be raised Catholic.[17] My grandmother's silence about her father was profound. Her stubborn refusal to discuss any narrative history about her parents created a kind of wall that no one in the family really understood. It was as if a sectarian divide existed in our family around who these ancestors were, a barrier no one could pass.

Before Irish independence in 1921, around seven million people emigrated from Ireland to North America.[18] Kerby Miller, in his comprehensive book about Irish emigration, writes that many emigrants leaving Ireland believed that they were "involuntary exiles" cast out by the harshness of English rule.[19] The Penal Laws were enacted in the seventeenth and eighteenth centuries to disenfranchise Catholics and make it difficult or impossible for them to own land. Most farmers were thus tenant farmers, barely able to support and feed their families; because of the ensuing poverty, many chose to emigrate. Since most of the English living in Ireland were Protestant, a fault line arose around religious identity. Miller observes that by the mid-nineteenth century "virtually the entire Catholic and Protestant communities were ranged in hostile opposition," and Irish society was "almost totally divided into two bitterly hostile camps."[20] A natural disaster in the form of a rapidly spreading potato fungus decimated the main dietary staple, potatoes, from 1845 to 1850, when 1.8 million Irish left the island for North America.[21] My research indicates that my grandmother's maternal side as well as her paternal ancestors almost all immigrated to Canada in the nineteenth century before the famine years. Sadly, I never heard detailed stories about these people from my grandmother, who nonetheless saw herself as wholeheartedly Irish and who taught us many Irish habits and customs, including a belief in "the little people" or fairies—an invisible world that affected everyday life. We celebrated St. Patrick's Day every year when I was growing up, and I was warned not to wear anything orange on that day—the color signifying Protestants and unionists—unless I wanted to be pinched.

Children are usually sensitive to pinches as well as to possibilities of an invisible world, and growing up with stories about who might inhabit that world can be quite stimulating to the imagination. I am not implying this imaginative pull is solely true for immigrant families, or that this example from my family somehow illustrates a wider phenomenon. Still, when family stories are cloaked in either lies or omissions, secrets frequently come to take on a strong valence of forbidden knowledge and children often want to know more to clear up the mystery. They like being detectives. Somewhere between the lessons about Adam and Eve—when too much knowledge leads to being cast out—and those about Oedipus—when too little curiosity results in prideful tragedy—there exists a zone of getting it right, where we know just enough to satisfy curiosity and resolve family mysteries to insure a sense of historical continuity. This "just right" zone can help children deal with feelings of confusion, anxiety, and dread that otherwise are associated with unbridged gaps in family narratives.

Children of immigrants and even subsequent generations often contend with trying to make sense of such gaps because they linger. Sometimes their imaginations run wild. I am not just thinking about what Freud called "family romances," in which children imagine their true parentage to be royal, magical, famous, or supernatural. Rather, I suggest that when secrets born of lies and omissions confound an immigration story, there is often a psychic vacuum into which children project fantastical contents. They use their imaginative powers to construct an alternate story to explain what's missing in their parents' tale of immigration. For many, this occurs unconsciously, for example, within nighttime dreams. Others may have daydreams or waking fantasies about what might have happened that their parents or grandparents do not want to tell. As mentioned in previous chapters, studies about intergenerational trauma typically confirm the unsettling aspects of this process. However, even absent any known history of traumatic events, other secretive behaviors within families complicate what can be known and shared among them; children are particularly sensitive and vulnerable to this because it affects what they feel they can know about themselves and their families. Almost all the immigrant stories covered in earlier chapters show elements of mysteries that derive from secrets that cannot be articulated because of deep anxieties about what might happen if the truth is revealed. In this situation, knowledge itself becomes conflicted, charged with unpleasant psychic attributes, defended against, and likely to affect how stories get told. Or not.

Perimeters of culture and group functioning

In Chapter 6, I mentioned how various perimeters can define us, whether we choose them or not. These perimeters operate to concretize human life when external things dictate categories that are poor substitutes for representing what an individual experience has actually been. For instance, there have been several examples in prior chapters of legal perimeters that affect immigrants. Hans (Chapter 1) would have been denied a visa because of his HIV+ status. Arturo (Chapter 5) was greatly surprised to learn that he was not a US citizen when his mother prevented him from going on a school field trip across the border. Ichiro's story (Chapter 5) shows the effects of government violence as discrimination to imprison someone singled out for reasons of heritage and race. Nasir (Chapter 4) struggled with aspects of German life even as he hoped for a future in Germany while making his way through a complex asylum process as a refugee to gain permanent status. Mariam (Chapter 8) faced her refugee history with a mix of shame and denial because of all that her family lost when they were forced to flee. In each of these cases, the state and government defined them, told them what their "status" as a citizen was, and as a result, either bestowed or withheld basic human rights. They were superficially "seen" but not individually acknowledged.

Some of the perimeters that are portrayed in the other stories in this book are cultural and pertain to family traditions, language, and social perceptions.

Miguel (Chapter 5) had to cross perimeters of nationality, race, and religion as his family resettled into life in a state where they appeared to stand out because of their ethnic differences and Central American heritage. Religion served as a kind of bridging device to span some of those differences in his family. Ursula (Chapter 6) found the United States unsuitable because she did not want to adjust to cultural norms about the obvious value this country has placed on business and economic transactions. Similarly, Marco's parents (Chapter 10) did not feel at home in the United States and expressed a longing to move elsewhere because of cultural differences that were difficult. Ifemelu (Chapter 10) had a story somewhat like theirs as she found American life all too strange, confusing, and not always as welcoming as it seemed. These reactions describe the effects of cultural perimeters around how people interact as well as how racial and ethnic differences are perceived and talked about.

Adam (Chapter 10) faced complicated issues such as a manic attitude at work, his wife's isolation and unhappiness with social life in the United States, and his wish to not be his father while still beating him at what Adam believed to have been his father's game. These perimeters are not just cultural but also familial, especially when they describe generational conflicts that separate us from our parents and grandparents, although they are often influenced by cultural traditions. Galit (Chapter 8) experienced many disruptions in her young life that made for a choppy narrative at best about herself and her family. An intergenerational component of cultural conflicts and tragedies became part of her family's restlessness in moving around a lot. Language turned into a problem area for her because it represented how disrupted her life had become—a new language in each new place. Likewise, David (Chapter 8) portrayed elements of how language and culture mix inexplicably to give a child a sense of perimeters, especially around what is understandable and what is not. Family perimeters are typically internalized across generations, and they can create isolation when a family relocates because they may not be easily translatable to the new conditions.

Cultural perimeters seep into us, mostly unconsciously, through exposure to art, literature, and music, our education, socialization, established family narratives, and early learning about our immediate surroundings. As mentioned in Chapter 10, Didier Anzieu, a French psychoanalyst, wrote about this level of a cultural perimeter with his idea of a group skin-ego.[22] This is an addition to his earlier concept of a personal skin-ego, which in French is termed *le moi-peau* (thus occasionally translated as *ego-skin* rather than *skin-ego*). The group skin-ego is an enclosure or wrapping for groups just as the personal skin-ego represents an enclosure for the individual psyche.[23] A key difference between Anzieu's skin-ego and my exploration of perimeters is that his skin-ego is representational; it is an idealized container to symbolize how we form a boundary to our psyche, or with the group skin-ego, to a group. My notion about how perimeters affect us refers to our taking inside actual physical boundaries—internalizing them, or in the case of laws and culture, to taking inside textual and pedagogical lessons and rules that enter into us whether we like them or not. For example, in Chapter 6, I referred to the Berlin Wall as a real construct that carried multiple meanings about economics and government, and ideas about freedom, history, and movement. It would have been difficult for a person in Berlin at that time to see the Wall and not have a visceral reaction to it; that is one example of how a perimeter gets inside us.

Anzieu, who was a trained group psychotherapist and wrote about groups, believed that what applied at the individual psyche could also be true for groups: "the bodily wrapping [i.e., skin-ego] is an unconscious psychical organizing factor in groups."[24] Further, Naomi Segal, in her recent translation of *The Skin-Ego*, writes in an introduction that Anzieu posited a "group psychical apparatus": "A group is a wrapping that holds individuals together ... a living wrapping, like the skin that regenerates itself around the body, like the ego which is meant to enclose the psyche...."[25] Thus, Anzieu saw groups as having something like a living membrane around them to hold them together and regulate their boundaries, much like cultures can do. This group skin-ego creates order, like the ego in the individual psyche, and it has a containing function to filter, direct flow, and provide protection. Aspects of it include the rules of the group, procedures for entry and exit, expectations for behaviors, and guidelines for membership. Again, many of these qualities apply to a culture as well. Using Jacques Lacan's concepts of real, symbolic, and imaginary, Anzieu finds that groups invoke the real by their requirements about space, time, and place; the symbolic by employing rituals and signs of belonging; and the imaginary by expression of group fantasies and metaphors.[26] Like culture, the group skin-ego offers members cohesion, an interface with those not belonging, and passage to other groups. Although "group skin-ego" and "culture" are not exactly interchangeable, they have many similarities; yet we might consider the term *culture* as being more extensive and including more than group skin-ego.

When I worked as the director of the Oakes Children's Center, a mental health center and school for children with emotional challenges, I often found principles of group theory and practice helpful for organizing different aspects of the day treatment program, which was based on a milieu approach. The children at the center were frequently in groups, and ideas about group cohesion, scapegoating, inclusion/exclusion, contagiousness of group emotions, and the roles of group leaders were beneficial not only for understanding many processes we all experienced in working with the children, but also for designing interventions to help lower group anxieties, promoting the development of relationships, and labeling group feelings that were troubling. Although I had not read Anzieu at that time, his concept of a group skin-ego has since occurred to me on numerous occasions when I recall certain events at the center. For example, the children were transported on local school buses—the typical yellow American kind—from home to school and back. Because of dangerously disruptive behaviors during the ride, we had to hire bus aides to supervise the children and keep them occupied with different kinds of activities and games. When the aides were first introduced, there were many unanticipated problems, and behavioral outbursts on the buses worsened. With a little sleuthing, we learned the children were talking about "aides on the bus" as meaning "AIDS," the infectious and then fatal disease. There had been a group panic coming from a misinformed belief that led to much acting out, such as opening the emergency door while the bus was in motion. Once we cleared up the misunderstanding with a bit of psychoeducational material, the children riding the buses calmed down. The aides were accepted and no longer sources of anxiety as disease-ridden and dangerous, a fantasy that destabilized the group and made the group skin-ego feel attacked.

Anzieu notes that many groups become unhinged if they share a delusion of "a parchment in common" in which reality gets lost because there is a mutual belief of "a single mind for several bodies."[27] His choice of "parchment" emphasizes the skin factor of groups, but it also describes a sheet used in a writing process, when things are written down—or at times metaphorically inscribed on us. This is similar to my idea of perimeters being internalized from pieces of external reality. This kind of delusional group skin-ego process (single mind for several bodies) seems applicable to most far-right authoritarian groupings, social media extremism, and cults. These groups typically resort to binary in/out judgments about people, can be concrete in their reasoning, and fear contamination. Thus, for them, xenophobia can be a defensive posture to ensure a primitive fantasy of a closely patrolled boundary.

Sectarianism can also illustrate what happens when a group skin-ego portrays a fantasy of Anzieu's parchment in common. As I described briefly, such division can occur when religious factions combat one another, as occurred in Ireland, and it can penetrate the dynamics of families when these perimeters are believed to have been wrongly crossed. The violation is based on a breach of faith as understood by group members who do not tolerate mixing or interfaith contacts. Often, sectarian strife can be a reason for immigration, although immigrants may only encounter newer and stranger forms of sectarianism in their receiving countries. Nasir and several of the adolescents from Syria and Afghanistan whom I met in Berlin in 2017 described this experience when they encountered xenophobia among Germans who were antagonistic toward them—recall the camping trip that had to be cut short because of safety concerns. Sectarianism can also, as illustrated by my grandmother's refusal to discuss her parents, contribute to the avoidance of even considering a subject; such a conversation could have been met with hostility because the topic was felt to be too hot to handle.

Another example from Oakes Children's Center pertains to the ways groups display a shared identity, what Anzieu might describe as their having tangible signs of belonging to a common group skin-ego. Each July, at the end of the school year, we took the children for a picnic at a local park for a day interspersed with group activities, crafts, and games. In the morning, before leaving for the park, the children each received a tee shirt that graduating students had designed, with the help of a teacher, and that the Center distributed to everyone, staff included. The tee shirts were identical except in size; students were very fond of them and proudly wore them in the community months after a picnic. Once, someone had the idea that each student or staff member would design their own tee shirt using fabric markers to decorate it. That year, on the day of the annual picnic, the mood among the children was notably tense, and unusually, there were a couple of children whose acting-out behaviors prevented them from attending the picnic. At the park, many children argued and shouted at one another, and a small fight broke out among several older students. During this fight, the two sides argued about which shirts had been drawn better and which ones had "stupid" and "loser" pictures on them. That year, staff had to end the picnic early and return to the school.

Later in the day, a few tee shirts were discovered in a garbage can. It was as if they had been judged to be useless because they had upset a tradition that denoted an important time in the children's lives. The idea of creating their own individual tee shirts had badly misfired by removing a marker of common identity, a sign of a group skin-ego that each one of us could wear and show collectively at the end-of-year celebration. Everyone sporting that identical tee shirt was the basis of an event that, for this day, made us all alike (in one way). Unlike in the Robbers Cave experiment (see Chapter 6), in which the children organized themselves to compete against one another, here the loss of a valued group symbol invited fragmentation and led to shows of individual aggression. This fragmentation represented a group panic at a time of transition when a familiar ritual usually held the school together. Students felt the school culture was threatened when an important wrapping—literally everyone in an identical tee shirt—was taken away. In subsequent years, the school kept identical tee shirts for staff and children at the picnic, and there was no repeat of what had happened that one year when the shirts were all different.

Anzieu's concept of a group skin-ego helps me to appreciate the kinds of biases and obstacles immigrants face in coming to a new country. A group skin-ego gives theoretical contours to how othering can happen when people fear outsiders are infiltrating a safe space that is vigorously defended—like with the arrival of the bus "aides." It also illustrates a social process for how real perimeters operate to separate or unite us—like tee shirts showing team affiliation. Our reactions to these social processes reveal how perimeters come to live inside us, which I illustrated in Chapter 6, when I described how I felt to have been included among "we Germans." These interactions occur over time, for the most part outside consciousness, and end up often enough surprising us. Some immigrants find this experience of internalization edgy and unpleasant. Like Ursula or like Marco's family, they might attempt to make do for a while looking for a tolerable compromise in a new country, but like me, they might also conclude they do not want to become part of "we" and choose to leave, either going back to their home country or to a different one.

In the United States, and perhaps in any country with substantial historical inflows of immigrants, there are multiple group skin-egos that can be found throughout the country. Some will be hostilely defended, others simply impermeable, and others more porous and accepting of new members. I would call the latter multicultural and embracing the dynamism that immigrant communities can offer. Those that are multicultural will not have rigid perimeters, not insist on assimilation, and not judge backgrounds based on a hierarchy of worthiness. Having enough of these places will make a country sufficiently welcoming for immigrants to locate a place to resettle and make a home for their families. Can unfriendly and belligerent groups be avoided? Probably not, at least in a democratic country with freedoms of assembly and speech. Monica Luci discusses Anzieu's concept of group skin-ego by applying it to Israel as a way to understand the polysemous significations of the Western Wall; that collective symbol represents a revised experience of group skin-ego offering healing potential.[28] She makes the important point that if individual psychic skin can heal, as Anzieu believed, then group psychic skin should be able to also. This perspective gives hope to immigrants for finding reparative contacts in their new countries as well as dealing with the rejections they might encounter.

Uncanny

Anzieu, in his book *The Skin-Ego*, makes a point that threats to the integrity of the skin-ego, in which its borders are tested, can evoke terror of the uncanny—another idea that links to Freud.[29] When the perimeters of the individual or group skin-ego are intruded upon, surprised by unanticipated incoming contacts, or even attacked, then a person or group typically feels an eerie disturbance that creeps unwelcome into their being. Webster defines *uncanny* as "having a supernatural basis; mysterious; arousing superstitious fear or dread; uncomfortably strange."[30] Uncanny, a complicated word, thus means many different things. It implies contact with the supernatural, to which the rationally minded as well as those who see themselves as hard-core realists might immediately object. From those readers, I ask for a little leeway. Supernatural beliefs have been with humankind for ages; they form a central foundation for myths and folklore as humans evolved and tried to comprehend a world that felt mysterious and inexplicable at times. Supernatural can be construed as what is beyond, or above, nature—what, within the realm of explanation, cannot be accounted for by observable cause and effect, by what our senses perceive, or by otherwise testable experimentation—by science. Thus, the mystery. There are definite gaps in a story about what has happened, although these gaps do not fall into the category of lies or omissions. Instead, they are things for which we do not have a handy model of understanding and thus belong to another category of the unexplainable.

Feelings associated with the uncanny are distinct: dread, fear, horror. These often have to do with a loss of control, which could merely be a loss of logic and reason to explain something. Often, such feelings are ascribed to the irrational as though that provides enough of an explanation. "Oh, that's irrational" as in "That's nonsense." But labeling an event or occurrence as irrational is also a defense against our limits to understanding it. We might not like that limitation to reason and then resort to a kind of name-calling, as in grasping for words like *superstition, hocus pocus, delusion, fallacy.* William James, the eminent American psychologist, long ago made a philosophical point that what belongs to the human mind is a part of human experience, no matter how we deride or devalue it, and he further notes that what is considered objective truth is determined by fairly relative standards.[31] Uncanny often evokes strangeness because it does not fit what is expected or what is remembered from prior learning and experiences. This strangeness can cause great discomfort and lead to our fleeing the uncanny circumstances. In short, the uncanny is a radical piece of human life.

Virtually all the cases and examples in previous chapters report some aspect of the uncanny that pertains to migration, resettlement, or encounters with the natives in an immigrant's new country. I have already mentioned that natives too can regard their encounters with immigrants as uncanny and seek to distance themselves from further contact. This avoidance shows how disturbing the uncanny can be for people—that they must reinforce with extra vigor whatever borders in the group skin-ego appear to have been trespassed on. In Chapter 4, I discuss the example of what happened in Berlin when members of the Church of Scientology attempted to recruit adolescent refugees from Syria and Afghanistan. Hearing that story for the first time, I shivered thinking about how unknown this group was to the refugee youth and how vulnerable they were to exploitation by them. Although there is a rational explanation for what happened, I don't think that would have crossed these adolescents' minds before they were informed. No, it would have been uncanny for them to be greeted in a way that was intended to capture their attention and eventually them, like in a fairytale!

Hans (Chapter 1) had several uncanny experiences related to his HIV seropositivity, especially when he heard of someone he knew who was seriously ill. He often worried he was "on death's door" and was preoccupied that he might be hospitalized in the United States with no say over his medical treatment. He was afraid of being transported into another reality where he would have little control. Nasir (Chapter 4) lived a journey that was supernatural, from traveling at night to the final leg of his journey when he was confined in a dark truck, scared to death because he did not understand the language of the traffickers. These circumstances were totally extreme, apart from the relatively safe reality that most of us know; that difference also held for his life in war-torn Syria.

Arturo (Chapter 5) thought he could go on a field trip across the border, and he could not understand his mother's refusal until she told him he was undocumented. His reality shifted without warning as he realized his changed situation. Miguel (Chapter 5) was cast in a role as a Black person without anyone asking him if he wanted that. He felt this had to do with his skin color, and his reality was often jarred by such aggressive and racist acts. Galit (Chapter 8) found herself in a new country, and the only way to show her upset was to refuse to learn English. The language of her new reality, probably uncanny for her, became her way to protest coming to the United States. Mariam (Chapter 8) ended up in an empty apartment in suburban Virginia without her father. The contrast in her realities from Beirut to suburban Virginia was overwhelming and disorienting, and she had no control over it. Adam (Chapter 10) had to rush to prevent his wife from being deported because of forgotten paperwork. His unconscious slip led to a serious reconsideration of staying in the United States, as if fate, uncannily enough, were intervening to disrupt their plans. Marco (Chapter 10) did not know his neighborhood in San Francisco but could tell me about playgrounds in Madrid. He described feeling disoriented in San Francisco and found comfort in a past reality that felt easier for him to move in. Each of these people had uncanny experiences in which their current reality was no longer what it seemed. Reality shifted into an unfamiliar form. Encounters with shifting realities can seem supernatural and terrorize us with disorientation and dread. Something similar happened to me when I researched my grandmother's family and found out how much she had avoided telling us about them—what I learned stunned me. A new reality is difficult to take in.

Freud wrote about the uncanny using as inspiration E.T.A. Hoffmann's novella *The Sandman*.[32] This work, written in German in the early nineteenth century, encompasses a confusion about what is real and what is not real; it includes not only occult phenomena but also aspects of madness and dreams. The main character is a young man, Nathanael, who is a student engaged to a woman Klara, whose brother Lothar is his friend. Nathanael recalls a story told him as a child about the Sandman. The Sandman visits children who will not go to bed and fall asleep; he throws sand into their eyes. Their sandy eyes bleed until they fall out, whereupon the Sandman steals their eyes and takes them to his children on the moon so they can devour them. The child Nathanael believes that Coppelius, an alchemist who regularly visits his father, is the Sandman. One night Nathanael hides in his father's study to watch them but is discovered when he screams about Coppelius's sinister plans. Coppelius threatens to throw embers into his eyes, but after listening to Nathanael's father's pleas, instead twists the boy's ankles and wrists until he loses consciousness with pain. This incident—did it really happen, was it a dream/nightmare, or did he imagine it?—is never discussed by Nathanael and his father. A year later, when Coppelius again visits his father, there is an explosion in the study in which Nathanael's father dies.

The novella returns to Nathanael's student days when a man who reminds him of Coppelius shows up on the scene, an Italian named Coppola, who sells instruments like glasses and barometers. A university professor, Spallanzani, vouches for Coppola, calming Nathanael's conviction that he is the alchemist Coppelius/Sandman in disguise. Nathanael purchases a small telescope from Coppola, and when he moves into an apartment across from Spallanzani, he uses it to observe the professor's daughter Olimpia. He becomes enamored with her, but she turns out to not be human, but an automaton. Nathanael is haunted by gruesome fantasies about her eyes. "Everything, his entire life was like a dream and just foreboding."[33] He struggles to hold onto one reality while another encircles him. He even assures himself that Coppola might be a doppelgänger ("double") and not actually Coppelius. The role of doppelgänger as a double to stand in for what once seemed to belong elsewhere is central to the effects of the uncanny in *The Sandman*.

Nathanael walks in on an argument between Spallanzani and Coppola, who now seems to be Coppelius, and he sees the automaton Olimpia without her eyes. After chasing Coppola/Coppelius, he becomes insane. He is sent to an asylum and apparently recovers. Afterward, he and Klara climb a tower to view the surrounding area, and when he uses the telescope he got from Coppola, he confuses Klara with Olimpia and once more goes mad trying to kill her. Lothar saves her from Nathanael, who jumps from the tower to his death. Years later, the narrator reports that Klara is contentedly married with two boys.

Freud's essay notes that uncanny experiences are frightening and usually accompanied by horror and dread.[34] The German word for uncanny, *unheimlich*, literally means "unhomely," and it can also mean not native or familiar. Freud explains that the "better oriented" a person is to their environment and surroundings, the less likely it is that there would be an experience of the uncanny.[35] Uncanny is associated with another term discussed in this book, the word *xenophobia*. *Xenos* in Greek means strange or foreign. Freud is interested in the Sandman as a figure who is deeply associated with the uncanny, primarily around the notion that he can remove a person's eyes, which is especially terrifying for children.[36] He regards Hoffmann as a "unrivalled master of the uncanny in literature," although I would add Mary Shelley (Frankenstein) and Bram Stoker (Dracula) to that list.[37] The uncanny is not something pertaining to either cognitive or intellectual uncertainty that arouses anxiety. Instead, its psychological effects of horror, alienation, helplessness and fear of repetition distinguish the uncanny from more mundane circumstances of anxiety. The possibility of repetition makes something uncanny seem inescapable and fated, yet also arousing. The presence of a doppelgänger intensifies the uncanny beyond typical anxieties because we are conditioned to find and notice our doubles in mirrors, dreams, and look-alikes. The uncanny has some overlap with what Jung called *synchronicity*. Both Jung and Freud shared an editorial concern about writing about such topics because they imagined that skeptics would discredit them.[38] Whereas with synchronicity Jung is interested in how the psyche achieves meaningful connections between unrelated coincidental happenings, with the uncanny Freud focuses on the more affective underpinnings of horror and terror.

The uncanny often arises for immigrants as well as for people in the receiving country when they become disoriented, frightened, and lose a frame of reference. Hoffmann provides a depiction that this is a dramatic shift of reality from what is familiar to what is unfamiliar. Accompanying that shift, a person may feel terror at not understanding it, loss of rationality in accounting for it, and disorientation about what comes next. In such moments, the real becomes unreal. Those components—limited understanding, loss of reason, little or no control, and disorientation—characterize many encounters that immigrants have as they transition into a new life, and they can also describe how natives can get caught in social processes that are rejecting, xenophobic, and avoidant. In addition, the image of a doppelgänger can reflect how natives perceive an immigrant when they evaluate whether the person belongs—is familiar—or does not belong—is unfamiliar. When the doppelgänger, or double, is perceived as a threat, then they can be associated with the uncanny rather easily. Experiencing a doppelgänger is often momentarily unsettling even when a person does regain a sense of orientation, such as "Oh, they only look like so-and-so." A doppelgänger adds a fleeting temporal effect to the uncanny; reality shifts when we least suspect it and suddenly becomes threatening.

For Freud, Hoffmann's story about the Sandman's taking of recalcitrant children's eyes connects to his theory about the castration complex.[39] Importantly, he theorizes about the implications of a loss of bodily integrity when we feel threatened by attack and injury. Our rising terror over images of such scenes demonstrates the nonverbal process through which the uncanny gets inside us. It is not merely a feeling of worry, but rather an eerie shiver of potential and brutal harm that disturbs us viscerally. Something could be cut away, something fundamental to who we are, and thus we too have a terror that the Sandman could blind us, turning us over to darkness from which we can never wake up. A similar belief about physical threats and harm is often central to xenophobia. Fears of infection, violent attacks, and contamination can lead to xenophobic behaviors of avoidance and rejection. These might be dressed up as concerns about habits and cultural values, but at their core, they reach back in the psyche to a more primitive level of terror at losing a sense of bodily integrity.

Lost and found

The uncanny often emerges at edges of experience that are transitional, such as twilight, falling asleep, waking up, losing consciousness, changing perspective, sensory confusion, big moves, accidents, deaths, and natural disasters. Immigrants and refugees live through profound transitions, and as such, they may encounter the uncanny whether they want to or not. Winnicott wrote about transitional phenomena as belonging to an in-between realm of me and not-me, where pretend and uncertainty can be played with as a young child discovers a space that is entirely theirs.[40] Although he was describing the developmentally positive aspects of transitional phenomena, many parents know well that transitions can be difficult for children and adolescents. During times of change, children might react with fear and upset about not having control. Transitions perhaps gravitate toward the uncanny when they affect our orientation to reality. In other words, going to another country is very different than going on a camping trip to a destination two hours from home.

Hartmut was a gay man in his late twenties from a city in northern Germany who was in the United States on a student visa and compelled by finishing his studies to leave the United States—even though he worked in a field where more professionals were and are needed. He decided to immigrate to Canada. We had been working together for about a year when he learned of his approved date for moving to Canada, which left us with only months in his analysis. This was at a time when he was frustrated and angry about the United States, especially that he could not stay. He was sometimes angry at me for not being able to help with all the loose ends he experienced in his life at this moment. Hartmut, knowing that I knew German, mentioned the German word *Fransen*, which means fringes like on carpet or upholstery, as symbolizing the many threads he could not gather together. He wished that I would share more directly my feelings with him, which he thought would make me feel less like "fringe," and he worried I was withholding intentionally. I commented that I felt he needed a space that was just for him to express the many complicated feelings he was having so as not to feel crowded. He appreciated this remark as tolerating his anger and saying something about my feeling for him—that I was trying to offer what I thought he needed, that I cared about him.

Around this time in Hartmut's work with me, an uncanny event occurred, which also felt synchronistic for both of us. In a session before this, we were discussing whether to switch to German, a move that Hartmut thought might help him get closer to some material about his parents. I had said that I thought we could do so after talking it through, but I might have been too distant in how I expressed this.

Hartmut:	I guess you expect we'll discuss it. It sounded like you expected me to bring it up, and I felt confused by what you said.
RT:	Yes, maybe I sounded remote, expecting things of you, and that wasn't helpful because I do want to know what you want here.
Hartmut:	I have this story that you were defensive because it made you angry when I asked if we could switch, so you went cold.
RT:	I could've handled it differently, said that it felt important to me, and that I wanted to talk it through with you. You felt pressured to guess about what was going on with me.
Hartmut:	Yeah. I'm relieved you said that. Like I can be angry and you won't come after me for that. (Pause) It makes me sad that I'd think you'd be angry with me, like I was turning you into the bad guy. Over the last months, you've really helped. I've been sad with a pain in my heart, but with you, I've felt I've had a place to bring it.

Hartmut had grown up in difficult childhood circumstances. Not only was he left alone too much but he was also overwhelmed by his mother's emotional outbursts. It was a confusing mix of alternately being emotionally abandoned and being intruded upon. He worried about risks with trust and vulnerability in relationships, and he wondered whether someone would really put his interests first. The image of the fringes seemed powerful at this time of impending transition for Hartmut. Fringe is decorative and thus not supportive. I thought Hartmut worried that I might not have wanted to hear his feelings about me as we were ending soon—would I instead protect myself by keeping a distance from him? In other words, would I keep to the fringes?

On the day of this event, I remember parking my car on a cross street near my office. I had pulled into an open parking spot and thought myself a little lucky on that day because parking in the neighborhood where my office was could be challenging. Briefly, I saw Hartmut ride by me on his bicycle. I got out of the car and walked toward the front of it where I happened to notice a piece of paper tucked partly under a front tire where the curve of the tire met the ground. I bent over and picked it up. It looked like a check, and when I unfolded it, I saw that it belonged to Hartmut, was dated that day, and made out to me. I shook my head in disbelief. It felt like a dream. How had his check gotten there? How had I even noticed it? And how had I come to be holding it? I went to my office, and as I passed Hartmut in the waiting room, I saw that he seemed troubled and was looking through his pockets. A minute or so later, Hartmut came into my office. I had placed his check on the couch for him to see.

Hartmut:	What? (Looks at his check surprised.)
RT:	Yes. I'm not sure what to say. I found it on the street tucked under one of my tires.

Hartmut:	That is really strange! (Continues to be surprised and amazed.)
RT:	I don't know what happened. Do you have any ideas?
Hartmut:	It was in the pocket of my jacket when I left this morning. When I got here, I reached for it and thought, damn, I lost it.
RT:	(There's a short silence.) What feelings come up now?
Hartmut:	Relief, and I feel thankful. Man, you saved me a headache of having to call the bank and deal with them. I was starting to worry about biking back home to look for it. What a coincidence!
RT:	[I really didn't know what to say, so I remained quiet.]

Hartmut spoke some about his work and the struggles he had with it. He mentioned a wish he had to be saved and referred to the found check. He spoke about a cough that he could not shake.

Hartmut:	Well, what do you make of what happened with the check?
RT:	I'm not sure. It's something of a synchronicity. I'll have to give it more thought.
Hartmut:	I saw your car on Tuesday [day of the previous session] when you were turning onto California Street. I noticed the PL [Poland] sticker [on the bumper]. That was significant because I hadn't put your name in Poland. And I saw the J sticker [for neighborhood parking in San Francisco] and figured that must be where you live. Is this creeping you out? That thing with the check ... it's like when a teenager does something stupid and their parents save him. I guess the J sticker, nice to know where you live, but I don't want you to feel like I'm prying and invading your privacy.
RT:	You're worried about my reaction to what you're saying, that you'll be too much for me.
Hartmut:	Well, I don't know exactly where you live. I'm aware I'm more curious. The longer we work together, you know me, and I know some of you, and it seems safe. Like last session when you shared how you felt. That shook something up. [Hartmut goes on a little about his work.] ... I'm noticing I can let the positive into my experiences more .... I'm jumping a little today.
RT:	Well, something unusual and exciting happened earlier. I imagine you wonder how the check ended up with me.
Hartmut:	Yes. It's nice hearing you say that. I feel closer to you now. As we talk, I'm feeling more open. [Pause] For me, it's difficult now to let go of you.

In the next session, Hartmut spoke about how many sessions we had until he moved. He reported *a dream in which he was jumping from a building and someone shot him in his right shoulder, although he survived, found a group to blend in with, and escaped.* He associated the dream with our termination and spoke about different endings he had experienced. Hartmut reflected that he was not dead in the dream and that he was still able to act; he had never had a dream in which he had been shot like this. He wondered whether I, as his rescuer (by finding his check), would have a Mr. Hyde side (*The Strange Case of Dr. Jekyll and Mr. Hyde* by Robert Louis Stevenson) like the shooter in his dream. He spoke some about the view out my window, which he liked. As we talked more about termination, he mentioned he wished we did not have to stop.

In this highly unusual fragment from an analysis, themes of change, transition, and relatedness surface at a pivotal point for someone who had already immigrated once and who was having to do so yet again. The "fringes" form an image that speaks to a contrasting wish for psychic containment at this turbulent time—for something durable and steadying. An uncanny event occurred at a time of transition for Hartmut, one involving me and depicting some of the "lost and found" aspects of our work together. In the preceding session, Hartmut wanted me to know that he felt I had lost him when I suggested we have a fuller discussion about using German in his sessions. Although there was nothing wrong with my suggestion, I probably put it awkwardly, as though it were a formality we had to address first. This exchange contributed to Hartmut's feeling that I had lost him. This sense of lostness resonated both with the upcoming termination and with Hartmut's feelings about his immigration to the United States, which did not end how he had hoped.

Jung's idea about synchronicity certainly describes a portion of what happened with Hartmut's check that turned up under one of my tires. However, it does not capture the strangeness of this event, like suddenly being in another reality. It was uncanny in that neither of us could quite believe our eyes, and I suggest there was something terrorizing about it, which perhaps Hartmut's dream about the shooter represented. I felt in the countertransference a sort of weight around having found the check and trying to account for that. When I gave up on trying to explain it—relatively quickly—I still felt that a trick had been played on us because it was too strange to believe, a little like the Sandman. On the one hand, it was a lucky stroke that saved Hartmut from dealing with his bank and me about a lost check. He was spared excess effort in sorting this out as well as needlessly carrying recriminations of self-blame. On the other hand, it seemed to invoke another reality, which shifted us into incomprehensible roles. Hartmut's framing of the incident as an adolescent mishap that a parent and son have to deal with was helpful in placing us in a more accessible transference-countertransference situation that we could both comprehend. That idea grounded us in a more familiar reality.

His associations about my car also seemed like a meaningful way to locate me as I moved (in the car), first by the reference to Poland (about my nationality) and second by the neighborhood where I might live (about my residence). Hartmut thus "found" new aspects of who I was to him, and I believe at this time of transition, these discoveries were not just facts about me, but rather they held meaning for how he would remember me and keep me in his mind. Lost and found had been a recurring theme during Hartmut's analysis, in which he found parts of himself that had felt lost to him until he rediscovered them. The lost check mysteriously landing under my tire was somewhat like a different reality imposing itself and announcing, "Now deal with it." This episode put us together with something lost. Interestingly, Hartmut's dream about the shooter led him to wonder about my doppelgänger: did I have a violent Mr. Hyde as a shadow of Dr. Jekyll, who could recover lost checks? I too felt a doppelgänger quality to Hartmut in imagining that the man on the bike had not been him, but someone else instead. The imposition of another reality about a lost "paper" of value seems evocative of what immigrants deal with when there are visa problems with their "papers" and they have to leave.

I am not implying that such uncanny events are typical of psychotherapy or analysis with immigrants and refugees, although it would be interesting to know how many analysts and psychotherapists have had such experiences. I believe what happened between Hartmut and me offers a window into just how terrifying many transitions of migration can be, especially when our hold on the reality we believe in gets shaken. This sudden shifting of reality, like what happens frequently in Hoffmann's *The Sandman*, represents an eruption of something new and disorienting, calling into question what we have believed to be true. It can appear dream-like, and it can definitely be uncanny. Paying attention to the details surrounding transitional events like this can open us to doing the therapeutic work of integrating realities that collide unexpectedly—something immigrants often have to contend with.

Lastly, a critical part of what makes an experience uncanny is that all of a sudden we are put into a shared space in which perimeters lose their generally accepted meanings; it is as if those perimeters are upended. In such a space, we cannot find easy frames of reference or perceptible guideposts for what has happened to us. Thus, experiences of the uncanny upset established perimeters for how we categorize ourselves in relation to reality, and this typically is quite hard to fathom.

The Dirae called

Of course, myths and fairytales make abundant use of the uncanny. That is partially why we are fascinated by them. At the end of The Aeneid, which invokes the uncanny throughout, Jupiter agrees with Juno that the Trojans can remain in Latium (Italy), although they must give up their Trojan heritage and henceforth be known as *Ausonian* or *Latins*. As I mentioned at the start of this chapter, Juno must concede this and stop her meddling on behalf of Aeneas.[41] This is the final price for their migration. To settle the last battle that is playing out in Book 12 of The Aeneid, Jupiter then sends the Dirae, Latin goddesses of vengeance like the Greek Furies, to drive things in Aeneas's favor and end it. The Dirae are "His ministers of wrath, and ready still/The minds of mortal men with fears to fill"; later, they take the form of birds, which Turnus's sister Juturna sees: "to the boding bird she turns,/Which haunts the ruin'd piles and hallow'd urns."[42] These frightful entities are representative of death and the underworld. They drive Juturna away and bewitch Turnus who loses his advantage against Aeneas. As he struggles, he becomes disoriented and cannot fight: "The Fury flew athwart, and made th' endeavor void."[43] Even though Turnus now surrenders and begs Aeneas for mercy, Aeneas, who is initially moved toward compassion, sees Pallas's sword belt, which Turnus wrongly wears, and becomes enraged. He then kills Turnus ending the book.

Reality often shifts in The Aeneid as twists of destiny play out for mortals who cannot count on their plan's eventual success because of the whims of the gods acting as instruments of fate. The appearance of the Dirae is the last in a long line of uncanny interventions that usurp the plot of The Aeneid. The course of action abruptly changes, and the characters are confused, even frightened. Perspectives are clouded. The sensory impact of the uncanny seems otherworldly, driven by invisible agents that feel powerful, a little like me and Hartmut trying to fathom how his check got under a tire of my car. The uncanny is not simply a way to write something off as unexplainable. It invites us to seek meaning and to engage with what is mysterious, what is irrational, what defies our usual senses, what happens when the familiar turns unfamiliar. Avoidance of the uncanny is thus analogous to xenophobia when groups of people are shunned. At a minimum, we lose out on learning about the strangeness of life whenever we choose to avoid what gives us goosebumps and shivers.

The ending of The Aeneid is based on the Roman idea of absorbing those that became part of its empire. The Trojans become Latins who would make history. Yet, although the concluding message in The Aeneid is that the Trojans must assimilate and take on the culture of their new land, Virgil endeavors to connect Roman history with a Trojan heritage. He demonstrates that the past matters for migrants to understand who they are. His story about the Trojans coming to Italy is intentional for creating a historical and mythical tie with the ancient culture of the Eastern Mediterranean as described in other myths and Homer's Iliad. Their past is significant, for it contains stories that are meant to be repeated.

Ad astra

It is fitting for me to conclude this book by stealing Virgil's *ad astra* just once more—to the stars, or as he meant, to have a story that extends over a length of time into the future. This is what most immigrants and refugees want, namely a story about themselves that is not forgotten and that their children and descendants remember and tell. The stars in this sense do not only belong to the night sky but also are the children that come after a migration. They are stars in the vision of their parents who migrated, and they represent a universal faith in finding somewhere else that will offer more for them. Immigrants hope to have found that somewhere else where a better life happens.

The following list highlights many of the psychologically salient aspects of immigration that are also covered in earlier chapters:

- It remains to be seen if comprehensive immigration reforms are legislated by the US Congress; the outlook is uncertain at best and more likely to tend negative.
- Many of the Trump administration's policy changes to US immigration will take time to reverse.
- Policies regarding asylum seekers at the US–Mexico border may, for some time, continue many restrictive actions taken during the Trump administration.
- Xenophobia and anti-immigration sentiment will likely remain in American political discourse as long as populist and nativist appeals dominate one of the political parties.
- Most immigrants' stories have a mystery in them and sorting out the mystery can often seem like detective work.
- These mysteries are not always intentional; sometimes, they arise from omissions in how an immigration story is told or conveyed; other times, they result from conscious lies to avoid details that the storyteller feels strongly about.
- Such aversions often avoid emotional territory that brings up shame, humiliation, panic about discovery, grief, and trauma; these missing pieces frequently feel like secrets within families.
- When there are gaps in the stories that immigrants tell, those close to them, especially family members, will likely fill in the holes with imaginative elements, projections, and fantasies that can underpin interpersonal distance and alienation.
- Crossing real and definable perimeters is part of the immigration experience; Anzieu's concept of a group skin-ego helps us to understand the cultural perimeters that immigrants navigate in coming to a new country.
- Experiences of the uncanny often arise for immigrants as well as for natives when they encounter one another; the uncanny feels super-natural, upends perimeters as I've defined them, and belongs to the range of irrational human experiences that defy logic and normative patterns of reason.

- Eerie strangeness of the uncanny can escalate beyond anxiety to dread and horror when reality appears to suddenly shift into something else; this shifting of realities often accompanies many immigration narratives.
- A doppelgänger (double) can represent a projection about a threat violating our usual abilities to perceive what is around us, and immigrants can sometimes carry projections of such doubles.
- A case example illustrates how a time of transition, when reality does change in various ways, can amplify possibilities for the uncanny to burst out; psychological containment can be critically helpful at such moments.
- The Aeneid has multiple points of entry for understanding migration and extracting psychological meanings for the archetypal dimensions of immigration.

I refer in this chapter to many of the case examples that are discussed in more depth elsewhere in the book to help readers appreciate references to trauma, lies and omissions, the uncanny, and dealing with perimeters. These core themes describe what many immigrants and refugees go through when they relocate and resettle in new countries.

In closing, I especially want to thank everyone who has contributed to this book, which I hope shows that complicated and hard stories can be told, even when they have missing parts. Sometimes, those parts can be redis-covered and brought to consciousness, which helps us feel more whole and more integrated. I have probably undertaken some *ad astra* in writing this book—my own reaching for the stars, because of the immigrants in my background and because of the love and support so many immigrants have continued to bring into my life. They have been sparks of light—like stars at nighttime—in my family, education, and career. My hope is that enough of us can feel the effects from some of those sparks to strengthen a belief in why immigration is important to keep open and available. It will be a worthwhile accomplishment when immigration becomes easier and more accepted across the globe. As I mentioned in Chapter 5, Jung describes sparks of luminosity as *scintillae* (a Latin term like *ad astra*), and he writes that their light "illuminates consciousness ... shining forth from the darkness of the unconscious."[44] Immigrants represent sparks for our societies and illuminate areas that we do not typically see. As we think about our contemporary troubles, couldn't the world use a lot more of that?

Notes

1 Virgil, The Aeneid, trans. John Dryden (Project Gutenberg E-Book #228, 2008), 956. Hereafter, references to Dryden's translation of The Aeneid will appear as Dryden and page number.
2 Walt Whitman, *Leaves of Grass* (Project Gutenberg, E-Book #1322, 2008), 311.
3 Miranda Cady Hallett, "Severed Families, Raided Workplaces and a Climate of Fear: Assessing Trump's Immigration Crackdown," *The Conversation*, October 26, 2020.

4 Wendy E. Parmet, "Immigration Law as a Social Determinant of Health," *92 Temple Law Review* 931 (2020), Northeastern University School of Law Research Paper No. 380–2020, https://ssrn.com/abstract=3635513

5 Jean Galbraith, "Contemporary Practice of the United States Relating to International Law: Trump Administration Further Restricts Asylum Seekers at the Southern Border through the Migrant Protection Protocols, Asylum Cooperative Agreements, and COVID-19 Procedures," *American Journal of International Law* 114, no. 3 (2020): 504–511, https://doi.org/10.1017/ajil.2020.41

6 Editorial Board, "Undoing Trump's Immigration Policies," *New York Times,* October 11, 2020, 8.

7 David J. Bier, "Did US Policy Cause Half of 'Unaccompanied' Children to Separate from Parents?" *Cato at Liberty,* April 14, 2021, https://www.cato.org/blog/did-us-policy-cause-half-unaccompanied-children-separate-parents

8 David J. Bier, "Immediate Solutions for Migrant Children," Cato Institute, March 17, 2021, https://www.cato.org/publications/immediate-solutions-migrant-children

9 Xavier Devictor, Quy-Toan Do, and Andrei A. Levchenko, "The Globalization of Refugee Flows" (working paper, National Bureau of Economic Research, Cambridge, MA, January 2021), 17, DOI: 10.3386/w28332.

10 Muzaffar Chishti and Jessica Bolter, "Border Challenges Dominate but Biden's First 100 Days Mark Notable Under-The-Radar Immigration Accomplishments," Migration Policy Institute, April 26, 2021, https://www.migrationpolicy.org/article/biden-100-days-immigration

11 Ibid.

12 Marc Van Der Hout, personal communication, June 16, 2021. Mr. Van Der Hout was president of the National Lawyers Guild and a long-term board member of their National Immigration Project of the National Lawyers Guild. He has also served for more than thirty years on the board of the American Immigration Lawyers Association and has practiced immigration law in San Francisco for more than forty years.

13 Alex Nowrasteh and Benjamin Powell, *Wretched Refuse? The Political Economy of Immigration and Institutions* (Cambridge, UK: Cambridge University Press, 2021).

14 Ibid., 77.

15 Ibid., 283.

16 For details about Odysseus and Oedipus, see Edith Hamilton, *Mythology: Timeless Tales of Gods and Heroes* (New York, New American Library, 1969); and Timothy Gantz, *Early Greek Myth: A Guide to Literary and Artistic Sources,* vol. 2 (Baltimore: Johns Hopkins University Press, 1993).

17 See for example, Wikipedia, s.v. "Marriage in the Catholic Church," last modified July 3, 2021, 3:03, https://en.wikipedia.org/wiki/Marriage_in_the_Catholic_Church; or Edward Peters, "Master Page on the Pio-Benedictine Code of 1917," Canonlaw.info, https://www.canonlaw.info/masterpage1917.htm

18 Kerby A. Miller, *Emigrants and Exiles: Ireland and the Irish Exodus to North America* (Oxford: Oxford University Press, 1985), 3.

19 Ibid., 10.

20 Ibid., 42, 99.

21 Ibid., 280.

22 Didier Anzieu, "The Group Ego-Skin," *Group Analysis* 32, no. 3 (1999): 319–329.

23 Didier Anzieu, *The Skin-Ego,* trans. Naomi Segal (London: Karnac, 2016).

24 Ibid., 121.

25 Ibid., xxviii.

26 Anzieu, "The Group Ego-Skin," 321–322.

27 Ibid., 327.

28 Monica Luci, "The Skin between Collective and Individual States of Mind" (paper presented at the twenty-first Congress of the International Association for Analytical Psychology, August 25–30, 2019).

29 Anzieu, *The Skin-Ego,* 111.

30 *Webster's Unabridged Dictionary* (1997), s.v. "Uncanny."

31 William James, "Pragmatism and Common Sense," in *Pragmatism and Other Writings* (New York: Penguin, 2000), 74–86.

32 Hoffmann also wrote the story on which *The Nutcracker* ballet and music are based.

33 E. T. A. Hoffmann, "Der Sandmann," in *Spukgeschichten und Märchen,* 124–158 (Munich: Goldmann Verlag, 1959), 140. My translation.

34 Sigmund Freud, "The 'Uncanny,'" in the *Standard Edition,* vol. 17 (London: Hogarth Press and Institute of Psychoanalysis, 1919), 219–252.

35 Ibid., 221.

36 Ibid., 232.

37 Ibid., 233.

38 C. G. Jung, "Synchronicity: An Acausal Connecting Principle" (1952), in *The Collected Works of C. G. Jung,* vol. 8, *The Structure and Dynamics of the Psyche* (Princeton, NJ: Princeton University Press, 1968), 417–519. Hereafter, references to Jung's *Collected Works* will appear as Jung, title, date, and volume number in the *Collected Works* (CW).

39 Freud, "The 'Uncanny,'" 243.

40 D. W. Winnicott, "Transitional Objects and Transitional Phenomena," in *Playing and Reality* (London: Routledge 1953/1989), 1–25.

41 *Ausonian* was another Latin word for *Italy.*

42 Dryden, 1422, 1424.

43 Dryden, 1432.

44 C. G. Jung, "On the Nature of the Psyche" (1954), in CW 8, para. 389.

Index

Page numbers in bold and italics denote tables and figures, respectively.

For Product Safety Concerns and Information please contact our EU
representative GPSR@taylorandfrancis.com
Taylor & Francis Verlag GmbH, Kaufingerstraße 24, 80331 München, Germany

www.ingramcontent.com/pod-product-compliance
Lightning Source LLC
Chambersburg PA
CBHW050348270326
41926CB00016B/3648